Living with the Ancestors:
Kinship and Kingship in Ancient Maya Society

PATRICIA A. MCANANY

Living with the Ancestors

Kinship and Kingship in Ancient Maya Society

UNIVERSITY OF TEXAS PRESS
AUSTIN

This book has been supported in part by a grant from the
National Endowment for the Humanities, an independent
federal agency.

Library of Congress Cataloging-in-Publication Data

McAnany, Patricia Ann.
    Living with the ancestors : kinship and kingship in
ancient Maya society / by Patricia A. McAnany. — 1st ed.
        p.   cm.
    Includes bibliographical references and index.
    ISBN 0-292-75165-6 (alk. paper)
    1. Mayas—Kinship.   2. Mayas—Kings and rulers.
3. Mayas—Genealogy.   4. Ancestor worship—Mexico.
5. Ancestor worship—Central America.   I. Title.
F1435.3.K57M33   1995
972.81'016—dc20
                                            94-5469

For C. J.,
who taught me how to fight and how to laugh

Contents

Preface *xi*

ONE *A Point of Departure* *1*
    Philosophical and Geographical Frame of Reference *6*
    Primary Themes *7*
    Theory and Definition: Ancestor Veneration
      and Lineage *10*
    General Sources along the Space-Time Continuum *20*

TWO *Ancestor Veneration and Lineage Organization in the Maya Region* *22*
    Anatomy of a Lineage *22*
    Communing with the Ancestors *26*

THREE *Creating a Genealogy of Place* *64*
    Forest, Field, Orchard, and Dwelling in the Tropical
      Lowlands *64*
    Fields of the Ancestors *66*
    The Role of Boundaries in Tropical Lowland
      Farming *84*
    Lineage as Resource-Holding Group *95*
    Where the Ancestors "Slept" *100*
    Ancestors as Guardians of the Fields *109*

FOUR *Lineage as a Crucible of Inequality* *111*
    Voracious Appetite of Lineages for Land *112*
    The Concept of Descent in Maya Society *113*
    Ranking and Hierarchy of the Lineage *116*
    Inequality and Asymmetry at the Nexus of
      Production *118*

FIVE *Kin Groups and Divine Kingship in Lowland Maya Society* *125*
    Political Manipulation of Ancestor Veneration *126*
    Contrasting Kingship with the *Longue Durée* of
      Kinship *131*
    Conflict and Autonomy in the Maya Lowlands *144*

SIX   *Ancestors and Archaeology of Place*   157
                     Lineage and the Fallacy of the Two-Tier Model 158
                     Lineage and Land 159
                     Ancestors as Place-Markers 160
                     Inequality in Lineage and Residence 162
                     Forces of Divine Kingship 163

POSTSCRIPT   *The Future of the Ancestors and the Clash between Science
              and Human Rights*   167

                     Notes 169

                     References Cited 177

                     Index 205

Figures and Tables

1.1 Maps of the Maya region 2

1.2 Tombs of ancestors in the countryside of China 14

2.1 Photo of Tzotzil Maya around grave of an ancestor on Todos Santos 30

2.2 Codex Madrid, page 52c; representations of Chak and Goddess I presenting offerings of *Cacao* 34

2.3 Codex Dresden, page 27c; sacrificial offering of decapitated turkey 35

2.4 Codex Madrid, page 96d; use of a small hatchet to carve an image of a human head 37

2.5 Codex Madrid, page 97b; preparing icons 38

2.6 Codex Madrid, page 98a; cutting down tropical cedar trees to carve icons 38

2.7 Tikal (Stela 29); side profile of royal personage with "anchoring ancestor" in the sky above 41

2.8 Copán, Altar Q, showing the juxtaposition of Yax-Pac with the founder of the dynasty, Yax-Kuk-Mo' 42

2.9 Pakal's ancestors and their associated orchard species 44

2.10 Codex Madrid, page 95a; ritualized bloodletting from ear 45

2.11 Chert "eccentrics" worked into the form of a human profile, possibly of ancestors 46

2.12 Codex Madrid, page 107b, with crossed long-bones motif 47

2.13 Tikal, Altar 5, showing bones with a glyph band describing a female elite personage 48

2.14 Map of Southern Sector of K'axob showing "alpha" and satellite structures 54

2.15 Perspective drawing of "alpha" plaza group and surrounding satellite residences—B Group 56

2.16 Burial offerings from shrine burial 57

2.17 Ceramic vessel with quadripartite design, Late Formative shrine, K'axob 58

2.18 Late Formative ancestor shrine in stratigraphic cross section, K'axob 59

2.19 Commemorative cache covering Late Formative shrine plaza *60*

2.20 Disarticulated bone from shrine burial *62*

3.1 Fallow field in advanced high bush—*k'ax*. *70*

3.2 Fallow field in low bush—*UAYMIL*—and higher bush *71*

3.3 Field facility at a far field *72*

3.4 Orchards and fields in permanent cultivation in Veracruz, Mexico *75*

3.5 Lady Zac-Kuk *76*

3.6 Codex Dresden, Farmer's Almanac, page 42c *82*

3.7 Codex Dresden, Farmer's Almanac, page 43c *82*

3.8 Codex Dresden, Farmer's Almanac, page 44c *83*

3.9 Codex Dresden, Farmer's Almanac, page 45c *83*

3.10 Close-up of cross motif on Late Formative bowl from K'axob *86*

3.11 Postclassic incensario fragments from near the surface in front of Structure 18 *88*

3.12 Cross section of south section-wall of excavation at Operation 1 K'axob *98*

3.13 Histograms of number and size of platforms surrounding Pulltrouser Swamp *103*

3.14 Dedicatory cache vessels arranged in quincunx pattern *105*

5.1 Late Classic Maya vase with offering scene *134*

Tables

3.1 Multiple-Family Households on Cozumel Island, 1570 Census *108*

Preface

This book is about the practice of ancestor venera-
tion in ancient Maya society. Written while I was a visiting fellow at Dumbarton Oaks Research Library in Washington, D.C., this work metamor-
phosed from an earlier project on Maya economic organization. The more I
researched economic aspects of Maya society—land tenure and agriculture in
particular—the more I came to appreciate the strategic role played by ancestors in legitimizing claims to land and in the inheritance of everything from
field plots to orchards and houses. From this, I reasoned that ancestral Maya
burials and the ancient structures in which they were interred have the potential to tell us something about larger forces at work in society. They provide
a strong link between the material basis of life and the ideological framework
which both reflects and creates reality.

Ancestor veneration, as a creative social practice, is about naming and
claiming—naming progenitors, naming descendants, and by virtue of these
proper nouns establishing proprietary claims to resources. This point was
brought home to me one day during the Fellows' luncheon at Dumbarton
Oaks. John Yellen had joined us and I was describing this book project to
him. Given the fact that John has spent his entire research career either following African hunters and gatherers or mapping and excavating what little
they left behind, I was not sure that he would be particularly interested in my
research on the link between ancestors and land. Quite to the contrary, he
parlayed my rather stiff narrative with a story about fieldwork in the Kalahari
Desert that so perfectly characterizes the counterpoint to my thesis of Maya
perspectives on land and resource claims that I narrate it here.

In 1970, while he was conducting archaeological excavations in the northwest Kalahari Desert of Botswana, a Herero pastoralist informed John Yellen
that he "owned" the land and that further excavations would require his permission. It soon became apparent that permission really meant payment and
the terms were quickly agreed upon. When the Zu/twasi—a nearby

group of hunters and gatherers—heard of this arrangement, they became interested in establishing a similar one. Once again, John agreed to provide recompense to whoever the group agreed were the rightful "owners" of the lands on which he was working. This was acceptable to the Zu/twasi, and they sat down to a prolonged discussion during which they agreed, in general principle, to the criteria by which they might claim portions of the landscape, and they identified a very old woman as one of the probable "owners." By their criteria, however, the old woman "owned" everything and was the only member eligible for recompense. Since this situation did not provide a meaningful solution to the desire for multiple reimbursements, discussion broke down. In the end, because the Zu/twasi "way" did not include the social practice of claiming land, no one came forward to request reimbursement from the archaeologist.

The old woman, probably by virtue of a long and venerable personal history of land use, had the strongest claim to the land, but when she died, in all probability that linkage was severed rather than inherited by her children or designated heirs. Among the Mbeere of Kenya, once a highly mobile group, the dead were not used to further territorial claims until the colonial government legally recognized such linkages in land claim disputes. Glazier (1984:113) has termed this process "the domestication of death" due to the stark transformation he observed in burial practices. Within a wink of time by archaeological standards, disposition of the dead changed from surface exposure in the bush to interment in underground pits at strategic use-locales on the landscape.

A central thesis of this book is that lowland Maya society "domesticated death" or began the process of naming ancestors and claiming resources during Middle and Late Formative times. These names and claims are not preserved in hieroglyphic texts during the Formative or Classic periods; rather, these "stories" reside in the ancestral remains themselves and the successive refurbishing of residential structures into which ancestors were interred. These are stories long overlooked by the prevailing unitary, elite-focused view of Maya society, but they are narratives well worth telling and represent the first step toward a social history of the ancient Maya.

The practice of forging a link between ancestors and land is not a social process that promotes economic equality, however; by its nature, it is highly exclusionary and promotes inequities in access to resources and status at many levels, from the closeness of the household grouping to the larger arenas of lineage and state. This type of inequality and the power struggles between the forces of kinship and kingship receive close attention in the pages to follow, for they represented powerful forces within Maya society.

This volume has benefited from the support, consideration, and criticism of a host of scholars and staff members, both in the United States and in Belize. The ideas expressed in this book germinated over three seasons of archaeological field work at K'axob (1990, 1992, and 1993), where we have been investigating a case study of the emergence of ancestor veneration. I appreciate the many and long conversations on the topic with my staff and students, including Marilyn Masson, Mary L. Angelini, Hope Henderson, Valerie McCormack, Sandra López Varela, and Annabeth Headrick, and for the continued support and good humor of the landowner, Señor Concepción Campos. Funding for the K'axob Project has come primarily from the National Science Foundation, and I wish to thank John Yellen, review panelists, and anonymous peer reviewers for the vote of confidence in my program of research.

In the specific environment in which this book was written—Dumbarton Oaks—I came to benefit from the intellectual support and challenge of Pre-Columbian Studies director Elizabeth H. Boone and from the frank responses to my research by other fellows at Dumbarton Oaks: Kevin Johnston, Cecelia Klein, Dana Leibsohn, Jeannette Sherbondy, and Craig Clunas. The support staff at Dumbarton Oaks, particularly Bridget Toledo and Carol Calloway, deserve a special note of gratitude.

Portions of drafts of this manuscript have been read by Joyce Marcus, Richard Leventhal, and Stephen Houston, who all gave generously of their time and individual genius to reflect on the ideas of this book. Throughout the many hours of revision and "word-smithing" Joyce, especially, was a continued source of support and inspiration. Intellectual pedigrees often go unacknowledged in prefaces, but as a graduate student at the University of New Mexico I benefited from some of the most interesting and incisive minds in archaeology, and I would like to bow in their direction. First of all, Lewis R. Binford, who fueled my resolve to integrate theory and practice in archaeological research by declaring (often) that Mayanists "do nothing more than dig for chronology"; Robert S. Santley, who in a more finely honed critique of Maya archaeology taught me the importance of sampling and generated a forum for spirited debate among UNM graduate students of the early eighties; Peter D. Harrison, who introduced me to Maya archaeology and from whom I "caught the bug" due to the infectiousness of his ardent enthusiasm and innovative ideas; and finally, and most importantly, to Jeremy A. Sabloff, who has always been "gender blind" in his support of students and who imparted to me his wisdom and analytical acuity particularly in regard to a rigorous concordance between theory and data. While I was a Taft Postdoctoral Fellow at the University of Cincinnati, Rhoda Halperin and Barry Isaac shared with me their holistic vision of economic anthropology and eased my life transition from mentored to mentor. Finally, my eternal gratitude goes to my husband, Thomas W. Killion, from whom great ideas flow like water and who is always ready to discuss archaeology or soothe ruffled feathers.

Washington, D.C., 1993

Living with the Ancestors:
Kinship and Kingship in Ancient Maya Society

Author's Note: Yucatec Mayan orthography used in this work follows R. Blair and R. Vermont Salas. When Colonial Yucatec spellings are presented, they are either in small capitals or closely referenced as Colonial-period.

ONE

A Point of Departure

The Maya lived with their ancestors in a manner that departs radically from twentieth-century western mortuary practices. Rather than distancing themselves physically from the dead—sequestering the ancestors in cemeteries apart from living spaces—they maintained a proximity between the living and the dead. From 1000 B.C. to the early sixteenth century, this subgroup of the first Americans—Maya of the Yucatán Peninsula and Guatemalan highlands (Figure 1.1)—interred their ancestors under the floors of their houses, in residential shrines, and within large funerary pyramids right in the center of their cities and villages. Through a complex series of rituals and sacralization of places, the dead were not forgotten; rather, active lines of communication were maintained between the living and the dead. The deathway of the Maya did not emphasize the termination of life as does the Christian deathway (Metcalf and Huntington 1991); instead, Maya celebrated the continued and pervasive influence of the ancestors in the lives of both rulers and farmers—the life that arises from death (Carlsen and Prechtel 1991:26). Formerly referred to by the antiquated phrase "cult of the dead," this social practice is anything but that. On the contrary, it is about living descendants and their strategies and struggles to chart a course for the future. In this book, I use what I hope is a more appropriate phrase to describe this practice: "living with the ancestors." Communing with deceased progenitors was not a religious experience divorced from political and economic realities (as another antiquated term, "ancestor worship," leads us to believe); rather, it was a practice grounded in pragmatism that drew power from the past, legitimized the current state of affairs (including all the inequities in rights and privileges), and charted a course for the future. Ancestors resided at that critical nexus between past and future, and their presence both materially and symbolically lent weight to the claims of their mere mortal descendants. Because of the important role of ancestor veneration in the context of kin groupings and divine kingship (cf. Feeley-Harnik 1985), a greater understanding of the theory, practice, and material signature of ancestor

1.1a
The Maya region, showing modern political units, selected cities and towns, and major rivers (map drawn by John A. Walkey).

North (N compass indicator)

Inset map (upper left):
Nohmul
Cerros
K'axob
San Estevan
Cuello
Colha
Altun Ha
Lamanai

Main map:
Canul
Dzibilchaltún
Cupul
Mayapán
Chichén Itzá
Cobá
Sotuta
Uxmal
Sayil
Tulum
Tutul Xiu
Uaymil
Yucatec
Tixchel
Dzuluinicob
Río Bec
Calakmul
Nakbe
La Milpa
Chol
Palenque
Piedras Negras
Tikal
Tzotzil
Yaxchilán
Naranjo
Xunantunich
Lacandón
Tah Itzá
Caracol
Tzeltal
Ixil
Seibal
Dos Pilas
Lubaantun
Kekchi
Quiché
Utatlán
Quirigua
Copán
Cakchiquel
Chalchuapa
Ceren

0   100   200
KM

1.1b   The Maya region, showing selected archaeological sites, late
              Postclassic political geography, and Mayan language groups
              (map drawn by John A. Walkey).

veneration will lead to a wider comprehension of the economic, social, and political processes that structured Maya society—commoners and elites alike.

In this study, the first goal is to investigate the web of interrelations among ancestors, lineage, and land (Chapters 1–3). These nested relationships are then examined in reference to secondary variables of social inequality and political power (Chapters 4–5). Drawing upon ethnographic, ethnohistoric, and archaeological sources, I attempt to fashion a synthesis of the general characteristics of Maya ancestor veneration and lineage organization. Documentary texts are used as a point of departure to the "deep history" of the Formative and Classic periods. While the focus of documentary texts is human action, the archaeological record is largely the material "fallout" of human actions (Binford 1983). The wedding of the two often is a search for plausible matches between human action and material residue. My use of documentary sources is geared not toward establishing matches but toward isolating basic principles of lineage organization and ancestral veneration and envisioning methods by which such principles can be linked to their material consequences. The documentary record from the Maya region then helps to establish a range of analytical analogies that may be relevant to our understanding of archaeological patterns.

In the end, my goal is (1) to reveal rather than to reify, and (2) to examine diachronic and synchronic variability rather than to create a static typology of evolutionary forms. Although this book is about "change through time" (i.e., diachronic variability), I do not adopt an evolutionary stance in which I artificially segment ancestor veneration within arbitrary blocks of time associated with stipulated societal forms such as ranked society, chiefdom, or state. I have chosen not to conceptualize my topic in this way for several reasons. First of all, I give process priority over taxonomic concerns because I am examining transformational processes across traditional typological boundaries. Second, I focus on variability in organizational forms across space, e.g., comparing burial practices at the small Belizean site of K'axob to the large center of Tikal. Third, broad typological frameworks, while useful heuristically, often are discordant with specific historical processes, and the latter is given precedence in this study. In a similar vein, the term "state" is seldom used in this study, not because I do not believe that many parts of the Maya region were organized as autonomous states at various times but because I wish to focus on the interaction between areas of differing political centralization. My primary perspective is grounded in less centralized areas with stronger kinship structures; i.e., in this study you will not find a unitary, from-the-top-down perspective on Maya society. Quite to the contrary, I view the realms of kinship and kingship as an arena of conflict.

This book does not claim to be an exhaustive treatise on ancestor veneration; rather, it is an exploration by an archaeologist of what I perceive to have been "an ancient blueprint" (à la Freedman [1966:31]) for Maya living— one that encoded much information about *genealogies of places* (de Certeau 1984) including fields, orchards, and gardens as well as residences and funerary pyramids. If these *genealogies* can be recovered, then our ability to understand the Maya past will be enhanced greatly, whether that reading is based upon hieroglyphic texts, a stratigraphic profile, osteological remains, or macrobotanical specimens. In many respects this book sets up a series of arguments or a theoretical program amenable to further elaboration and "on-the-ground" testing. This research is applicable not only to the Maya lowlands but also to other regions of Mesoamerica, such as the Gulf Coast.

Often noted and frequently chastised for its intellectual parochialism and theoretical naiveté (Marcus 1983), the field of Maya archaeology nonetheless continues to grow, attract more students, and retain its aura of mystery and glamour among lay people. The paradigmatic basis for scholarly research in the Yucatán is diverse, embracing many different schools of thought from the materially based school of cultural ecology to the iconographic emphases of art historians and epigraphers. While paradigmatic clashes often produce growth within a field of study, competing schools of thought in Maya research more frequently result in "separate but equal" programs of archaeological research. It is time for a *rapprochement* between iconographers and anthropologists interested in ideology and economy. This research is one effort toward such a meeting of the minds insomuch as it links human thought and ritual practice with the material bases of life—land resources, boundaries, and so on—the latter being topics that often fall within the domain of cultural ecology. In short, this research represents the new fusion within Maya archaeology which is a hybrid of advances in both epigraphy and field archaeology (Freidel 1993).

Although this study is not cast within an evolutionary/typological framework, the research is spurred by the larger questions of anthropological theory regarding social formations, political power, the bases of factional conflict, and economic processes. Within the social sciences in general, there has been a trend toward the reevaluation of the role of technology and class conflict in noncapitalist contexts and a resultant reduction in the priority of these variables (Brumfiel 1991; Gailey 1987; Giddens 1981). Instead, greater emphasis has been placed on structures of domination grounded in social authority rather than technological superiority and on the dynamics of factional conflict (as opposed to class conflict). Within the theory and practice of archaeology, this reflection (referred to by a number of terms such as postprocessual archaeology, critical archaeology, and symbolic archaeology; e.g., Hodder 1982, 1986, 1987; Miller and Tilley 1984; Shanks and Tilley 1987; Tilley 1990) has engendered an emphasis on the expression of ideology as an active agent of conflict and change rather than an epiphenomenal expression of infrastructural arrangements. The present work represents a modified approach, employing a contextual-based analysis to explore the interweave of ideology, economy, and power. As such, this study is concerned not only with theoretical issues but also with how we frame our questions about the past and detect and read transformation and conflict in this postevolutionary and postprocessual era of methodological and theoretical reevaluation.

Although this book is not directly about change, it does address conflicts attendant upon the emergence of powerful lineages and centralized kingship among lowland Classic Maya. In the past, this type of change has been dichotomized falsely into voluntaristic and coercive scenarios, most notably in a seminal paper by Carneiro (1970a). Dismissing voluntaristic theories of state formation, Carneiro proposed that warfare was the primary mechanism of social inequality and supravillage political integration. The thesis of the present research is that other mechanisms (not so easily dichotomized into voluntaristic and coercive categories), such as the formation of lineal descent groups with their attendant ancestral-focused ritual practices, provided a vehicle for the emergence of social and economic inequality. In view of this perspective, warfare, as an extreme form of social conflict, represents the failure of other mechanisms of differentiation and confederation to promote the legitimacy and acceptance of a new social order. The rituals of ancestor veneration, on the other hand, mitigated social differentiation by providing a rationale of genealogical depth. In other words, the practice of ancestor veneration is one that bridges two kinds of social formations: egalitarian or weakly ranked on the one hand, and strongly ranked or stratified on the other.

PHILOSOPHICAL AND GEOGRAPHICAL
FRAME OF REFERENCE

In Maya research, areas termed "peripheral" to large centers or cities are often perceived as passive recipients of *dicta* issued by the elite *literati* of the big centers. Because elite Maya of the Classic and Postclassic periods left behind so much physical material relevant to their wishes, desires, edicts, building programs, and so on, often we have failed to note the fact that, in all probability, there were factional conflicts in every realm of Maya life. How do we investigate these hypothesized dissenting voices, particularly those of the commoners who did not participate in "elite" culture? Heads of nonelite lineages, for example, did not leave behind hieroglyphic texts because they did not attend the "schools" for elite children in which such skills were taught. Settlement archaeology is one approach that allows us to document the structures of both the "humble" and elite Maya

(Webster and Gonlin 1988), but modest structures and small settlements are more likely to be analyzed in terms of what they lack (i.e., stelae, inscriptions, standing architecture, polychrome vessels, and so forth) rather than what they have.

Here, rather than looking to the cities to explain the smaller settlements, I adopt a perspective in which villages and towns are the primary focus and the city is seen as the aberration. Particularly relevant to this approach is the archaeological site of K'axob, a place to which I turn for exemplary material periodically throughout this study. Located in northern Belize on a patch of high terrain between the New River and the southern arm of Pulltrouser Swamp (Figure 1.1), K'axob is a pioneer community with roots stretching back to 1000 B.C. The place persisted as a village of about one hundred structures well into the Terminal Classic (McAnany n.d.), with the construction of pyramidal architecture well into the Late Classic. Material remains from K'axob suggest that it was a community that was neither fabulously wealthy nor impoverished. With its ubiquitous pattern of multiplatform dwellings arranged around central patios, it seems to have been a community held together by the web of kinship (McAnany 1986). But it was not an egalitarian village; by 400 B.C. (and perhaps earlier) certain individuals were accorded special burial treatment while others were interred with simple grave goods under the floors of Formative structures. This pattern persists through the Classic period, leading one to ask how the inhabitants of K'axob dealt with the emerging differences in rank and stratification evolving at the large centers. Did K'axob maintain political autonomy, or did it become a dependency of the nearby centers of Nohmul, San Estevan, or the more distant Naranjo? Does the construction of raised fields along the western margin of the settlement (Turner and Harrison 1981, 1983) indicate (1) incorporation into a wider political economy with attendant taxation obligations, (2) population outstripping available land resources, or (3) some type of agricultural specialization (McAnany 1992)? K'axob provides a geographical and philosophical backdrop to this study: a small, perhaps politically autonomous place in the eastern Maya lowlands. In many respects, this book is a companion volume to an upcoming K'axob monograph in which a thesis of this study—that the practice of ancestor veneration is linked to the entrenchment of resource rights—is examined in light of archaeological data from Formative-period K'axob.

PRIMARY THEMES

The basic postulate of this work is that ancestor veneration was a critically important organizing force in all sectors of Maya society—among commoners and nobles alike. Among Mayanists, rarely has this force been discussed in contexts other than elite genealogies and royal succession; some scholars have even suggested that the social practice of ancestor veneration and concepts of the afterlife were lacking among the non-elite Maya (Carlson 1981:190; Coggins 1988:66). On the contrary, ritual practices attendant upon this institution provided a structural charter for the organization of social, political, and economic arenas of action. The following three themes of action and conflict structure my research.

(1) Ancestor veneration, through lineage organization, charted and legitimized resource rights through the mechanisms of oral memory, written records, and, most importantly, the continued physical presence of buried ancestors in domestic complexes which were, in effect, a type of *domestic mausolea*. Residences and their circumambient spaces were the repositories of ancestral remains. As such, these places were potent links to the past as well as important items of inheritance. Maya expressed their genealogies not only in hieroglyphic script but also in the physical use and reuse of places.

I propose that exclusionary and inherited resource rights go hand in hand with the genesis of ancestor veneration. In other words, strong links to past ancestors also provided nearly unassailable rights and privileges. These included access to land, water, tracts of "forest," and other inheritable goods, properties, and resources. Historical misinterpretations of lowland tropical agriculture, starting with the translation of Maya texts from the early Colonial period (see discussion in Chapter 3), have imposed a barrier to creating a synthetic theory of Maya agriculture, land tenure, and transgenerational inheritance. By approaching the topic of land tenure by way of ancestral veneration, it is possible to build a more holistic model of land and lineage in Maya society.

(2) The social practice of keeping ancestors within the realm of the living to legitimize the claims of their descendants also provided a rationale for emergent and existent social inequality. In reference to the Megaliths of western Europe, Renfrew (1983:159, 162) has termed these monuments "tombs for the living" and has noted that communities with such monumental territorial markers must have had an "adaptive advantage." Through ancestors, resource rights and privileges were viewed in the conservative light of precedents set by progenitors. This transgenerational quality is critically important to the crystallization of new social forms. It is what Giddens (1981:34) has termed "the problems of the generations—or how the dead make their influence felt upon the practices of the living."

In anthropological literature, lineage development is often viewed as a mechanism by which social groups are split into many segments (Fox 1987; Sahlins 1961; Southall 1957); however, ethnographic accounts also indicate that lineage structures promote the perpetuity of land tenure systems and, in doing so, augment the partial or total alienation of certain social segments from access to resources (Johnson and Earle 1987: 190). In Chapter 4, I examine how the corporate nature of lineal social structure provides a viable mechanism of societal differentiation which could, quite easily, become institutionalized.

(3) Maya lineage heads, variously called *ah kuch kabob, councilors,* or *regidores* in the ethnohistoric literature, were politically powerful heads of kin-organized groups that engaged in dynamic conflictive as well as accommodative relations with centralizing political forces in Maya society—the ruler or *ahaw* of the southern lowlands Late Formative and Classic periods and the *HALACH UINIC* of Postclassic northern Yucatán. This older form of lineage leadership, organizing commoners as well as nobles, persisted into the Postclassic and was an institution that crosscut rank and class. For the most part, organizational structures of this type have not been envisioned as part of Classic Maya society, yet ethnohistoric records (discussed below) document clearly that it was the *ah kuch kab* who organized production and collection of tribute in Postclassic northern Yucatán. Given the recent decipherment of hieroglyphic texts as well as the discovery of iconography suggestive of endemic interpolity conflict and cycles of conquest (Culbert 1991; Schele and Freidel 1990), we can speculate that the collection of tribute was not a practice foreign to Classic-period kings. In such a context, local leaders such as lineage heads would have played an important role in lowland Maya polities.

The hypothesis of persistent tension between "kinship" and "kingship" (Gailey 1987) is here applied to the Maya region (Chapter 5) with profound implications for our models of Classic-period geopolitics. The existence of this tension (centripetal vs. centrifugal) appears to have been highly variable across time and space in the Maya region. At any point in time, rulers and autonomous lineage heads existed side by side, while other lineage heads were subordinates of the rulers. This pattern certainly existed during the Postclassic period, and a case will be made here that this relationship prevailed during the Classic period as well. Fundamentally expressive of the conflictive relationship between kinship and kingship is the distinctive role of ancestor veneration within royal dynasties. That is, its ritual expression is *not* just veneration of lineage heads writ large but rather is structurally different in the manner in which genealogy was encoded in written texts and iconography. It is also distinct in that ancestors were invoked to substantiate claims to divinity as well as to the royal prerogative to tax and to draft labor and warriors. In this regard, royal ancestor veneration is an appropriation of a Formative social practice that emerged within an agrarian milieu. In Chapters 2 and 5, the contrastive role of ancestors among kin groups and divine kings is discussed in detail. Carlson's (1981:190) advocacy of the separation of "ancestor worship and funerary practices of the elite from those involving the common man" is correct in the sense that elite ancestor veneration was qualitatively different from that practiced by nonelite kin groups; however, he is incorrect in assuming that ancestor veneration and principles guiding ancestral interment were not present among the YALBA UINICOB or commoners (Roys 1943:34).

The intertwined topics of ancestor veneration and lineage structure have a history of impressive anthropological research in Asia, Africa, and the Americas. I am indebted intellectually to this corpus of work, and I hope this study amplifies and enriches earlier research. Below, some of this literature is examined in order to (1) establish a comparative base and (2) indicate the manner in which my research diverges from previous treatment of ancestors and lineage.

THEORY AND DEFINITION:
ANCESTOR VENERATION AND LINEAGE

In the first half of the twentieth century, the topic of kinship organization was particularly popular within social anthropology. As societies in Africa, Asia, and the Americas came under the scrutiny of European- and North American–trained anthropologists, it became clear that, for many of these groups, the practices and rituals of dealing with the dead assumed pivotal importance, not just for the duration of the funeral but throughout the life of the survivors. Transmission of property, rights, and privileges was as inextricably linked to death and ancestral veneration as was the crystallization, on a transgenerational scale, of inequalities in access to resources both within and among lineages. In this section, relevant aspects of seminal studies of lineage and ancestor veneration in Africa and Asia are discussed. Then, the manner in which these studies were adapted to the Americas (outside of the Maya region) using the medium of ethnohistory and archaeology is explored. The following chapter is devoted to the study of ancestor veneration in the Maya region exclusively.

Africa and Asia

Since ancestral deities and attention to ancestors are nearly universal social traits, more rigorous definitions have been sought for the practice of ancestor veneration. Drawing upon ethnographic field research among the Tallensi, Fortes (1987:79) defined the legal aspects of an institution that he called "ancestor worship" as "a body of religious beliefs and ritual practices, correlated with rules of conduct, which serves to en-trench the principle of jural authority together with its corollary, legitimate right, and its reciprocal, designated accountability, as an indisputable and sacrosanct value-principle of the social system." More importantly, Fortes (1987:72) goes on to clarify the distinction between "ancestor worship" and the so-called "cult of the dead" in the following way: "An ancestral 'spirit' is not thought of as a kind of nebulous being or personified mystical presence but primarily as a name attached to a relic . . . standing for ritual validation of lineage ancestry and for mystical intervention in human affairs." In other words, Fortes (1987:67) argued that the term "ancestor worship" or "veneration" should be limited to those groups who commemorate ancestors by name and not extended to those who display a general attention to spirits of the dead.

Freedman (1966:145) uses the term "cult of immediate jural superiors" to contrast groups who show concern with the dead (e.g., the Manus as studied by Fortune [1935]) from those who practice ancestor veneration. In a comparative study of Melanesian religions, Lawrence and Meggitt (1965:8) also distinguish between totemic forebears of named unilineal descent groups and totems from which no descent is claimed but which are adopted as badges by named groups because of some past association. Based on his studies of kinship in the Chinese provinces of Fukien and Kwantung, Freedman (1966: 153) has drawn a further distinction between "ancestor worship as a set of rights linking together all the agnatic descendants of a given forebear (the cult of the descent groups) on the one hand, and ancestor worship as the independent tendance [sic] and commemoration of forebears as it were for their own sake, on the other." For the purposes at hand, the following definition of ancestor veneration is employed: *rituals and practices surrounding the burial and commemoration, by name, of apical ancestors of kin groups.*

From ethnographic research on ancestor veneration in Africa and Asia, one point in particular is perfectly clear: only specific individuals within a descent line become ancestors (Fortes 1987:71; Freedman 1970). That is, the practice of ancestor veneration and the rituals surrounding the treatment of the dead are not extended equally to all members of a lineage; rather, they are employed preferentially when particularly important and influential members of a lineage die. This pattern is consistent throughout the Americas also, including in the Maya region.

From an archaeological perspective, a critical characteristic of ancestor veneration is that of protracted burial rites. A corpse may be interred only to be exhumed at a later date; Freedman (1966) vividly describes such practices in the "New Territories" of south China: hillsides were covered with pots containing skeletal material that had been exhumed from a primary burial. This secondary context may be the final resting place for less esteemed ancestors, while important forebears of powerful lineages would eventually be entombed in a tertiary burial crypt. At any one of these stages, skeletal parts may be lost or removed so that the final interment of skeletal material from an esteemed ancestor rarely contained 100 percent of the skeleton. Among the LoDagaa of Africa, Goody (1962) describes the elaborate ritual surrounding the protracted burial practices through which a once-living member of the community is transformed into an ancestor. Goody notes that the death of an important family member necessitates the transmission of property, rights, and duties to the inheritors, and, as the group dynamics of competition over inheritance are played out, burial rituals help to smooth over an extremely stressful time for the living. The complex rituals and practices of ancestor veneration have been characterized by Humphreys (1981: 268) in the following way: "secondary burial rituals increase the room for manoeuvre in those aspects of funerary rites which are concerned with renewing, reorganizing and relegitimising relations among the living." Furthermore, in the context of ancestor veneration, the physical remains of a powerful deceased person continue to have potency. Because of this quality, bones of ancestors are often curated by living descendants and can command a prominent place within the household, as Taylor and Aragon (1991) document for the outer islands of Indonesia. Ethnohistoric sources suggest similar practices for ancient Mesoamerica, yet the taphonomic effects of such practices on mortuary assemblages are seldom acknowledged in the archaeological analysis of osteological remains.

In China, the eventual entombment of important ancestors is carried out in accord with a type of geomancy called *feng-shui,* a technique for siting graves and buildings using astrological reckonings (Feuchtwang 1974; Freedman 1966 : 125). Thus, tomb placement on the landscape of China was not done in a haphazard manner. Once a tomb was built, periodic rituals were carried out at the tomb site; Freedman (1970 : 172) has described the public, male-dominated nature of rituals surrounding tombs of apical ancestors, contrasting them with the domestic practice of ancestor veneration in which the female is the principal actor. *Feng-shui* ensures not only that the tomb is placed appropriately but also that it is safeguarded. In interlineage rivalry "the surest way to destroy a rival for good is to tear open his ancestral tomb and pulverize the bones they contain. . . . bones *are* descent; without them one is cut off from the most powerful source of ancestral benefits" (Freedman 1966 : 139; emphasis added). According to Feuchtwang (1974), the bones of ancestors can become, literally, bones of contention in the conflict between the centralized powers of the Chinese state and rebelling factions; insurgencies were quelled by neutralizing the *feng-shui* of rebel factions through the pillage of their ancestral shrines. In reference to the Classic-period elite Maya, Carlson (1981), among others, has suggested that the skeletal remains of

Maya royalty were interred following a Mesoamerican variant of geomancy—an idea echoed by Ashmore (1991), who has examined the integration of Maya cosmology and cardinality with the placement of the deceased.

The truly universal aspect of ancestor veneration in Chinese society, however, is found in domestic shrines. Here, important ancestors of the preceding three to four generations, symbolized by ancestral tablets, are commemorated (Freedman 1970:164). In this context, it is the female who conducts the rituals of ancestor veneration, which include special commemoration of the birth date of the ancestor and offerings of preferred food and drink (Freedman 1970:173). Often a woman will intercede on behalf of an ancestor's descendant to ask the forebear to ensure protection or harmony. By gender of the agent of ritual, the domestic context of ancestor veneration contrasts with the ancestor halls of China, which are emphatically the domain of males. Built only by very successful lineages, these halls contain ancestral tablets of considerably greater genealogical depth than those contained in the domestic shrines. Freedman (1966:4) specifically refers to a hall with a record of ancestors stretching back forty-two generations. These halls consist of "a building put up and maintained by a patrilineal group to house their ancestor tablets and serve as the center of ritual and secular activities" (Freedman 1970:168). Essentially men's clubs, Freedman notes that few women ever set foot inside an ancestral hall and, not surprisingly, a low number of ancestral tablets of females are housed there.

In patrilineal systems such as China, a deceased male head-of-household who is a member of a wealthy lineage receives preferential treatment such that his bones are more likely to be entombed and his tablet more likely to be enshrined in the ancestral hall for many future generations (Freedman 1966). Despite this fairly strong gender bias, females do participate in these social practices, both as agents of ritual and as objects of veneration. Bones of important female forebears are entombed, particularly when the patriline desires to emphasize connections with the lineage of the female. In the domestic shrine, tablets of female and male forebears are displayed with equal reverence. Moreover, the female is the important agent of ritual in the context of the domestic shrine, while her male counterpart dominates the more public rituals conducted at the tomb and in the ancestral halls (Freedman 1970:173).

The practice of ancestor veneration is linked intricately with special considerations of place. In the "New Territories" of China, there were four physical locales of ancestral veneration (Freedman 1970): (1) domestic shrines, tended by women and containing tablets commemorative of both males and females; (2) ancestral halls of successful lineages, which were primarily male-oriented in commemoration and ritual practice; (3) the defleshing grounds of the dead, the final "resting place" for many of the deceased; and (4) burial

1.2   Tombs of ancestors in the countryside of China (from Freedman
        1966).

tombs physically disassociated from the residence, where the bones of important ancestors were interred and where public rituals were conducted by
males (Figure 1.2). Thus, the transport of skeletal remains from the defleshing ground to a tomb signifies the transition from a deceased relative to an
ancestor. In Mesoamerica, on the other hand, the common practice of interring dead ones within the heart of cities and villages not only blurred the
distinction between deceased relatives and ancestors but also promoted ritual
practices that lacked the gender hierarchy so explicit in the Chinese pattern.

    In studies of ancient Maya society, the importance of ancestor veneration
as an agent of legitimation is being recognized increasingly not only in hieroglyphic texts of royal dynasties but also in nonelite residential compounds.
Ancestor veneration, however, does not exist in a vacuum; rather, it is
the quintessential expression of lineage structure. As Freedman (1966:118)
notes,"ancestor worship . . . threw certain organizational principles of the
lineage into relief and expressed ideas central to the competition within, and
the unity of, the lineage communities." Likewise, Southall (1957:111) comments on "ancestor worship" among the African chiefdoms of the Alur: "It
is not surprising that the Alur ideas of the relationship of lineage and of their
development through time find more consistent expression in the ritual context of ancestor worship than in the welter of political activity." Finally, ancestor veneration has been identified as a unifying force in segmentary systems of exogamous localized groupings such as those documented in Africa

by the classic studies of Fortes (1965) among the Tallensi and Goody (1962) among the LoDagaa. Thus, ancestor veneration is a potent ritual through which lineage membership is expressed.

The writings of neo-evolutionists stress the importance of descent groups as a vehicle of social differentiation and the nexus of residential clusters (Fortes 1953; Fried 1967; Service 1971; Weber 1947). Service (1971:109) distinguishes between residential groups formed by unilineal descent groups (the "lineal tribe") and those formed by marital residence rules without descent reckoning ("bands"). Fried (1967:125) examined ranked societies held together by kinship ties among residential groups. While ostensibly not stratified economically, ranked societies nevertheless were noted to be somewhat exclusive in that lineages offered members shared access to restricted resources. The most commonly cited characteristic of residential descent groups, however, is a shared concern with genealogy, defined by Freedman (1966:31) as "a set of claims to origin and relationships, a charter, a map of dispersion, a framework for wide-ranging social organization, a blueprint for action . . . a political statement." Genealogies provide not only a means by which descent can be reckoned and the web of kinship defined in an exclusive manner, but they also provide a "blueprint for action" in terms of the intergenerational transmission of property, rights, and duties upon the death of powerful members of the lineage. The close linkage between genealogical reckoning and resource rights—in this case, land—has been emphasized by Southall (1957:65) in reference to the chiefdoms of the African Alur: "The few clans which have maintained or achieved complete territorial integrity have, not surprisingly, preserved or involved more highly consistent genealogical charters which are symbolic of it." Thus, although the lineage may not always have a spatial or territorial integrity, more often than not it is anchored both symbolically and materially to the use of a particular landscape.

The construction of genealogies that mitigate competition for resources has a resonance when applied to the Maya lowlands, where there was a striking increase in population over the first millennium A.D. and where the inhabitants employed a variety of strategies to encode and preserve genealogical information. These strategies included repetitive, transgenerational occupation and refurbishing of household compounds (in which ancestors were interred); successive interment of the dead in ancestral shrines and pyramids (Coe 1956); protracted treatment of the dead with display of skeletal parts and ashes in wooden and clay icons (Tozzer 1941); and iconography and script replete with references to ancestors (e.g., Ashmore 1991; Houston 1989; Lounsbury 1974; Schele and Freidel 1990; Schele and Miller 1986).

The rituals and rules of intergenerational transmission of resources, privileges, and obligations is an important part of lineage organization. Most ethnographers who have studied lineage structure have focused on this very public (and easily recorded) aspect of lineage. Upon the death of a leading lineage member, property and goods are passed down to the next generation according to the customs of the lineage (Freedman 1966; Goody 1962; Southall 1957). For instance, it was common among Chinese lineages studied by Freedman (1966:150) for all sons to inherit equal portions of land, but the eldest son inherited the residence and, along with the head residence, the ancestor shrine. In this way, there is generational continuity in the residence, a feature that, over the long run, is archaeologically visible as a sequence of occupation and refurbishing. Haviland (1988), in fact, has noted such characteristics in the residential groupings of Tikal. Lineages exist not in episodic but in durational time—the *longue durée* of Braudel (1980)—and thus are appropriate analytical units for archaeological research.

Given their potential for longevity, lineages are neither synchronic nor static social formations, even though the bulk of our knowledge about these structures derives from short-term ethnographic studies. Lineages can undergo rapid or slow cycles of growth, dissolution, or coalescence with other lineages. While less prosperous ones may die out altogether, generally due to demographic factors, other lineages enjoy a longevity that seems legendary by twentieth-century Western standards, such as the forty-two generations of commemorated ancestors documented by Freedman (1966:4). Smith (1959: 191), likewise, noted the antiquity of family ties in rural Tokugawa-period Japanese villages by observing that relatively new immigrants had found that older, established families (who monopolized all the good agricultural land) had been in the village for several hundred years. These ethnographic examples further clarify the notion that lineages, rather than being ephemeral social formations, can persist on a scale of time that is long enough to be detected *archaeologically,* given that our phases often span two hundred years or more.

Americas

In the Americas of the Pre-Hispanic and Colonial periods, the critical role of the ancestors in social practice and resource rights has been recreated from a fragmentary archaeological record; ethnohistoric accounts of *entradas,* missionization efforts, and land litigation; and a core of principles and cosmological perspectives that survived the Spanish invasion. Outside of the Maya region, research focused on the practices of "living with the ancestors" has been most prominent in the Andean region of South America and in the Oaxacan (Zapotec) area of Mesoamerica.

We have long known that ancestral veneration was an important aspect of imperial Andean societies, since a mummified ancestor carried on a litter was one of a host of potent images of royal Inka culture provided by Guaman Poma (1980; see also Zuidema 1973). It is increasingly clear, however, that ancestors also played a fundamental role in *ayllu* organization (nonroyal, landholding corporate groups of the Andes). The Huarochirí manuscript, a colonial document compiled by Father Francisco de Avila "who seems to have used it as secret intelligence for his assault on American deities from 1608 onward" (Salomon 1991 : 1) is especially relevant here. The *ayllu* defined itself most clearly in terms of its ancestor-focused kindred; it included lineages but was not always unilineal (see Spalding 1984 : 28–29) and frequently formed a portion of a multi-*ayllu* settlement (Salomon 1991 : 22). As suggested in the Huarochirí manuscript, inclusion within an *ayllu* was open to political negotiation and not based on hard-and-fast kinship reckoning. Specifically, "One can see in the myths of Concha *ayllu* . . . that genealogical connection alone was insufficient to bestow land on the two Concha lineages that had become politically disconnected. But adoption combined with political or marital alliance was seen as sufficient to create *ayllu* entitlements even when there was no genealogical tie" (Chap. 31, Sec. 403; Salomon 1991 : 23). In short, the *ayllu* was a political entity with the ancestor-focused imagery and *huacas* (superhuman persons, shrines, or holy and powerful objects) serving as "framing activities" (Douglas 1966 : 63–64) for economic matters.

As Sherbondy (1982 : 22) notes, water rights and canals in the Cuzco area were controlled by the *ayllu* rather than by individual families. The manner in which ancestors were invoked to substantiate these claims again clarifies the inextricable linkage between ancestors and proprietary resource rights:

> These rights are based on claims that their lands and waters were originally distributed to them by the founders of the *ayllus*. Whether the founding ancestors are deities or real human beings is not important for defining rights. It is only essential to be able to make a claim to lands and waters by citing an ancestor. In the case of a conflict with another *ayllu*, the older ancestor has precedence.
>
> . . . the ancestors who were responsible for giving the source of water to the *ayllu* or who constructed the canal system are called the "owners" (the *"dueños"* in Spanish).[1] (SHERBONDY 1982 : 22)

So, although the *ayllus*, strictly speaking, are not descent groups, the rights to water are passed down to descendants through *ayllu* membership.

Based on passages in the Huarochirí manuscript, Salomon (1991:19) addresses the manner in which *huacas* are the "spacial [sic] foci of superhuman and human genealogy," particularly as that genealogy is "symbolized by shrines called *pacarinas* or 'dawning places' that represented founders' and heroes' appearances on earth." Thus, physical landmarks within the territory of an *ayllu* embody the social identity of a group and their genealogical history within such a territory much in the same way as the *warabal ja* or lineage shrines of the highland Quiché Maya establish a charter for local resource use (see Chapter 2).

According to the Huarochirí manuscript, mummified ancestors were kept in caves or special stone structures (Chap. 11, Sec. 155, Salomon 1991:20), establishing a sacred geography that linked territorial places to ancestral time. "The pre-resettlement scheme of territoriality, a mental map of social groups attached to place-deities and localized ancestors, still formed a complete and intelligible shadow-geography projected onto the landscape that colonial organizations had already reshaped *de facto*" (Salomon 1991:23). Likewise, the Quechua word for village, *llacta*, is not simply a function of demography and geography. Rather, the term encompasses what Salomon (1991:23) refers to as a triple entity of a "localized *huaca* (often an ancestor-deity), with its territory and with the group of people whom the *huaca* favored."

The *ayllu* was not an institution of equality; ranking was omnipresent within the structure of the *ayllu*. So deeply did the ideology of inequality permeate the *ayllu* that deviations from rank ordering required long explanations. Such a qualifying description occurs in Supplement 1 of the Huarochirí manuscript, which contains a long description of "the birth of human siblings whose rank order closely approached equality—that is, twins" (Salomon 1991:21).

The recording of ancestral genealogies is a leitmotif of hierarchically organized groups both in South America and in Mesoamerica. In the latter region, particularly among the Zapotec and Mixtec, genealogies were key to the maintenance of elite status. Such constructions of history continued into the Spanish Colonial period as elites strove to maintain their noble status through petitions to the Colonial authorities (Whitecotton 1990:133). So intertwined was the scribal act of writing with the recording of genealogy that "the Zapotec word for book or document—*quichi tija colaca* (Córdova 1942:244v)—means 'paper of old lineage people' or simply 'paper of my ancestors'" (Whitecotton 1990:133). One preserved document of Zapotec genealogy, that of the Hispanic Society of New York City, indicates the temporal depth of such systems of ancestral reckoning; in a series of bands "fifteen generations of paired individuals (females on the left, males on the right)" are portrayed (Whitecotton 1990:15). The metaphor of ancestors as emergent from the trunk of a tree is shown in the Codex Vienna (Marcus 1992:274) and is also usefully employed in royal genealogies of the Maya ruler Pakal. Further information specific to ancestor veneration comes from a reinterpretation of the accounts of early chroniclers and missionaries in the Zapotec area who collected the names of local "deities" often by reference to material icons which Spaniards termed "ídolos" (idols). Marcus (1978; Marcus and Flannery 1994) has challenged the notion that the diversity of names given to these icons represents a Zapotec cosmos inhabited by a pantheon of gods in the sense of Classic Greek and Roman pantheons. Rather, she suggests that many of the names of revered individuals recorded by early chroniclers and missionaries were actually the names of apotheosized ancestors. Ancestor veneration is deeply rooted among the Zapotec, where the practice may have emerged as long ago as the Early Formative (1150–850 B.C.) and was represented by figurines (referred to as *penigolazaa* or "old people of the clouds") which have been found at the sites of San José Mogote, Tierras Largas, Abasolo, Huitzo, and Tomaltepec (Marcus and Flannery 1994).

Significantly, the transition from the village-based ancestral veneration of the Formative to the veneration of royal ancestors within the context of a state religion centered at Monte Albán was not a seamless fusion; rather, the process is marked by the disappearance of the small solid figurines and the transformation of the fire-serpent and were-jaguar motifs (Marcus and Flannery 1994). In other words, state appropriation of ancestor veneration was not simply an amplification of village-based practices but was symptomatic of a fundamental restructuring of the power relationships to which certain ancestors lent tacit consent. That is, the salient links between ancestors, lineage, and land were weakened at the same time that a smaller subset of royal ancestors became increasingly important in providing a bridge between generations in the transmission of political power.

With the emergence of the Zapotec state, "ancestors" were increasingly associated with large, elaborate residential structures (Caso 1938, 1969; Winter 1974). Tombs at Monte Albán were family crypts, reopened and repainted several times (Flannery and Marcus 1983). In residential complexes at nearby Lambityeco, Lind and Urcid (1983) have found iconographic as well as burial evidence which supports the notion that ancestral veneration was central to the Zapotec. Excavations at one elite residential locale (Mound 195) in particular revealed the remains of six successive elite houses with three associated tombs, one of which was fronted by a frieze (Lind and Urcid 1983:79). The iconographic content of the frieze illustrates the importance of ancestral depiction: "Each of the male figures in the lower friezes carries a human femur in his hand—the femur of his ancestor, a symbol of his hereditary right to rule" (Lind and Urcid 1983:80 and their Fig. 5). This complex also contained a two-meter-high altar complex and a family mausoleum (Tomb 6) built on top of a 1.5-meter-high stone-faced platform. Osteological analysis served to support the iconography; that is, femora, in particular, were underrepresented in the multiple and secondary burials of elite Tomb 6 (Lind and Urcid 1983:81). This conflation of residential, ritual, and burial contexts is characteristic of much of Mesoamerica. Although the Spanish missionaries of the sixteenth and later centuries forced the separation of the dead from the domiciles of their descendants, ancestors are still perceived as residing in the house among the highland Quiché (Bunzel 1952). Among the highland Mixtec, the word *vehe* refers to both "house" and "grave" (J. Monaghan, pers. com. 1992).

Examination of ethnographic, ethnohistoric, and archaeological research among societies of the Americas as well as Africa and Asia indicates that the rituals of ancestor veneration knit the political and economic spheres together with the ideological sphere in a way that very few social practices have the capacity to do. This summary, not intended as a comprehensive literature review, establishes the intellectual "common ground" of the themes of ancestors, lineage, land, power, and kingship. As applied to the Maya regions, this avenue of research is capable of producing a more holistic view of Maya society. This expanded perspective can provide a basis for modeling expectations of the archaeological record not only in regard to investigations of elite, architectural contexts.

GENERAL SOURCES ALONG THE
SPACE-TIME CONTINUUM

Subsequent chapters follow the themes of ancestor veneration, lineage, land, inequality, and power into the Maya region. In doing so, a concerted effort has been made to consult major references in four categories of Maya scholarship relevant to these topics. These categories are (1) ethnographic texts; (2) ethnohistoric texts; (3) Maya texts such as the books of Chilam Balam and the Dresden, Madrid, Paris, and Grolier codices, as well as legal disputes and boundary settlements; and (4) archaeological literature, including analyses of artifacts, structures, and settlement as well as transliterations and interpretations of hieroglyphic texts and iconography.

Each category has its own geographic and, of course, temporal strengths; for instance, ethnographic sources are rich for highland Chiapas, Guatemala, and northern Yucatán, whereas ethnohistoric texts are abundant for sixteenth-century northern Yucatán, the Chontalpa, and highland Guatemala. While the exact provenience is unknown for the Maya codices, it is generally accepted that they are all pre-Hispanic, and except for the Codex Grolier, which apparently came from a dry cave in Chiapas (Coe 1973), the codices originated in the Yucatán-Campeche area. While Thompson (1972: 15) favored a date of about A.D. 1200–1250 for the Codex Dresden, suggesting that it was a Postclassic version of a Classic-period document, Paxton (1986) has argued that a more recent date is also possible. The lion's share of archaeological data comes from survey, excavation, and iconographic documentation at sites in the Petén region of northern Guatemala, along the Usumacinta River, modern-day Belize, and the southeastern zone of Copán. Areas such as northern Yucatán, the western riverine regions of Chontalpa, and the Guatemalan highlands are underrepresented because less archaeological research focused on the Classic and Formative periods has been conducted in these areas.

Some readers may be startled by the manner in which archaeological examples from the Formative period are juxtaposed, within the same breath, with documentary materials from Colonial times or recent ethnographic observations. While not denigrating the importance of temporal control in Maya studies, I do believe that social practices can be studied both in their historical specificity and across the space-time continuum. As the title of this book suggests, the boundaries between the past and the present are rarely as absolute as the western positivist perspective would suggest. There are certain societal structures—"armatures," as Hunt (1977:248) referred to them— that persevere and, in fact, transcend historical incident. The coalescence of lineage and locality in the practice of ancestor veneration is one such cosmologically robust and temporally pervasive structure.

TWO

Ancestor Veneration and Lineage Organization in the Maya Region

Ancestors and lineage are ubiquitous themes that pervade the ethnographic and ethnohistoric literature of Yucatán. The extent to which these themes exerted a powerful influence on everything from dynastic succession to the placement of fields and orchards will be demonstrated in this chapter and those to follow. Here, principles, practices, and places of ancestor veneration and lineage organization throughout the Maya region are discussed in order to establish the presence and importance of these institutions.

ANATOMY OF A LINEAGE

By A.D. 1547, Spaniards had succeeded in gaining a foothold in northern Yucatán. One of their first actions was to divide the land into *encomiendas* that were bestowed as spoils of conquest on the Spanish adventurers (Farriss 1984).[1] Shortly thereafter, the Spanish Crown asked for detailed descriptions of the occupied lands: geography, hydrology, crop production, crop potential, and presence of metals and precious stones, as well as descriptions of the population and political history of the current occupants. Having very limited knowledge of the partially subjugated Maya population, many of the *encomenderos* relied on the literate Maya Gaspar Antonio Chi to "ghostwrite" the historical portion of their reports or *relaciones geográficas*. The following excerpt from the *Relación de Cansahcab*, a document compiled between 1579 and 1581, reveals the importance of both lineage and ancestral funerary pyramids in pre-Columbian Yucatecan society:

> This land appears to have been well populated, because throughout it there is not a palm [*sic*] of land which has not been cultivated and occupied by large and medium buildings of stone and vaulted houses,

very well built. And according to what the Indians say, and as it appeared from their histories, the natives descend from those who made the said edifices. And there is in the land the lineage of them, who descend in direct line from the said ancients. Others say that they [the builders of these structures] were foreigners who settled in it [the land], and that the natives put an end to them and killed them. And both [natives and foreigners] were heathen and were buried under great hills which they made of stone and under pyramids and edifices that they made for them.

(TRANSLATION BY ROYS 1962:54)

Lineage and ancestry, likewise, are extolled in the opening chapter of the *Chilam Balam of Chumayel,* entitled "The Ritual of the Four World-Quarters," which contains a listing of the first lineages and the names of their founding ancestors: Ah Canul of the Canul lineage, Ix-Kan-Tacay of the Puch lineage, and so forth (Roys 1967:64–66; Scholes and Roys 1938:609). Michael Coe (1965:105–106) has suggested that this passage is a *précis* of the Uayeb or New Year Ceremonies in which named lineages from the four quarters of a settled place rotated responsibility (in the office of *holpop*) for the processionals, banquets, and care of one of the four icons of the New Year. His suggestion is supported by the fact that from three to five patronymics are listed for each direction (M. Coe 1965:105); even more significant, this interpretation of the Uayeb ceremonies suggests a territorial dimension to lineages.

In Yucatec society, founding lineages held a dominant position, and a specific term, *yax ch'ibal* or "first lineage," was used to refer to them (Roys 1957:12) and to distinguish them from the numerous lines of lower-ranking lineages. The nature and number of lineages in northern Yucatán has been provided by Roys:

A very important feature of Yucatecan Maya society was what might be called the name group. Every person of either sex had a patronymic, and the bearers of the same patronymic constituted a recognized group. This was called *ch'ibal* ("lineage in the male line"), and *the Maya thought of it and called it, a lineage.* Some of these lineages certainly, and probably many of them, had their own patron deities, a number of whom seem to have been *deified ancestors.* . . . More

than 250 Maya patronymics have been collected from
the colonial records and those of more recent times,
as well as from the Maya manuscripts.

(ROYS 1957:4; EMPHASIS ADDED)[2]

Among elite sectors of Yucatec Maya society, lineage structures persevered throughout the ravages and population dislocations of the Colonial period. Thus, in 1662 when Juan Xiu petitioned the representative of the Spanish Crown for the right to carry a musket, he testified that "this should be granted to me because it was we, the people of my *lineage,* who brought back the bones of Mirones and the chalice which they took in former times with the church furnishings" (Morley 1941:507, Doc. 35; emphasis added).[3]

As Roys (1967:5) has noted, the lineage name was a patronymic and passed through the male line, but Maya society was not a patriarchy in the strict sense of the word since importance was given to matronymics, referred to as *naal* or "mother's name." Furthermore, the term for noble, *almehen,* was a compound of *al* ("a woman's offspring") and *mehen* ("a man's progeny"; Roys 1943:33). Patronymics seldom described the occupation of lineage members in the way that European surnames, such as Mason or Carpenter, did. Rather, Maya lineages adopted the names of plants, mammals, insects, reptiles, and fishes (Roys 1957:45, 1967:9 and his Table 1). There is no ethnohistoric evidence, however, that these animals or plants were considered representative of the essence of the lineage in the same way that Houston and Stuart (1989) have interpreted the meaning of the *way* glyph as representative of a naturalistic co-essence of elite individuals named in hieroglyphic texts.

Variation in the titles of the heads of lineages suggests the presence of royal and subordinate lines or elite and nonelite lines much as Carmack (1981) has observed among the highland Quiché. Roys (1957:7) has suggested that the title/role of *hol pop* or "head of the mat" referred to the leader of the most important and politically powerful elite lineage within a given area (cf. M. Coe 1965). Another title/role that occurs with great frequency in the ethnohistoric records of Yucatán is that of the *ah kuch kab,* which has been defined as a council member or *regidor* (Farriss 1984; Roys 1943; Tozzer 1941:87), a lineage head and collector of tribute (Barrera Vásquez 1980:44; Ciudad Real 1984), a *principal* (M. Coe 1965:104), and finally simply as a wealthy commoner (M. Coe 1965:104; Freidel 1983:54). Thus, in the Yucatec political system, there was an office/title for a recognized lineage leader who was not necessarily a high-ranking noble. Although the specific roles of the *ah kuch kab* are not altogether clear, this position demonstrates an institutionalization of the lineage in the political process. Through the leadership of an *ah kuch kab,* many households within a polity might be organized and mobilized, thus creating a strong dynamic of intrapolity factionalism—a much-neglected topic in Maya archaeology.

Lineage organization is a major theme in ethnohistoric research; this social formation, for example, is acknowledged to be a building block of settlement structure even in the poorly understood Cehache area of southern Campeche (Scholes and Roys 1968:69).[4] From sources such as these we learn that lineages were not dichotomized into simple categories of elite and nonelite, but rather were richly textured and complex groupings with significant internal variation in status and wealth. In the family papers of the Xiu lineage there is specific documentation of ranking within lineages as exemplified by the coexistence of *hidalgo* (elite) and non-*hidalgo* lines (Morley 1941:349, 444–446).[5] The economic and political inequality extant within lineages is also indicated in the Xiu family chronicle by the fact that it was the junior and cadet lines of the *hidalgo* branch that throughout the Colonial period migrated away from the Xiu heartland of Maní as the Spaniards successively reduced the wealth and political influence of this preeminent Yucatec family.

For the Maya highlands, Carmack's (1981) study of the Quiché Maya is very explicit regarding lineage structure. Essentially, the Quiché were organized into patrilineal descent groups of subordinate and major lineages with exogamous marriage customs (Carmack 1981:160). Today, Quiché Maya use the term *xe'al* (meaning "root") to refer to lineage (Tedlock 1982:25). While major lineages occupied the large central sites such as Utatlán, the subordinate lineages were located in the rural countryside in *amac,* described as "pueblo pequeño extendido como están las piernas de las arañas" (Ximénez 1929:130). These small settlements with spidery extensors were apparently tied to the major lineages through political obligations of taxation and corvée labor; nevertheless, Carmack (1981:161) tells us that the rural lineages retained some measure of independence and shared many of the structural characteristics of the ruling lineages. This observation highlights one of the limitations of applying a strictly class-based model of social organization to the Maya region. Population factions split or segmented along lineage lines is a more appropriate model than a class-based nobility-and-peasantry model. If the Postclassic highland Maya were not organized into a simple class-based system, then it is doubtful that the lowland Classic Maya were organized in such a simplistic fashion.

Among the Quiché, a lineage head is known as *chuchkajaw* (mother-father) or *c'amal be* (leader) and is both a religious and political leader (Carmack 1981:161; Tedlock 1982:35); the dual gender translation of the term *chuchkajaw* indicates that the contribution of the female to lineage leadership and ritual is deeply encoded linguistically. The segmentary structure of the Quiché lineages as documented by Carmack has been elaborated by Fox (1987), who has described the Quiché as a segmentary state. Carmack has stressed the territorial and residential focus of the Quiché lineages, a focus expressed ritually through ancestor veneration. This practice is echoed in the ethnographic work of Bunzel (1952) among the Quiché of Chichicastenango.[6] Significantly, both Carmack and Fox have utilized a model of segmentary lineage organization as a guide to archaeological research at highland Maya Postclassic sites and, by doing so, have focused on the material signature of lineage structure. Employing ethnographic analogy in the highlands of Chiapas, Vogt (1964:402) too has attempted to forge a link between the present and the past by reference to the funerary-and-temple pyramids of the Classic Maya as "lineage mountains" analogous to the natural features venerated by the contemporary Tzotzil.[7]

Archaeologists and epigraphers increasingly are looking for material evidence of lineage organization in the Classic Maya lowlands. Architectural groups with freestanding architecture, multiple courtyards, and bench features are increasingly interpreted as the compounds of elite lineages. This explanation of architectural patterns is offered by Haviland (1968:109), who refers to "patriclan buildings" and specifically identifies the following excavated structures at Tikal as the loci of patriclans: 3F-12, 4E-31, and 5G-8. Haviland (1968:Table 2) also presents a list of unexcavated structures as other probable clan buildings. At Copán, Group 9N-8, commonly known as the "House of the Bacabs," is thought to have been the residence of a lineage of scribes (Fash 1991; Schele and Freidel 1990; Webster 1989). Schele and Freidel (1990:329−330) have interpreted the dedicatory inscriptions at this compound as containing the name of the lineage leader, *Mak-Chanil*. Ancestor shrines at other residential compounds, such as Group 10L-2 (Andrews and Fash 1992), indicate the plurality of lineage compounds at Copán. From the Mundo Perdido structures at Tikal, Laporte and Vega (1986:129−132) have interpreted this Early Classic complex and the many burials interred therein as the focus "del linaje Garra de Jaguar" (of the lineage Jaguar Paw). Likewise, Group IV of Palenque is now known to have been the long-term residential focus of the lineage of Chac-Zutz', a *sahal* and warrior (Schele 1991).

COMMUNING WITH THE ANCESTORS

In a reference to what appear to have been ancestor shrines in Yucatán, Landa (Tozzer 1941:130−131) describes a plethora of "idols" in homes and temples. Tozzer (1941:9, n.44) suggests that, in fact, the "idols" were icons of ancestors; he further notes that many of them were female. In fact, so many of these icons were female that the name Isla de Mujeres was given to the island north of Cozumel, due to Francisco Hernández de Córdoba's observation (in 1517) of lots of female "idols." Marcus (1978) also has noted that in Zapotec ethnohistoric sources, the term "idol" often refers to a named ancestral representation; thus, many of these figures were material manifestations of ancestor veneration and were displayed to establish the genealogical depth of a lineage. The wooden "idols" are described by Landa as "the most important part of the inherited property" (Tozzer 1941:111). In this sense they are analogous to the genealogical tablets of Chinese ancestor veneration. As Welsh (1988:196) and others have noted, some of these "idols" were, in fact, partial or cremated remains of the ancestors themselves; the heads of important HALACH UINICOB were apparently not an uncommon sight at the shrines of important lineage groups.[8] Landa suggests that some form of preferential treatment of skeletal remains, which resulted in their incorporation in shrine displays (and therefore not with the actual burial interment), was common for "people of position" (Tozzer 1941:131).

Early chroniclers consistently interpreted the plethora of icons as indicative of a pantheon of deities. While some of them undoubtedly did represent Maya supernaturals such as Chak or Kukulkan, many others were representations of important ancestors. Note the reverence to named ancestors in the following passage from the *Chilam Balam of Chumayel:* "These were the four lineages from heaven, the substance of heaven, the moisture of heaven, the head-chiefs, the rulers of the land: Zacaal Puc, Hooltun Balam, Hochtun Poot, Ah Mex-Cuc Chan" (Roys 1967:147). Elsewhere, Roys (1957:130) identifies don Juan Kauil, a leader of the important lineage of Cupul, as a descendant of "Kukum Cupul, Sacalpuc (a deified lineage ancestor)" (also see Roys [1939:147, 1943:78] and Scholes and Adams [1938:153] for more generalized references to deified ancestors of Yucatec lineages). The principle of quadripartition in reference to founding lineages is also found in the *Popol Vuh* of the highland Quiché, which names the four founding ancestors whose power and authority are expressed by the nagualistic association of the ancestors with the fierce jaguar: Balam Quitze, Balam Acab, Mahucutah, and Iqui-Balam.

The importance accorded to ancestors and the reverence given to their representations/remains constituted acts of heresy in the eyes of proselytizing Spanish friars who acted to suppress this "cult." The tenacity with which Yucatec and highland Maya groups continued to revere these icons in which their identity—past, present, and future—was vested is attested by the number of individuals tortured and killed during the Spanish Inquisition. Bishop Diego de Landa showed perhaps the greatest zeal in rooting out these "pagan" practices. Records of his interrogation and torture of the inhabitants of Maní during the terrible summer of 1562 can be found in Scholes and Adams (1938:1:153).⁹ Through these interrogations we learn, for instance, that the

> lineage cult was one of the subjects commemorated in their hieroglyphic books. *Hunixquinchac* (Hun-ix-kin-chac?) was said to be the god of the people named *Puc,* and *Chocunquinchac* was the deity of the *Kumun* lineage. "The greatest of these gods" was *Zacalpuc,* with whom we are more familiar; but unfortunately we are not told with which lineage he was associated. . . . Indeed, he still figures in the Maya prayers of modern *yerbateros* as the first man to offer posole to the *Chacs.* (SCHOLES AND ROYS 1938:609)¹⁰

This information, extracted under torture to which even the Spanish Crown could not turn a blind eye, resulted in the temporary removal of Bishop Diego de Landa from the Yucatán and the permanent removal of don Diego de Quijada from his position as alcalde mayor of Yucatán due to his role in the interrogation, torture, and imprisonment of uninformative or uncooperative Maya (Scholes and Roys 1938). Both Clendinnen (1987) and Tedlock (1993) question the veracity of these confessions on the grounds that they were extracted under torture and many of them were later retracted. One thing is certain, however: this harsh repression of indigenous Maya religious practices speaks not only of the extreme importance of ancestral lineage figures to the integrity of the Postclassic Maya way of life but also of the threat that the continuation of these practices posed to the Spaniards. Landa, in particular, was obsessed with the desire to demonstrate the existence of European Medieval-style sacrilegious behavior on the part of newly proselytized Maya (Clendinnen 1987:122; Tedlock 1993:146–147). In reference to this clash of ideologies, Scholes and Roys (1938:610) hazard the opinion that "in times when the worship of the old gods was attended with so much danger, only those who were most important to the welfare of the people would receive sacrifices. These may have been the rain and wind gods and the tutelary divinities of the lineages."¹¹

Highland Maya groups, such as the Tzutujil, Quiché, and Cakchiquel, made similar images of deified lineage leaders—images referred to as *chajal* ("guard" or "guardian") by the Cakchiquel (Orellana 1984:96). This reference indicates the extent to which ancestors were perceived as serving to protect their descendants and, by extension, guard their resource entitlements from encroachment. The linkage between ancestors and land is further established by reference to the placement of ancestral shrines by Quiché lineages. According to Carmack (1981:161), the lineages were closely linked to tracts of land upon which there were "sacred spots where altars are built, the most important of which are the *warabal ja* ('sleeping house') for the ancestors." [12] The Quiché venerated their ancestors at these locations within the landholding area of their lineage, thus affirming the explicit linkage between ancestors and resources.

The continued importance of ancestor veneration in the Maya highlands is suggested by the ethnographic work of Bunzel (1952), Tedlock (1982), Colby (1976), and others. Among the Ixil Maya, Colby (1976:75) states that "the Ixil pray not only to their immediate lineal forebears but also to the departed souls of town leaders (*b'o7q'ol tenam*), native town priests (*b'o7q'ol b'aal watz tiix*), calendar priests (*7ahq'ih*), curers (*b'aal wat tiix*) and possibly other individuals not directly related to the praying individual." This list thus consists of the principal leaders of the community, and it corroborates the pattern noted by Freedman (1966) that ancestor veneration is a selective process and does not extend equally to all deceased progenitors. The selectivity of ancestral veneration is echoed by Landa (Tozzer 1941), who states that only lineage heads or people of position were venerated after their death and that only their remains were treated preferentially. In a provocative thesis, Colby (1976:76) suggests that benevolent nagualism—the belief that powerful individuals can transform themselves into animals such as the jaguar for the purpose of magic—is compatible with ancestor veneration, since ancestors are seen as an empowering force of life. Witchcraft and homicide, on the contrary, are negative guises that ancestors are capable of assuming, and Colby notes that accusations of such behavior are rare among the Ixil, who prefer to perceive the ancestors as enabling spirits and the source of rights and privileges.

Colby contrasts ancestor veneration with tonalism: the Mesoamerican notion that humans have guardian spirits, also mostly animals, and that an individual's fate is determined by the character of the guardian spirit rather than by the power of a lineage or a group of ancestors. Tonalism includes the naming of persons after a given day name (usually a number and animal or object from the 260-day calendar) rather than after their lineage association. Very common among the Aztecs, tonalism was increasingly adopted in the Maya highlands immediately prior to the Spanish invasion, and Colby notes that the final two Quiché rulers had day names rather than lineage names.

Ethnographic sources from both highland and lowland Maya settings document the fact that rituals and places relating to ancestor veneration have retained an importance in Maya society, particularly in the "universal" domestic setting (Bunzel 1952:35–36; Gossen and Leventhal 1993; Holland

Photo of Tzotzil Maya around grave of an ancestor on Todos
                              Santos (from Collier 1975: Figure 11; courtesy of University of
                              Texas Press).

1964:302–303; Thompson 1976; Vogt 1964:37–38; Wauchope 1938;
Wisdom 1940). Domestic ancestral shrines in particular differ from those
recorded archaeologically and in early historical documents in two important
ways: (1) they seldom contain osteological or carbonized remains of the ancestors—rather, ancestors are buried in cemeteries at the edges of town; and
(2) ancestors are more frequently invoked in a generalized fashion rather
than by reference to a specific, named apical ancestor (Nash 1970:22, 45;
Vogt 1969; Watanabe 1990:139). Quiché and Ixil practices provide excep-
tions to this generalization in that named ancestors are invoked during rituals
(Carmack 1981; Holland 1964; Tedlock 1982:25, 65). Where the commemoration of named ancestors still exists, the ritual is often subsumed
within the christianized structure of All Saints' Day (Figure 2.1; Collier
1975:91; Morley 1941; Redfield and Villa Rojas 1962:202–204; Watanabe 1990:137, 140, 145). The following example illustrates this point.
During the early part of this century, Sylvanus G. Morley conducted ethnographic interviews among the descendants of the illustrious Xiu dynasty of
Maní. Morley's informant, Cenobio (Xiu) of Tixcacalcupul, stated that he

had been instructed by his paternal grandmother, Dominga Kumul, to pray for the "important dead" on All Saints' Day. She had recited to him the names of prominent ancestors, particularly those in the senior line, spanning four generations (including all the sons of a prominent ancestor, Antonio Xiu II, by his first wife). The specificity of this commemoration is remarkable because Dominga Kumul was related only affinally (through marriage) to a son of Antonio's second wife (Morley 1941:369, 384). While the genesis of ancestor veneration may not be well understood for the Maya region, its presence and importance during later periods is amply documented. This information provides insight to the social conventions associated with this reverential treatment of select deceased relatives, a topic to which we now turn.

Practices of Ancestor Veneration

Active propitiation of ancestors is a vital part of ancestral veneration and is implemented through feasting, processionals, and other commemorative and dedicatory rituals (practices that Marcus [1992:263] has described as "performance reaffirmation rituals"). The importance of banquets, in particular, cannot be overstated, although the archaeology of feasting has not been addressed in the Maya region with the same vigor as it has been studied in Andean archaeology (see Morris and Thompson 1985; Murra 1980). Nevertheless, the encyclopedic observations of Landa intimate that banquets played a critical role in commemoration of ancestors in Postclassic Yucatán.

FEASTING. As Feeley-Harnik (1985:288) has observed, "ritual and politics meet in food." The term *prestation economy* is often applied to social systems in which a significant amount of wealth was circulated and political alliances were defined through the mechanism of feasting. Among the Maya, ritualized feasting and prestations were undertaken upon many different occasions: marriage, significant calendric events, victory in war, and to "celebrate the memory of the deeds of their ancestors" (Tozzer 1941:92). In addition to lavish foods and gifts, these banquets also included varied entertainment in the form of musical bands (Miller 1988), dancing, and apparently some comic performances. So important was feasting that the Motul dictionary defines the honored lineage leader title of *hol pop* as "head of the banquet" (Roys 1939:44), a definition that is in accordance with Cogolludo's description of the entertainment duties of the *hol pop* as head singer and keeper of the musical instruments (Roys 1939:46). In the context of ritualized feasting (generally prefaced by periods of fasting), a range of social and political issues were addressed and resolved. Feasting does not seem to have been an activity restricted to the elites, but rather it operated within all sectors of Maya society and was encoded strongly in memory through the gifts that were distributed during feasts. Of this memory, Landa notes that "they have strong friendships and they remember for a long time these invitations, although they are far apart from one another" (Tozzer 1941:92).

Landa was impressed and scandalized by the opulence of this feasting behavior and by the copious amounts of *balche'* which were drunk:

> And often they spend on one banquet what they have earned by trading and bargaining many days. And they have two ways of celebrating these feasts; the first, which is that of the nobles and of the principal people [*ah kuch kabob?*], obliges each one of the invited guests to give another similar feast. And to each guest they give a roasted fowl, bread and drink of cacao in abundance; and at the end of the repast, they were accustomed to give a *manta* to each to wear, and a little stand and vessel, as beautiful as possible.
>
> (TOZZER 1941:92)

The types of food and gifts listed by Landa are interesting for several reasons. First of all, they demonstrate unambiguously the contribution of female labor to feasting and prestation in the form of woven *mantas* and the consumption of fowl—dooryard animals raised by women (Pohl and Feldman 1982; Nimis 1982). Second, the phrase "as beautiful as possible" suggests that the gifts distributed at feasts were exquisite, distinctive items that would be curated and that served to encode materially a memory of the feast. Of the items mentioned by Landa, the most durable are the vessels. In this regard, recent research on the epigraphy and clay sourcing of Late Classic ceramic polychrome vessels is particularly relevant. Neutron activation analysis of these containers indicates redundant patterns of transfer of vessels from their locale of production to the place where they enter the archaeological record (R. Bishop, pers. com. 1991; Bishop et al. 1985), usually as burial accouterments. This pattern is not an economic one; rather, it is consistent with the circulation of ceramic vessels in the context of ritual feasting.[13] Those polychrome vessels with a band of hieroglyphic script, the so-called Primary Standard Sequence, often contain glyphs which recently have been translated as the words for "painting" or method of decoration, vessel class, contents of vessel, and vessel ownership (Houston, Stuart, and Taube 1989:720; Grube 1991).[14] Thus, these well-made polychromes, so indicative of Classic Maya society, probably circulated in the context of gift-giving at feasts, one of the few contexts in which the programmatic specificity of the hieroglyphic bands would make sense. It is likely that many of the vessels interred with deceased individuals (who later assumed the status of ancestor) were in and of themselves a chronicle of ritual feasts attended by that individual (see Appadurai [1986] for a pertinent discussion of the social life of things). The banquets per se are relevant to the issue of ancestral veneration, since some of them were organized to commemorate ancestors. The wide distribution of polychromes, in both elite and nonelite burial contexts, suggests that most sectors of society participated in such feasting (although polychromes from nonelite contexts seldom feature hieroglyphic texts) or had otherwise acquired access to polychromes. Finally, feasting activities are important because they represent a ritualized context in which rulers and *principales* (*ah kuch kabob*)—who represented different factions—feasted together. This type of interaction will be pursued in greater detail in Chapter 5.

DOMESTIC RITUALS. During the Postclassic, women apparently played important roles in attending to and "feeding ancestors of a household." Once again, through Landa's eyes, we glimpse at the richness of domestic rituals performed at ancestor shrines: "They [women] were very devout and pious, and also practiced many acts of devotion before their idols [ancestors], burning incense before them and offering them presents of cotton stuffs, of food and drink and it was their duty to make the offerings of food and drink which they offered in the festivals of the Indians" (Tozzer 1941: 128). This passage is strongly reminiscent of Freedman's observation that, in China, the female was in charge of the domestic commemoration of the ancestors, and likewise reminiscent of Feeley-Harnik's (1985:299) discussion of the female as tomb-guardian in many African kingdoms. The strong association between females and ancestor shrines/tombs clashes strongly with Sanders' (1989:97) interpretation of an ancestral shrine from the House of the Bacabs at Copán as a male domain. Unlike the physical separation between ancestor shrines and skeletal remains in Chinese society, ancestral remains among the Maya were not spatially separated from domestic commemorative shrines. Rather, the two were conflated at one locale, particularly for nonelite Maya and probably for many elite as well. In this way, the spatially segregated gender-linked hierarchy of Chinese ritual participation that Freedman (1966, 1970) noted—women in domestic ritual and men in public ritual—was somewhat ameliorated among elite and nonelite in the Maya region. In the Codex Madrid, representations of female and male standing "head-to-head" and presenting offerings (Figure 2.2) suggest complementary oppositions (Joyce 1990) rather than a hierarchical rank-order. Underlying this complementarity may be the fact that the status of women in Maya society was never diminished by the total subjugation of kin-organized leadership roles to a state entity (cf. Gailey 1987; Silverblatt 1987). Because of the environmental and social forces opposing political centralization and favor-

2.2

Codex Madrid, page 52c; representations of Chak and Goddess I presenting offerings of *cacao* (*Codex Tro-Cortesianus* [*Codex Madrid*] 1967, courtesy Akademische Druck-u).

ing smaller-scale polities in the Yucatán Peninsula, in many areas lineage structure as well as the physical locale of the residence may have retained its integrity and political power throughout the Classic and Postclassic periods.

BLOODLETTING AND SACRIFICE. Landa recounted in detail the ways in which "they offered sacrifices of their own blood" (Tozzer 1941:113–114)—a ritual means of honoring ancestors. This passage has been quoted frequently in the interpretation of Classic-period iconography, discussed below. Landa does not specify the periodicity of auto-sacrifice, but he does state that women did not engage in bloodletting (Tozzer 1941:114, 128). The graphic iconography on Yaxchilán Lintel 24 of Lady Xoc pulling a thorny cord through her tongue is a vivid refutation of Landa's assertion that women did not let blood. But Lady Xoc was a royal woman, and Landa may have been referring primarily to nonroyal women. As Marcus (1978: 185–186, 1983:471) has suggested, the extent to which women engaged in rituals such as bloodletting was probably a function of social standing rather than gender.

The perceived power of the sacrifice of blood (human or animal) in propitiating the ancestors, mitigating the adverse auguries of a New Year, and

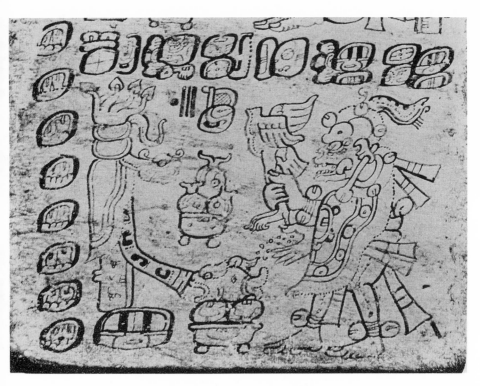

2.3   Codex Dresden, page 27c; sacrificial offering of decapitated turkey (Deckert 1989, courtesy Akademische Druck-u).

dealing with ad hoc crises was very strong among the Maya. Many scenes of
the Dresden and Madrid codices are images of sacrificial offerings, both human and nonhuman, such as the decapitated turkey shown in pages 65a and
107b of the Codex Madrid and on pages 34a and 27c of the Codex Dresden
(the latter is shown in Figure 2.3). Maya offerings to their "idols" (many of
which were apotheosized ancestors) included endless variations on body
parts and blood: complete entities, specific organs only (especially the heart),
or blood of a human or animal, as well as cooked and prepared foods of
animals and plants (Tozzer 1941:114).

                         CREATING IMAGES OF THE ANCESTORS. From the early
chroniclers, from the "idolatry" trials conducted by the Spaniards in northern Yucatán, and from the images in the codices, we can surmise that the
carving of wooden representations of progenitors for placement in both domestic shrines and within larger-scale ritual contexts was a prevalent practice
among Yucatec Maya. During the summer of 1562, there was a public *auto*

da fé which included the burning of books, the disinterment of the bones of dead "idolatrous" Maya, and the conflagration of thousands of "idols" that had been collected during the Inquisition (Scholes and Roys 1938:595). Clendinnen (1987:83) has suggested that this number was greatly inflated due to the fact that, under torture, Mayas confessed to whatever number of "idols" their inquisitors suggested and then later had to "beat the bushes" in order to produce the requisite number. The claim of having destroyed many "idols," however, is widespread and occurs in every chronicle of every *entrada* well into the seventeenth century.[15]

Although the humid climate of the Yucatán Peninsula and the conflagration of the *auto da fé* of Bishop Landa and others have together conspired to limit severely the recovery of such perishable ancestral icons, human images with distinctive features that were rendered in clay and stone have survived the ravages of time. From the cenote of Chichén Itzá, furthermore, where the conditions of preservation are unusually felicitous, a modified human cranium coinciding with Landa's description of the protracted curation of the bones of ancestors was dredged, as well as examples of wooden (ancestral?) icons that had been painted blue (Coggins and Shane 1984:Figs. 174–176, 199).

> The rest of the people of position made for their [deceased] fathers wooden statues of which the back of the head was left hollow, and they then burned a part of the body and placed its ashes there, and plugged it up; afterwards they stripped off the dead body the skin of the back of the head and stuck it over this place and they buried the rest as they were wont to do. They preserved these statues with a great deal of veneration among their idols. . . . They kept these together with the statues with the ashes, all of which they kept in the oratories of their houses with their idols, holding them in very great reverence and respect. And on all the days of their festivals and rejoicings, they [earlier specified as women] made offerings of foods to them, so that food should not fail them in the other life, where they thought that their souls reposed, and where their gifts were of use to them.
>
> (TOZZER 1941:129–31)

These observations by Landa, probably provided by the informant Gaspar Antonio Chi, suggest that the carving of wooden representations of immediate forebears (particularly paternal ones) was an important part of ancestral veneration among Yucatec Maya. Indeed, in another chapter Landa returns to the wooden figures and emphasizes their heirloom quality and the fact that they were inherited property. This statement comes as no surprise given that property, privilege, and authority were vested in descendants through their ancestors; thus, the material icons of progenitors were potent symbols of the rights of inheritance. Even among the refugee Yucatec Lacandón population of the nineteenth century, images evocative of ancestral gods were prized and passed down through the generations (Tozzer 1907).

Elsewhere in this *relación,* Landa discusses the carving of wooden "idols" (*kulche'*) during the month of Mol. The work was done by relatively specialized males, in designated locations, and under various restrictions and taboos; apparently, images were generally carved from cedar (Tozzer 1941: 159–160), a wood called *k'uche'* in Maya. In botanical nomenclature, this tree is *Cedrela mexicana* Roem. and is a wood that is not available everywhere throughout the peninsula. The passage suggests that the specialist carved images for the rest of the community and was compensated for his labor and work "with birds, game, and money" (Tozzer 1941: 160).

During Late Postclassic and early Colonial times, images often were carved using "little hatchets of a particular metal" (Tozzer 1941: 121). The use of a small hatchet to carve a representation of a cranium is depicted in the Codex

2.4   Codex Madrid, page 96d; use of a small hatchet to carve an image of a human head. Note elaborate cloak, necklaces, and ear spools worn by carvers (*Codex Tro-Cortesianus* [*Codex Madrid*] 1967, courtesy Akademische Druck-u).

2.5   Codex Madrid, page 97b; preparing icons (*Codex Tro-Cortesianus* [*Codex Madrid*] 1967, courtesy Akademische Druck-u).

2.6   Codex Madrid, page 98a; cutting down tropical cedar trees to carve an icon (*Codex Tro-Cortesianus* [*Codex Madrid*] 1967, courtesy Akademische Druck-u).

Madrid on pages 95 through 98 (Figures 2.4 and 2.5), with subsequent use of a bone awl to bore out the eyes shown on pages 98, 99, and 100. The act of cutting down the prerequisite cedar tree may be the subject of 98a (Figure 2.6). In the codex, the carvers are represented as Maya supernaturals who wear large ear spools, jade necklaces, and special patterned cloaks. They are often shown working under canopies or roofed structures.

It may be significant that the type of wood specified by Landa as appropriate raw material for ancestral images—cedar—is present throughout the macrobotanical record of Formative- and Classic-period K'axob despite the fact that there is an overall and dramatic decrease in tropical forest species from the Middle Formative to the Terminal Classic periods (Miksicek n.d.). Cedar was also valuable as building material; individual trees or stands of cedar, which thrive in moist soil, must have been protected and probably inherited by the Maya to ensure the continued availability of this resource.

Iconography of the Ancestors

Postclassic and Colonial descriptions of the rituals of ancestor veneration are complemented by Classic-period political iconography and hieroglyphic script, both of which depict the central importance of royal ancestors to the continued power and position of ruling lineages and divine kings. It was Proskouriakoff (1960) who first recognized that the range of calendrical dates carved on monuments set up in discrete groups associated with individual structures at Piedras Negras matched those of human life spans, and from this insight she reasoned that the texts of the monuments recorded events in the lives of a sequence of rulers who lorded over Piedras Negras, Yaxchilán, and other sites as well (Proskouriakoff 1961, 1963, 1964). Now it is recognized widely that the agenda of many hieroglyphic texts was the creation and strengthening of the ties of descent in the dynastic lines of divine Maya rulers. The texts and iconography of monuments (particularly those erected during Cycle 8) often explicitly link a central protagonist with an apical and often deified ancestral figure, who may have been a founder of a dynastic lineage (Marcus 1976:32, 1978; Stuart 1988:221). As expressed by Schele and Miller (1986:14), "the purpose of art was to document the bloodlines of Classic Maya kings. . . . records of parents and ancestors transferring power to their children consume a large part of Maya pictorial imagery and writing." In Maya iconography, ancestors are often indicated through special markings or particular costume accouterments (Schele and Miller 1986:43, 275, Fig. VII.3). The topic of ancestor veneration as it is depicted in Classic Maya iconography and texts is highly politicized, with complex linkages between kinship and political power. The subject deserves a comprehensive study in and of itself. Here, I do not attempt such an all-encompassing treatment. Rather, I discuss some of the more salient examples of ancestral representations in iconography and text with two purposes in mind: first, to demonstrate the centrality of the ancestors to Maya statecraft; and second, to provide a point of departure for a later discussion of the appropriation by Classic-period elites of ancestor veneration, and its transformation from a kinship ritual tied to land entitlements to a ritual legitimizing kingly prerogative (Chapter 5). Here, the following expressions of royal ancestor veneration are examined: (1) presence and strategic placement of named ancestors on carved/painted monuments, (2) ancestor cartouches, (3) images evocative of ancestors, and (4) hieroglyphic texts recounting genealogies and genealogical connections.

PRESENCE AND STRATEGIC PLACEMENT OF IMAGES.
On Classic Maya monuments—be they carved stelae, lintels, or altar/ thrones—canons of style and composition are often highly programmatic. Generally, the main protagonist (often a single male) is placed compositionally within a sequence of rulers of a particular dynasty that is indicated not only in hieroglyphic text but also through images of named progenitors. From the Early Classic onward, ancestors are placed at the top of a composition (Marcus 1976, 1978; Schele and Freidel 1990:372). For example, the early stela from Tikal (Stela 29) shows a side profile of a king, possibly named Scroll-Ahau-Jaguar (Figure 2.7). Above him floats the head of what is generally considered a dynastic ancestor, an early Jaguar-Paw; this composition is cited by Schele and Freidel (1990:140–141) as an early example of the "principle of the anchoring ancestor," essentially the juxtapositioning of images of current rulers with those of previous ones in order to legitimize the current state of affairs.

At Palenque and Yaxchilán, current rulers and their dynastic forebears are depicted as interacting dynamically in rituals of royal succession in which an ancestor hands over a symbol of power and authority, such as a staff or headdress, to his or her descendant. Through this artistic convention, in which time is compressed, an image is created of direct and unequivocal transmission of power. In reality, progenitors depicted often have long since passed away. The extent to which this image of direct transference of power is overstated suggests that dynastic succession and interregnum periods may have been fraught with tension and conflict. At Yaxchilán, for instance, the ruler Bird-Jaguar is shown on Stela 11 conducting a flapstaff ritual with his father, Shield-Jaguar, whose age would have been ninety-three years. Bird-Jaguar's parents (Shield-Jaguar and Lady Eveningstar) are named and shown on the obverse side of the monument above the "sky" register; Bird-Jaguar and three captives are shown below (Schele and Freidel 1990:86, 272–275, 479). At Copán, presentation of images of dynastic forebears in dynamic interaction with their descendants is elaborated on Altar Q and the sculptured bench panel of Temple 11. On the four sides of Altar Q, a seated representation of Yax-Kuk-Mo', founder of the Copán dynasty, is shown along with

J.A.LABADIE '94

2.7   Tikal (Stela 29); side profile of royal personage with "anchoring
       ancestor" in the sky above (drawing by John Antoine Labadie
       after Figure 49 in Jones and Satterthwaite 1982, courtesy of The
       University Museum, University of Pennsylvania).

fifteen descendant *ahawob*. The final ruler depicted, Yax-Pac, sits facing as
if in conversation with his ancestral progenitor, Yax-Kuk-Mo' (Figure 2.8).
A similar scene is repeated on the sculptured bench panel of Temple 11. Most
noteworthy is the fact that the progenitors of Yax-Pac are not represented as
generalized ancestors; rather, they are carved as individual and distinctive

J.A. LABADIE '94

2.8 Copán, Altar Q, showing the juxtaposition of Yax-Pac (sixteenth ruler in a Copán royal lineage) with the founder of the dynasty, Yax-Kuk-Mo' (drawing by John Antoine Labadie after Figure 100a in Robicek 1972 and Figure 8.3 in Schele and Freidel 1990).

portraits and with a sense of "spontaneity [that] imparts the idea that these deceased kings were physically present at the accession rite [a physical impossibility], thus permanently demonstrating in stone that all the past kings of Copán participated in [and sanctioned] Yax-Pac's accession" (Schele and Miller 1986:124).

In a similar and well-known example from Palenque, the sides of the sarcophagus of the ruler Pakal are carved with the busts of six generations of claimed ancestors preceding him. Named ancestral figures appear to be sprouting from an earthline register around the four sides of the sarcophagus. This metaphor of an "ancestral orchard" (Schele and Freidel 1990:221; Figure 2.9) [16] is provocative not only due to the organic way in which the sculptors depicted Pakal's royal pedigree but also because the species represented (cacao, nance, guayaba, chicozapote, mamey, and avocado) are transgenerational, inherited resources. The orchard species, therefore, are used as a metaphor of divine kingship; i.e., cacao trees are passed down through the generations just as was the throne of Palenque. In other words, Pakal appropriated a potent symbol of agrarian inheritance and used it to anchor his genealogy (more on this in Chapters 3 and 5). To this day, highland Maya peoples, the Tzutujil in particular, continue to use agrarian metaphors of life, death, replacement, and continuance (such as the term jaloj-k'exoj) to express renewal of an ancestral form (Carlsen and Prechtel 1991).

ANCESTOR CARTOUCHES. A slightly more stylized way of presenting royal ancestors, and one that is midway between an image and an abstract hieroglyphic sign, is the ancestor cartouche. For example, this convention was employed at Palenque (western wall of House A of the Palace complex), where a row of thirteen stuccoed, painted cartouches or medallions are thought to have contained images of ancestors (Robertson 1985: Figs. 112–138). Schele and Freidel (1990:503) present a summary of the iconographic ancestral imagery of Classic and Terminal Classic monuments, tracing the initial recognition of ancestor cartouches at Yaxchilán to Proskouriakoff. The cartouches of Yaxchilán are now thought to relate to the association of ancestors with celestial bodies such as the sun and moon (S. Houston, pers. com. 1992). In its Terminal Classic form, the frame around an ancestor may be represented as a Sun Disk as known from Chichén Itzá (Schele and Freidel 1990:372) or, alternately, as the open mouth of a feathered serpent from which a human head emerges, such as appears at Chichén Itzá and many of the Puuc sites (cf. Houston and Stuart [1989] for a nagualistic interpretation of the imagery, particularly as it co-occurs with the way glyph).

2.9

Pakal's ancestors (six ascending generations) and their associated orchard species (drawing by John Antoine Labadie after Figures 174–177 in Robertson 1983).

EVOCATIVE IMAGES. Classic and Postclassic iconography is replete with images of auto-sacrifice: that is, the representation of elite individuals piercing fleshy parts of their bodies with obsidian blades, stingray spines, thorn-covered ropes, and so on. While the images are quite graphic, the reality and frequency of these practices is more difficult to evaluate from iconography (Leventhal 1990). Depictions of bloodletting have been linked to ancestors because images, argued to be those of ancestors, are revealed emerging from the body of a serpent after bloodletting takes places. Royal Maya women seem to have played an important and public role in bloodletting rituals. Interpretable as a highly ritualized form of ancestral veneration are the images from Yaxchilán of Lady Xoc pulling a barbed rope through her tongue (Lintel 24) and of Lady Balam-Ix pulling a rope through her tongue (Lintel 17). The bloodletting image is not exclusive to the medium of carved stone; the Codex Madrid contains images of both male and female supernaturals in the act of bloodletting (Figure 2.10), as do the Jaina ceramic figurines.

The association of clouds with ancestors is also seen in the frequent occurrence of the dotted scroll motif, particularly as it appears at the tops of stelae

Codex Madrid, page 95a; ritualized bloodletting from ear
(*Codex Tro-Cortesianus* [*Codex Madrid*] 1967, courtesy
Akademische Druck-u).

2.11   Chert "eccentrics" worked into the form of a human profile, possibly of ancestors (courtesy of Dumbarton Oaks Research Library and Collections, Washington, D.C.).

from Ucanal and Jimbal. Stuart (1988:221) suggests that "ancestor imagery . . . [and] a cosmological framework . . . were the principal forces behind the vast majority of ancient Maya public art." The medium of chipped stone may also have been used to represent ancestors, namely the so-called eccentrics, many of which feature a human profile (Schele and Miller 1986:73; Figure 2.11). In this regard, the documented Late Formative origin of "eccentrics" (Gibson 1989) is particularly interesting since ancestors come to play an important role among both kin groups and divine kings during this period.

Another image directly linked to the ancestors is the skull-and-crossbones motif present in Maya and, in fact, all Mesoamerican iconography. From a European perspective, this image suggests a morbid fascination with death, but Carlson (1981:193) has noted that its meaning actually is quite the opposite: the motif "signified more than death and decay. It was a sign of completion and rebirth from the ancestral bones." Symbolic of generational continuity and the rights and privileges that are inherited from the previous generation, crania and/or long bones are potent images symbolic of social order and orderly successions, be they transmissions of royal power or of the

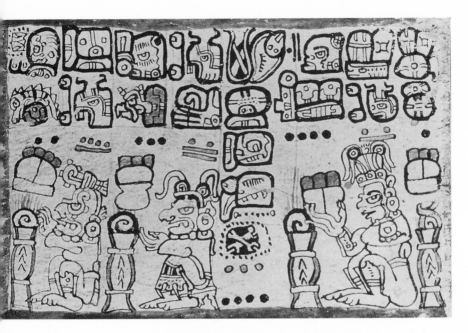

Codex Madrid, page 107b; note crossed long-bones motif in lower center of frame (*Codex Tro-Cortesianus* [*Codex Madrid*] 1967, courtesy Akademische Druck-u).

fields and orchards of wealthy commoners. Thus, this motif crosscuts a range of social contexts; it is found in the pages of the Codex Madrid (107b and pages following; Figure 2.12) as well as in the highly orthodox royal iconography of Altar 5 at Tikal, in which a skull and a stack of four long bones are shown with an underlying glyph band describing a female elite personage (Jones and Satterthwaite 1982:38; Figure 2.13). The glyph band encircling what appears to be an exhumation scene contains a verb that has been deciphered as *pasah* ("was opened") at position 26 (D. Stuart and S. Houston, pers. com. 1992).[17] The two dates on the text indicate that eight years passed between death and exhumation of this important female personage from Topoxté. Altar 5, therefore, directly indicates that some elite individuals underwent complex and protracted burial rites which included exhumation from a primary burial. Moreover, the iconography from both Tikal and Yaxchilán demonstrates that royal women were both actors and subjects in ancestor-focused ritual.

HIEROGLYPHIC SCRIPTS RECOUNTING GENEALOGICAL CONNECTIONS. Many hieroglyphic texts are concerned with documentation of royal parentage (Houston 1989:52). Thus, named individuals and

0 |___|___|___|___|___| .50M.

2.13   Tikal, Altar 5, showing a skull and a stack of four long bones with an underlying glyph band describing a female elite personage (from Figure 23 in Jones and Satterthwaite 1982, courtesy of The University Museum, University of Pennsylvania).

their titles represent a large portion of the deciphered hieroglyphic corpus. The dynasty of Tikal, for instance, boasted a genealogy of thirty-nine sequential rulers who followed the quasi-legendary lineage founder, Yax-Moch-Xoc (Schele and Freidel 1990:140), although few of the thirty-nine rulers are recorded in hieroglyphic texts (J. Marcus, pers. com. 1992). The parentage and accession of the Late Classic king of Tikal (Ruler A), buried under Temple I, is recorded in hieroglyphic text on Lintel 3 of Temple I (Jones and Satterthwaite 1982:98). At Palenque in the Temple of the Cross Group, elaborate texts and pictorial imagery were designed to legitimize the break in lineage succession through the male line as the staff of office passed twice through the female line, once from Lady Kan-Ik to Ac-Kan and once from Lady Zac-Kuk to Pakal (Schele and Freidel 1990:222–228). Scenes of deceased parents taking an active role in handing over the scepter of office recur throughout the triad of the temples of the Cross, the Foliated Cross, and the Sun (Robertson 1991). Also, the hieroglyphic staircases of cities such as Copán, Dos Pilas, and Tamarindito were built to commemorate the sequence of dynastic rulers (Fash and Stuart 1991; Houston and Mathews 1985; Marcus 1976, 1983). The use of hieroglyphic script in conjunction with sculpture in order to accommodate changes in the dynastic lineage of Tikal is discussed in light of the problematical inscriptions on the headless statue of Tikal recovered from Structure 3D-43 (Fahsen 1988). Although there exist no extant pre-Hispanic codices in which specific genealogical records are listed, Thompson (1972:8, 1978:23), for one, argues that books of genealogy/ history, similar to central Mexican codices, probably existed.

Classic and Postclassic Maya iconography is replete with references both to specific named ancestors and to abstract motifs evocative of the important role of lineal descent in Maya society. The pictorial medium of iconography and the explicit script of hieroglyphic texts lend themselves to an appreciation of the pervasive role that the ancestors played in Maya society. Less explicit but equally compelling is the medium of architecture, which provided a physical structure or "house" for the ancestors.

PLACES OF THE ANCESTORS
These places are the house, the church, and the cemetery. The house is the everlasting home of one's own ancestors, where they are invoked as private persons, as family men and women maintaining order in their homes. . . . In the church at Chichicastenango a man may invoke his own ancestors, but especially he goes there to invoke those who in their lives held offices or practiced professions and who now hold authority in the world of the spirits. (BUNZEL 1952:270)

In the earlier part of the twentieth century, even though deceased relatives were interred in cemeteries, the Quiché of Chichicastenango (as cited above) venerated their immediate familial ancestors in the domestic setting and invoked those who held significant status within the community at the place of public ritual, the church. In the deeper history of lowland Maya Formative and Classic periods, venerated ancestors were interred principally in two locations: in a residential/ritual context (be it elite or commoner) or in a nonresidential and exclusively ritual context such as a funerary pyramid. In both contexts, the physical remains of ancestors stayed within the city or settlement, in contrast to the Chinese pattern of ancestor entombment in the countryside (Figure 1.2). Here, I emphasize the physical places where ancestral remains and residential remains come together rather than places such as caves that were evocative of the link between the living and the "other" world of forebears (e.g., Brady 1989; Carlson 1981).[18]

A striking difference between ancestor veneration in China, as documented by Freedman, and ancestor veneration in the Maya lowlands (as we understand it for the Classic and Postclassic periods) lies not so much in the rituals and practices of ancestor veneration but in the way in which the landscape was used to hold the skeletal material and the commemorative shrines of the ancestors. In the Chinese examples cited in Chapter 1, the ultimate entombment of an ancestor and the public rituals enacted at the location of entombment were physically removed from the household, where only a commemorative shrine and tablet symbolizing the ancestor were kept. According to Freedman (1970:164–173), rituals enacted at these two separate locales were gender-specific in terms of the principal actors in the ritual. In the Classic Maya lowlands, on the other hand, residential contexts often provided the *curational envelope* for ancestors of both elites and commoners. In this way, the two realms—physical interment and ritual commemoration—were conflated. In view of Freedman's and Feuchtwang's comments regarding the importance of safeguarding the bones of important ancestors, the Maya convention of intracompound interment of ancestors could be viewed as a type of safeguard insuring that ancestors were kept on the land where their descendants lived.

The identification of residential compounds as domestic mausolea (or sepulchres, as Coe [1988:235] has called them) is a logical consequence of the increased attention that "household archaeology" has received during the last three decades. As more residential structures and their subfloor burials and caches were excavated, archaeologists noted variations on the practice of interring the dead: within the core of the dwelling itself, under adjacent patio spaces, or within shrine platforms. Such interments and accompanying and sequential commemorations were largely family or lineage affairs, and the number of individuals participating in such ceremonies may have usually been under one hundred. Upon the death of an important leader of a large, powerful Maya lineage, on the other hand, as many as a thousand people

(Sanders 1989:103) may have been incorporated into lineage-based mortuary rituals.

The small size of the family group contrasts with the large-scale public gatherings that undoubtedly accompanied the interment and commemoration of a royal ancestor buried in a funerary pyramid in the epicenter of Classic Maya cities. With population estimates for these cities and their immediate hinterlands ranging from ten thousand to sixty thousand (Culbert and Rice 1990), rituals enacted in memory of royal personages were akin to large public performances or state theater (Geertz 1980; see also Demarest 1992). That Maya public ritual had a strong performance aspect to it is suggested by the architectural geometry of the city epicenters, in which large plazas capable of accommodating thousands of people are flanked by steeply sided mortuary pyramids that are akin to stage scaffolding. In visual media, the sharp duality in clothing worn by royalty (the simple cotton loincloths of men and plain, white *huipiles* of women, as opposed to elaborate headdresses, jade ornamentation, pectorals, and belts for men and heavily embroidered *huipiles* for women) is implicative of a strong emphasis on stage costuming.

Initial recognition of the fact that the "temple-pyramids" of the Maya were, in fact, royal funerary shrines was a consequence of the discovery in 1952 by Alberto Ruz Lhuillier (1973) of the tomb of Pakal, the powerful ruler of Palenque who was buried within a funerary pyramid constructed under his supervision. Unlike Pakal's Temple of the Inscriptions, at which there is little evidence of later expansions or interments, many funerary structures display long sequences of reuse and expansion. This pattern prompted Coe (1956:388) to note that

> If the only function of temple-pyramids (and "palaces") in the Maya Classic was ceremonial, why were they covered over with new constructions with such bewildering frequency? Why were the superstructures razed again and again to make way for superimposed buildings? Except in times of political and religious disturbances, sacred structures in other parts of the world were never treated in such a seemingly cavalier fashion.

In reality, this behavior was extremely reverential and indicative of the continued interaction of the lowland Maya with their ancestors and the places where ancestors were interred. The perpetual cycle of death and inheritance (rebirth) was played out in the pattern of burial interment and structure remodeling. In this way, Maya monumental architecture was very different from the Western tradition of large commemorative shrines that, once constructed, tended to become fossilized in time—such as the obelisk in Washington, D.C., which commemorates the first U.S. president. Monumental architecture of the Maya had a plasticity and flexibility and the sanctioned potential to change and grow as the array of ancestors changed and expanded through time.[19] In Chapter 3, I argue that the same relationship holds true for domestic architecture.

There is probably no single location in the Maya lowlands that so typifies this flexibility in commemorative, monumental architecture as does the North Acropolis at Tikal—a necropolis where ancestors were interred for over a thousand years, from the Late Formative through the Classic period. The complex archaeological cross section of the trench through the North Acropolis (Coe 1990: Figs. 9–11) shows clearly the long sequence of construction, modifications, and refurbishings that took place at this place of the dead. The direction of north has associations with the dead in Maya iconography and prose (Ashmore 1991; Schele and Miller 1986:277); thus, it is no surprise that later constructions are erected to the south of this complex of ancestral interments. Temples I and II frame the east and west sides of the Great Plaza located immediately to the south of the North Acropolis, and the Central Acropolis, which flanks the southern side of the plaza, completes the frame. In the Classic city space of Tikal, important founding ancestors of the Tikal dynasties were interred on the northern side of the Great Plaza at the center of the city.

This positioning was certainly no accident; Carlson (1981:187) and others have suggested that geomancy (Chinese *feng-shui* or the positioning of burial shrines with respect to the principles of directionality, solar cycles, and primal forces such as wind) probably existed among the Classic Maya.[20] The public location of royal burials in funerary pyramids and the tremendous amount of periodic ritual associated with these funerary structures is somewhat analogous to the public contexts of Chinese tombs and ancestral halls. Carlson (1981:145), further, has noted two parallels between cosmological systems of China and pre-Columbian Mesoamerica: "the quadripartite pattern of the cosmologies and the interactive role of ancestors or ancestral deities in the lives of men." With good reason, therefore, the North Acropolis of Tikal (plus Temples I and II; Coe 1990), Mundo Perdido of Tikal (Laporte and Vega 1986), the Temple of the Inscriptions at Palenque (M. Coe 1965; Ruz Lhuillier 1973), and El Grupo May of Oxkintok (Rivera Dorado 1990) have been interpreted as important ancestor-mortuary complexes. From Palenque to Copán, the significance of these structures to royal ancestor veneration is demonstrated by virtue of associated hieroglyphic texts and richly furnished burials and by the monumental scale of building construction.

Although the importance of royal ancestor veneration is expressed unambiguously in Classic Maya architecture, scripts, and iconography, it is the thesis of this research that the genesis of ancestor veneration is in formative and nonelite agrarian contexts. Furthermore, the agrarian-linked practice of ancestor veneration persists through the Classic period alongside the highly derived and politicized elite form. As Freidel and Schele (1989:242) have noted, the convention of interring ancestors under the floors of residential structures is rooted in the Formative and is temporally antecedent to any known pyramid-tomb complex. In residential contexts, the expression of these practices tended to be more subdued, particularly in reference to archaeological remains. Two- or three-meter-tall shrines and subfloor burial pits replace towering pyramids; hieroglyphic texts and the carving or painting of complex iconography is absent; and ancestors of nonelite lineages tend to be buried with shell necklaces, modest amounts of jade, and a few treasured ceramic containers. As a result of these differences in burial treatment, more refined archaeological methods of sampling, data collection, and analysis are necessary to infer social practices regarding the treatment of ancestors in residences.

In the Maya lowlands, ancestor veneration existed in a variety of social and physical settings: among both nonelite and elite sectors of society and in both domestic ritual and public ritual contexts. A great deal of field research has resulted in the identification of small Late Classic pyramidal platforms (sometimes referred to as *oratorios*)[21] as a component of residential units. These modest structures (usually one of several platforms arranged around a central plaza) are present at sites throughout the Maya lowlands—e.g., Copán (Leventhal 1983), Tikal (Becker 1971; Haviland 1981), and Seibal (Tourtellot 1988), as well as Mountain Cow, Benque Viejo, Holmul, Dzibilchaltún, and Altun Ha (Welsh 1988:88), to name a few published examples. For the Postclassic, Thompson (1954:124) has described the presence of ancestor veneration and family ossuaries at the site of Mayapán. The ubiquity of this pattern of ancestral shrines is not surprising. In reference to ethnographic data from China, Freedman (1970:164) referred to the veneration that took place at the residential shrine as the universal aspect of ancestor worship.

Classic-period ancestral shrine structures are often located on the eastern side of plaza groups, although, as Welsh (1988:Tables 105, 106) demonstrates, there is considerable variability in shrine cardinal location and orientation across the Maya lowlands. Many residential compounds, particu-

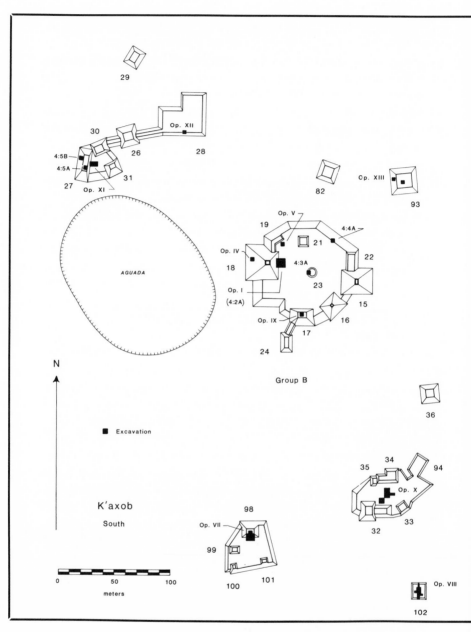

2.14   Map of Southern Sector of K'axob showing "alpha" and satellite structures; note location of Operation I on eastern side of Structure 18 (drawing by author and Ingrid Martonova).

larly smaller ones, contain no shrine structure whatsoever—a variation that may be explained by reference to developmental cycles of residential growth (Haviland 1988; Tourtellot 1988) or simply by differences in wealth and status. Analyzing a sample of over four hundred burials from sixteen lowland Maya sites, Welsh (1988:190) has observed that burials (of both male and female adults) in shrine contexts tend to be better furnished than comparable burials located in residences (under floors or in platform or plaza construction fill). This locational and contextual pattern strengthens the interpretation of shrine interments as indicative of ancestor veneration. Both Haviland (1988) and Tourtellot (1988) have attempted to establish links among the following archaeological variables: the size of residential complexes, the number of renovations and expansions, presence of shrines, and the social organizational variables of household and lineage developmental cycles.

EXAMPLE: FORMATIVE ANCESTOR SHRINE AT K'AXOB. Ancestor shrines as ritual foci for lineage and household groups is linked with the progressive sacralization of place at K'axob. One locale in particular, the ancestral heartland of the community of K'axob, demonstrates this pattern quite clearly. Following more than five hundred years of occupation and domestic structure renovation during the Middle Formative and the early part of the Late Formative, a clear change in construction type and burial practices occurred within the six-by-eight-meter excavation locus called Operation I (Figure 2.14). Located in front of pyramidal Structure 18, which defines the western side of a large plaza, stratified deposits from this excavation span the full range of pre-Hispanic lowland Maya time: Late Postclassic back to the Middle Preclassic or Middle Formative. The pyramid itself is Early Classic in construction and rises just over four meters off the plaza surface. This plaza complex is composed of four pyramidal structures (between two and six meters in height) and several lower platforms (Figure 2.15). There are no structures on the northern side of this plaza, allowing an unobstructed view of a larger northern plaza group that contains a thirteen-meter-tall pyramid also constructed during the Late Classic.

During the later part of the Late Formative, locally known as the K'atabche'kax ceramic complex, burial patterns changed from extended individuals interred in long burial pits to seated or tightly flexed individuals deposited into circular pits. Within Operation I, a series of circular pits intruded into a low, apsidal platform structure lacking a plastered surface. All around the structure, a thick, plastered plaza floor was laid down. Just shy of the western edge of the excavated area, two extremely deep burial pits were then prepared: an oblong trench and a circular pit. The trench intruded down

2.15   Perspective drawing of "alpha" plaza group and surrounding satellite residences—B Group. Structure 18 is located on the extreme right side of the platform: Operation I was exca-

2.16   Burial offerings from shrine burial (photo by Mary L. Angelini).

through Middle Formative deposits to terminate at the soft, limestone bedrock. Judging from the condition of the collar lining of the trench and the stratified nature of the interred deposits, the trench was reopened several times and secondary burial interments placed within. The ancestors interred at this specially prepared locale were buried with a formidable array of jewelry and accouterments: a marine bivalve amulet, shell "tinklers," carved bone (possibly fan handles), jade beads, and several ceramic vessels (Figure 2.16). The vessels represent a variety of forms from a miniature Sierra Red spouted jar to a large bowl with a streaky Society Hall slip, a flamboyant outflaring rim, and a large cross painted on the interior of the base (Figure 2.17). Two of the vessels from the trench feature contain this motif. The small circular pit immediately adjacent to this ancestral burial locale also contained more than one individual, and two of the three vessels from this circular pit were also painted with the cross motif. The oblong pit, containing a wealth of burial goods and a concentration of vessels bearing the quadripartite motif, was sealed by a low platform creating the first formalized ancestor shrine at K'axob (Figure 2.18).

At the end of the Formative, the shrine complex was buried and two dedicatory caches deposited into the fill: (1) a single Society Hall flaring-rimmed

2.17   Ceramic vessel with quadripartite design, Late Formative shrine, K'axob (photo by Matthew Bobo).

bowl and (2) a deposit of three vessels and seven pecked-and-shaped lime-stone spheres (Figure 2.19). The lowest, barrel-shaped vessel was filled with a collection of jade and shell beads and fragments of a possible mosaic. There was no further significant construction at this locale until the Early Classic, when the Structure 18 pyramid was built (Figure 2.15). The pyramid capped this Formative locale of domestic structures, subfloor ancestral burials, and a Late Formative burial shrine. Although only the basal course of the staircase risers was found intact, fragments of painted plaster excavated amidst the rubble reveal that the pyramid was painted red.

The large temple-mortuary complexes of major Classic Maya cities and the small residential shrines, such as this Formative shrine from K'axob, both indicate differences in the placement of the dead based on social status, po-litical power, and wealth. In residential contexts, as well as exclusively regal/ritual contexts, commemorative shrine and burial site were literally super-imposed. This spatial conflation elevated the status of the living individuals, both male and female, who were involved in the rituals of the ancestors. It also resulted in an emphasis on the long-term occupation of places, punctu-ated by frequent refurbishings, as well as the progressive sacralization of burial places within the domestic compounds (see Haviland [1981] on Tikal elite residential group 7F-1). This pattern of sequential refurbishing and sac-

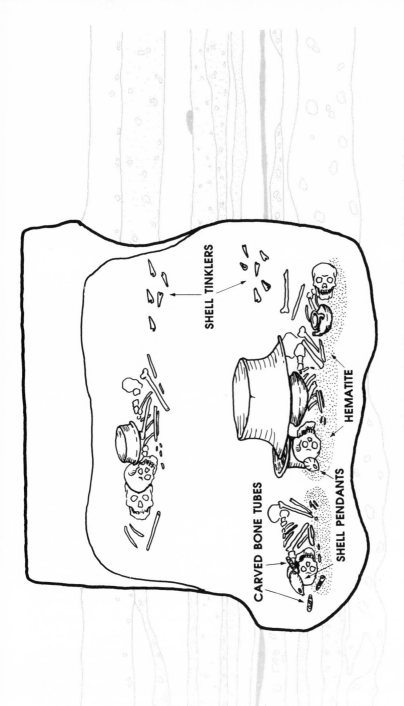

2.18   Late Formative ancestor shrine in stratigraphic cross section, K'axob (drawing by John A. Walkey).

2.19   Commemorative cache covering Late Formative shrine plaza
                        (photo by author).

ralization also has been observed in the Operation I deposits of K'axob. The
residential-ancestral shrine pattern, previously identified for the Classic period, is not in fact restricted to that time period and can also be found in
Formative contexts where sufficient horizontal excavation permits the recognition of such features.

Material Remains of the Ancestors
        From an archaeological perspective, two basic princi-
ples of ancestor veneration are particularly compelling in that they directly
affect the sex and age composition as well as the taphonomy of ancestral
remains. The first is that an ancestor is a cultural construct and, therefore,
the product of a selective process; the second is that the bones of revered
dead are generally part of a protracted series of rituals that do not always
terminate in the placement of a full skeleton at the final burial site.

        The fact that not all deceased family members become ancestors—the role of
ancestor being reserved for leaders and prominent lineage members—means
that many individuals are never interred in domestic or monumental mausolea. This fact introduces gender and age bias into archaeological samples,
such as exists in the burial record of Seibal, where females are grossly under-

represented (Tourtellot 1990). As a point of comparison, in patrilineal systems such as in China, a deceased male head-of-household who is a member of a wealthy patrilineage receives preferential treatment; his bones are more likely than those of a female relative to be entombed and his tablet more likely to be enshrined in an ancestral hall for future generations to revere (Freedman 1966). Using very conservative criteria for the lowland Classic Maya, Welsh (1988: Table 111) identified eleven burials that were directly suggestive of ancestor veneration due to reported missing skeletal parts. Specifically, the face or skull had been removed. In light of questions regarding the extent to which a gender hierarchy was expressed through burial treatment, a breakdown of these burials by sex is informative: three burials contained males only, one burial contained a male and a female, and two burials contained females only. (For five burials sex could not be determined.) From Tikal, of the shrine structures in plaza arrangements (Type 2 plan), only 22 percent of the thirty-two known burials were identified as male (Becker 1971). These data, though from an admittedly small sample, suggest that in both elite and commoner contexts both males and females were viable candidates for ancestor status. This pattern exists despite the tendency toward patrilineal descent and inheritance within Maya society. The dual sexes of engendered ancestors were encoded linguistically not only among the Quiché but also among the Tzotzil, who refer to ancestral deities as *totilme'iltik* or "fathers-mothers" (Vogt 1964: 32). The Maya, therefore, deviated in a significant way from known Chinese ethnographic examples; thus, the issue of engendering ancestors must be approached independently in the Maya region.

Practices related to communing with and drawing power from ancestors invariably coexist with protracted treatment of skeletal remains and the retention of certain skeletal elements (particularly crania and long bones) and heirlooms among the living, who used them as potent symbols of inherited power. The Quiché, for instance, are said to have migrated with sacred bundles called *pizom c'ac'al,* which were handed down from the founding lineage leaders to their successors and contained unspecified relics of the founding ancestors (Carmack 1981: 63). Bundles are a recurrent motif of Classic-period iconography in the lowlands as well, and some of them have been linked to glyphic expressions for the inheritance of political power and accession to office (Berlin 1968; Proskouriakoff 1960; Schele and Miller 1983). Other bundles are known to have contained bloodletting paraphernalia used to invoke revered ancestors. These iconographic representations are complemented by archaeological burial data such as elite Burial 85 from Tikal, which lacked a cranium and femora (W. Coe 1965).

The explanation of missing elements from burial contexts, however, is of-

2.20   Disarticulated bone from shrine burial (photo by author).

ten phrased not in terms of veneration but rather in terms of ritual human sacrifice. In fact, Maya burials missing anatomical parts (particularly the crania) are generally considered to be *prima facie* evidence of ritual human sacrifice (Fowler 1984; Robin 1989; Schele 1984; Sharer 1978). This automatic attribution of missing parts to the ritual of human sacrifice is due partly to the more sensational attraction of this explanation (as opposed to that of ancestor veneration) and partly to the inherent ambiguity in archaeological methods for ascribing meaning to burials with missing skeletal parts. Welsh, for instance, labels as evidence for human sacrifice any burial falling into the following categories: multiple interment consisting of an adult(s) and child(ren); multiple interments of an apparently complete skeleton accompanied by an incomplete skeleton (usually decapitated) or a secondary urn interment; interments at locations in which caches usually occur, such as under stelae, altars, or temple stairs; and finally, any interment with missing skeletal elements, such as "headless bodies, bodies without femurs or lower legs, skulls without bodies, legs without bodies" (Welsh 1988:171). In light of general ethnographic and ethnohistoric Maya sources describing the ritual behavior associated with the disposition of dead ancestors, all of these burials could equally well be the result of reverential rather than sacrificial behavior.

ANCESTRAL REMAINS IN A K'AXOB BURIAL SHRINE. The oblong trench underneath the low shrine platform described above contained skeletal remains that some archaeologists would interpret as indicative of human sacrifice—that is, the remains of multiple, disarticulated individuals (Figure 2.20). Closer attention to context, however, quickly dispels this notion. The burial locale is in a focal location, the multiple "collar" linings around the top of the pit indicate that it was opened and resealed several times (rarely the practice in sacrificial contexts), and the individuals were interred with a rich and diverse variety of grave goods. The bones of these individuals (estimates of the minimum number of individuals vary from eight to twelve; R. Storey, pers. com. 1993) bear no recognizable evidence of cut marks indicating decapitation or dismemberment, suggesting that a period of time elapsed (during which defleshing occurred) before the disarticulated remains were interred in the shrine.

Comparative material comes from the site of Cuello, where a large population of Middle and Late Formative burials have been excavated. Robin (1989) has found a significant increase in partially or totally disarticulated skeletons during the transition between the Middle and Late Formative periods. She ascribes this difference to the onset of human sacrifice, but other explanations, such as protracted burial rituals associated with ancestor veneration, are equally plausible. This ambiguity in the interpretation of skeletal material indicates an area of research in which advances in methods of interpretation are urgently needed while we still have access to the skeletal remains of the ancestors of the contemporary Maya.

THREE

Creating a Genealogy
of Place

*Y*ahau ah nohol u chun u uinicil Ah Noh<Ix>-Kan-
Tacay u kaba u chun u uinicil A<h> Puche. Bolonppel yoc
haa u cananmaob, bolonppel uitz u cananmaob.
                              (*Chilam Balam of Chumayel*)
The lord of the people of the south is the first of the men of
the Noh family. Ix-Kan-Tacay is the name of the first of the
men of the Puch family. They guard nine rivers; they guard
nine mountains.   (TRANSLATION BY ROYS 1967:64)

ti yet . . . u [mah]antic kax u manab tu than lae yume hex
talbal kax.   (*The Titles of Ebtun*)
This, lord, is an inherited forest . . .
                      (TRANSLATION BY ROYS 1939:265)

In a document of 1561 and another on the reverse of the
same sheet . . . is recorded an individual title to a tract of
land and its conveyance "to the principal men of the town
here at Ebtun." The vendor states that it is the "title of the
forest of my ancestors." (ROYS 1943:37; EMPHASIS ADDED)

FOREST, FIELD, ORCHARD, AND DWELLING
IN THE TROPICAL LOWLANDS

Statements such as those given above suggest that the
Yucatec Maya of the Colonial period perceived of their land tenure system as
one in which rights were inherited through an ancestral line and boundaries
of lands were carefully noted and sometimes guarded. We turn now to the
realm of land, lineage, boundaries, and inheritance in order to investigate
how Maya farmers configured themselves on the landscape to facilitate production. These variables are critical ones because they not only determined
how production was organized, but they are also powerful determinants
of archaeologically detectable settlement structure. In this chapter, ethnographic, ethnohistoric, linguistic, and archaeological data are examined in

order to characterize land use in a tropical lowland setting and to examine the relationship between land tenure and residential structure. Here, I am not attempting to reconstruct a static pattern of land tenure; rather, I am exploring the variable arrangements that may have existed during pre-Hispanic times among families, lineages, and land. Not all land was appropriated by the rulers, just as not all land was communal-use lineage land or land locked into a chain of hereditary successors within a single family. Rather, the tropical lowland pattern of land use and tenure was complex and varied, with a pronounced tendency toward nonadjacent plots (as a hedge against risk factors, among other reasons). Moreover, one can detect from contemporary studies of lowland tropical agriculturalists a relationship between the intensity with which land is used (intensity as measured by length of time lands are left in fallow) and proximity to residence. Thus, lands adjacent to residences (the "vacant" spaces of archaeological settlement-pattern research) take on particular importance because they are spatially proximate to burial sites of ancestors. A central thesis of this research is that burial places of the ancestors create a genealogy of place that links descendants to that land. In this sense, the creation of ancestors, as a social practice, is an indicator of the enclosure of land into exclusionary tracts with inherited entitlements.

Since our knowledge of Classic-period land tenure patterns is so poor, this discussion cannot fail to break new ground and, I hope, to destroy some old myths. As we shall see below, current and past reconstructions of land use and tenure based upon the ethnohistoric record from northern Yucatán contain a fatal flaw which has resulted in the underestimation of the importance of land tenure and the undervaluing of the role of kin group leaders in structuring agricultural production. I suggest that this problem stems from the simplification, in translation, of the Yucatec Maya word KAX (or k'ax), which has been translated simply as "forest" when in fact it has other more applicable meanings, such as fallow land, weedy lands, and monte or bush land.

An understanding of the linkages among the variables of land and lineage is dependent upon a consensus on the starting point of such an investigation. For this reason, the first part of this chapter is concerned with defining the nature of Maya agriculture as it relates to land use, boundary maintenance, and inheritance. I will make the argument that, at many times and places, the lineage was the resource-holding group—the "glue" that held together a multicomponent farming system with spatially extensive as well as intensive patterns of land use. As "guardians" of their resources, lineage leaders were positioned in a relation of dynamic interaction with the more centralized forces of kingship from the Late Formative until well into Colonial times; variations on this relationship are explored in Chapter 5.

The final part of this chapter focuses on the place where the ancestors "slept"—the residential compound and the surrounding fields and orchards. The dwelling is seen as a place of convergence. It is here that ancestral shrines are located as well as the physical remains of progenitors, who by their presence bear witness to the successional chain of resource rights. The multistructure nature of many Maya residential complexes and their temporal depth reflect their transgenerational and multifamily character. Following Haviland (1988), I suggest that the frequent recourse to remodeling residential complexes is indicative of descent rights and the process of inheritance. In a very real sense then, archaeologically defined stratigraphic sequences of burial interment, structure renovation, and special dedicatory deposits are ultimately genealogical sequences.

FIELDS OF THE ANCESTORS

When a Missouri corn farmer fallows a field, the first-year growth will be grasses and short, stubby plants. If the field is allowed to "rest" for two to three years, a mat of prairie grass or chest-high saplings can be expected to establish themselves. A full cycle from fallow field to mature temperate hardwood or conifer forest can take several decades. In the tropical Yucatán Peninsula, on the other hand, a fallow field will produce chest-high saplings during the first year and three-meter-tall trees during the second year of fallow. Within five to seven years, both upper and lower canopy species will be present and, to an untrained eye, this growth will look like a virgin tropical rain forest. As one moves south along the peninsula, the rate of succession quickens, as does the compositional complexity of the mature rain forest. This difference between the rate and composition of plant succession in tropical fields as opposed to temperate fields has created a cognitive dissonance as temperate-climate dwellers frame classification systems to describe tropical agriculture. This difficulty is apparent in studies of Maya land use, which have combined the unconsciously denigrating and ahistorical attitude of "colonialists" vis-à-vis "the other" with the perceptual limitations of early twentieth-century Maya scholars. A specific example of a linguistic translation of Maya prose will illustrate my point.

The middle quotation listed above as "*ti yet . . . u [mah]antic kax u manab tu than lae yume hex talbal kax*," translated as "This, lord, is an inherited forest . . . ," is taken from the *Titles of Ebtun* (Roys 1939:265), a collection of Colonial-period documents (1600–1823) maintained by people of the eastern Yucatán town of Ebtun. These records chronicle a series of land agreements and surveys defining (1) the contested provincial boundaries between Cupul towns and those of Sotuta and Cochuah; (2) the boundaries separating town or lineage lands of Ebtun and Kaua from those of Cuncunul,

Tekom, and Tixcacalcupul; and particularly (3) the 182-year legal battle for the recovery of the Tontzimin tract sold to an outsider (Roys 1939:51). The quote cited above is from a testimony given by Lorenzo Tus in 1713 regarding his claim to two tracts of inherited land in lieu of supporting legal documentation. The term "inherited" as used by Colonial Maya is meant to convey a precedent of prior resource rights to certain agricultural fields, going back several generations and probably to pre-Hispanic times. Yet the phrase is translated simply as "This, lord, is an inherited forest . . . ," with the word *k'ax* being translated simply as "forest." The same translation (*k'ax* = "forest") is employed hundreds of times throughout the translation of this and other documents. In using the word "forest," Roys evokes an image of unspoiled wilderness, a great place to go deer-hunting, for instance, but not an image of agricultural lands that may be in various stages of fallow. Is this an accurate translation of what Lorenzo Tus meant when he used the word *k'ax*? Or is it a translation that so simplifies this term as to obscure the subtle complexities of Maya land use, tenure, and inheritance? The Yucatec Maya Cordemex dictionary (Barrera Vásquez 1980:387) suggests multiple meanings for the term *k'ax*, including *bosque* (forest or woods), *arboleda* (grove), *montaña o monte* (mountain forest or thicket), *campo donde hay monte* (an agricultural field in which there is thicketlike regrowth), and *selva* (rain forest). The variety of definitions suggests that the word *k'ax* has many meanings, only some of which are what in English we call a "forest." Furthermore, the expression *u k'ax kah* is used by Yucatec Maya to refer to *ejido* (Barrera Vásquez 1980:387), or the agricultural lands controlled by a cooperative unit. In the Cordemex dictionary, another expression, *u k'axil kab*, is taken directly from the earlier Motul dictionary. This expression is defined similarly in both places: Cordemex, *asiento de colmenas, sitio de colmenas* (Barrera Vásquez 1980:387); Motul, *monte para colmenas, bueno para colmenas* (Martínez Hernández 1929:241)—a fallow field in which the characteristics of regrowth make it a good place for beehives. My main point here is that *k'ax* has several meanings, and most of the appearances of *k'ax* in documents should be translated as fallow field, not forest.[1]

Because *k'ax* has no satisfactory equivalent expression in Spanish or English, there is a cognitive dissonance to the thought and translation process—a dissonance that, I suggest, resulted in grossly oversimplified theories of both the structure of lowland Maya agriculture and principles of land tenure. Scholars of the early part of the twentieth century, in fact, often displayed a colonial-imperial attitude toward Maya agriculture, delighting in a denigrating contrast of the sophistication of Maya hieroglyphic script with the purported simplicity of contemporary and past farming techniques (e.g., Roys 1943:38). Did these scholars actually believe that five hundred years of slavery, servitude, debt peonage, and massive population reduction and relocation had not altered patterns of land use and tenure and stripped them down to all but the essential human/land relationship? The authorized attitude of agricultural simplicity engendered many generations of mis-reconstructions of contact-period Yucatec Maya farming practices and, by analogy, of farming practices of the southern lowlands during the Late Formative and Classic periods. A salient part of this misrepresentation is the false polarization of the terms "forest" and "field." In temperate latitudes these words connote oppositional states (present or absent); in the tropics, however, due to an accelerated rate of regrowth facilitated by a frost-free climate and, generally, ample seasonal rainfall, forest and field are the endpoints of a biotic continuum that encompasses great diversity in strategies of land use. The European conception of "forest" is of an area unsuitable for agriculture, defined as communal land used to feed livestock, for hunting, and for resource gathering. As a result, the lowland tropical "forests" of the Yucatán were equated with communal lands despite the fact that Maya witnesses themselves referred to them as "inherited," suggesting that the lands were part of a *fixed-plot* system and were as carefully anchored in time and space as were most other aspects of Maya life. In other words, a translation that captures the sentiment of Lorenzo Tus might read something like, "this is an established field that I inherited from my father and grandfather; at present, it lies fallow."

From Forest to Field

Lowland tropical agricultural systems are frequently structured into multiple components which together yield a highly textured landscape. Over the past twenty years, significant research effort has been expended in the identification and documentation of past and present techniques of lowland tropical farming that coexist with or replace swidden agriculture (Harrison and Turner 1978; see McAnany 1992:184–190 for a review). Here, the emphasis is not on the identification of different components (which has already been accomplished) but on reintroducing human organization to this highly textured landscape. In shifting the focus to human use of tropical lands, I hope to initiate a discussion of the kinds of land tenure relationships that existed in the past and to highlight the role of transgenerational inheritance as a mechanism that promoted fixed-plot farming, affected the use of lands around the dwelling, and resulted in ancestral interments within the dwelling itself.

Hanks (1990:316) has observed that among the Yucatec Maya, "the homestead and the milpa . . . [are] two embodiments of a single spatio-temporal system." Thus, lowland tropical agriculture has a spatial dimension as well as a biological and labor process dimension. The variable-fallow plots (*kax*) are spatially the most remote from the residence and are the places at which "forest" and field are temporally sequential. As one moves closer to the residence, the practice of fallowing fields may drop out altogether as continuously cropped and fertilized plots become more common. Landscape modification or capital (as per Blaikie and Brookfield 1986) and raised and canalized fields and terraces are also more likely to occur close to the residence. Below, I present a model of this biotic continuum starting with the "pristine" rain forest, moving through the fields, and ending with the residential heart of Maya farming. At each point along this continuum, however, strategies of land use may differ significantly, yielding a complex and multi-component farming system.

There is very little documentation of the composition of a pristine lowland rain forest in the Maya region. Analysis of macrobotanical and pollen remains from archaeological as well as lacustrine core contexts indicates a high rate of deforestation during the Classic period and earlier in most areas suitable for agriculture (Brenner, Leyden, and Binford 1990; Leyden and Brenner 1992; Rice, Rice, and Deevey 1985; Stein 1990; Vaughn, Deevey, and Garrett-Jones 1985). We do not yet know whether the Classic Maya maintained "refugia" of high canopy forest in the interstices of their field plots, or whether the only "refugia" remaining were in nonarable, nonreclaimable areas—for example, swamps with seasonally variable water levels and steep slopes, such as those of the Maya mountains. The rain forest plays an important role—that of an environmental thermostat—in regulating rainfall, temperature, evapotranspiration, and particularly nutrient flow. The contemporary Lacandón, as Nations and Nigh (1980:20) observe, "farm *in* the forest, they do not replace the forest." Recent palynological evidence from central Petén, however, indicates that the ecologically sensitive farming habits of the Lacandón may not be relevant to agricultural practices of the first millennium A.D. Vegetation changes of the Classic and Postclassic periods were so severe that reestablishment of the historically known tropical rain forest only slightly preceded Spanish incursion into the Petén (Brenner, Leyden, and Binford 1990; Leyden and Brenner 1992).

Moving away from virgin rain forests, we come to lands that are part of a fixed-plot farming system with varying rates of fallow. In such a system, there may be many fields in mature stages of fallow; this "high bush" is the KAX or *k'axil* that Roys translated as "forest" (Figure 3.1). These areas are not really "wild," however, because economic species, interspersed with the natural succession species, change the fundamental nature of the biota. Nations and Nigh (1980:15) comment that the *acahual* (*k'ax*) contains a species structure and biomass distribution that differs from both field and forest—an ecotonal

3.1   Fallow field in advanced high bush—*k'ax* (photo by Peter D. Harrison).

band along the continuum from forest to field. Furthermore, these areas were and are intensively used as a source of pharmaceuticals, herbs, wild game, raw materials for construction and manufacturing, and other resources. In an environment in which game is not plentiful, the *k'ax* is like a managed wildlife preserve. Rich in primary productivity, the *k'ax* is attractive to deer, coatimundi, armadillo, tepesquintle, and other sources of protein (see Nations and Nigh 1980: Table 5). These are also the lands on which the apiaries are located in Yucatán. Tending bees is largely a male activity today (Redfield and Villa Rojas 1962: 48) although females may have been more involved in the past when the hives of stingless bees could have been located closer to the domicile. AH MUZENCAB (the Maya bee protector or supernatural), however, is generally described in Maya prose in male, gender-specific terms (Roys 1967: 63–65; cf. Pohl and Feldman 1982).

In his treatise on Maya ethnobotany, Roys (1931) documents the fact that the Maya *k'axil*, in part, constituted a medicine chest (see also Hanks 1990: 306). Compiling Colonial-period medical prescriptions and incantations from Yucatán and adjoining Campeche and Quintana Roo, he shows that the Yucatán is the only "part of America where we find a considerable body of medical literature written by the Indians in their native language" (Roys 1931:xix). Furthermore, he notes that "a surprisingly large percentage of the Maya medical texts [are] devoted to the treatment of symptoms and based on objective observations of the effects of certain plants in the human system" (Roys 1931:xxi). The *k'axil* or fallow fields are used extensively as apiaries, for pharmaceuticals, and as the locale in which economic species, particularly arboreal ones, continue to grow and to be harvested throughout the fallow cycle. Moving along the continuum from forest to field, we investigate early fallow fields (sometimes called *UAYMIL* in Yucatec Mayan; Figure 3.2). Even this area is never completely rested, however, since quick-return tree species such as *achiote*, and today banana, are generally planted in such areas—thus the term *pak che kol* or "planted tree *milpa*," which is used by the Lacandón for these "fallow fields" (Nations and Nigh 1980:15 and their Table 4).

Next are fields currently in cultivation but prone to intermittent fallow, the length of which depends on a variety of natural, political, and demographic

3.2   Fallow field in low bush—*UAYMIL*—in foreground and higher bush in background (photo by Peter D. Harrison).

Field facility at a far field (photo by Peter D. Harrison).

factors. These fields are not those near the residence (the infields; Turner and Sanders 1992:266–267) but rather are those fields located at a distance of an hour or more (without the aid of modern transportation). Today, in the Tuxtlas region of the Gulf Coast and the Petexbatún region of the Maya lowlands, Thomas W. Killion (1990, pers. com. 1992) has found that when fields such as these are worked, facilities are built in the field for resting, eating, and sometimes storing harvest (Figure 3.3; see also Sheets 1992:113). This far-field component of lowland farming is a logical outcome of an ex-pansive and complex system of tropical agriculture. In this regard, the follow-ing excerpt from the once-lost *Relación de Nicolás de Valenzuela* that re-counts the conquest of the Lacandón is particularly interesting: "The huts of the milpas, although smaller (than the houses of the town) are as well built. And in the milpas they have mud-daubed granaries of maize" (Hellmuth 1977:425–426). Storage of grain in the fields and the construction of field houses indicate that the Lacandón, too, were engaged in outfield agriculture and that they built facilities in this managed landscape. Smyth (1990) has documented the existence of a similar pattern in the Puuc Hills today, as has Sheets (1992:Fig. 2-2) in the Zapotitan Valley.

These far fields often are described as "milpa," which in popular usage is synonymous with "corn field." A Nahuatl term, *milpa* is actually a com-pound of *milli* or "cultivated land" and *pan* meaning "on the surface" (Kart-tunen 1983:147, 186). Hellmuth (1977:44) argues that, among sixteenth-and seventeenth-century Maya and Spaniards, the term more frequently used was *milpería*, which he interprets as "sown field of a variety of crops with a little hut." The intimation is that *milpa* does not refer, by definition, to a monocropped maize field but to a polycultural field distant enough from the residence to require a field hut.

The species composition of these fields was probably variable. While the role of maize in the constellation of lowland cultigens was and remains extremely important, polycultural fields and orchards in this lowland tropical environment provided a diversified culinary base and represented a strategy of risk reduction and wealth enhancement. To assert that Maya agriculture of the past was based primarily on maize production, as it is today, is to ignore a complexity and diversity that is apparent in iconographic representations and palaeobotanical remains.

To be sure, maize has been discovered in the earliest Middle Formative deposits at Cuello (Hammond 1991) and also at K'axob (Miksicek n.d.). A storable staple such as maize, furthermore, did play an important role in the political economy of the Classic Maya. Maize is symbolized by a handsome young male in both Classic iconography and in the Postclassic Codex Dresden (Taube 1985). Processed maize, such as tamales, is frequently depicted on Classic Maya vessels in food presentation scenes (Taube 1989). But would a time traveler crossing the base of the Yucatán Peninsula in A.D. 700 have seen rolling hills covered with acres sown purely in maize? Probably not. As Hellmuth (1977:436) has pointed out, monocropping maize in the rich but exhaustible limestone-derived tropical soils of the peninsula can quickly deplete soil fertility. The continued occupation through nearly two millennia of many areas of the Yucatán indicates that soil conservation was not a foreign notion to pre-Hispanic Maya farmers. The weight of ethnohistoric evidence indicates that the Maya of the contact period, at least, mixed cultigens together in many of their plots.[2] This agricultural technique requires more labor, skill, and in-depth knowledge of compatible plants and planting schedules than does monocropping (Nations and Nigh 1980:11).

Within this type of fixed-plot, variable-fallow regime, the length of time any one field was cultivated and the number of times it could be cropped per year varies, because this rhythm is so closely linked to very local environmental and pedological conditions which change considerably across the peninsula. Some cultigens suck nutrients out of the soil faster than others—maize is particularly culpable in this regard—and this factor also affects cropping frequency. At the base of the peninsula, plots could have been cultivated between five and eight years (Hellmuth 1977:436). Farther north in the Puuc Hills, an in-depth study of spatial variation in soil classes indicates that length of fallow varied locally between one and twenty-one years depending upon edaphic characteristics (Dunning 1989:Table 2). In wetter areas of the Petén, such as Poptún and along the Usumacinta drainage, double-cropping (two harvests per year) was possible (Culbert, Magers, and Spencer 1978:158; Hellmuth 1977:425–426; Nations and Nigh 1980:13), while in the drier north, only one harvest was possible (Dunning 1989:13).

In many areas of the Maya lowlands for which extensive survey data have been collected, the distribution of Classic-period residential units is dispersed but continuous across all sections of arable land. This settlement distribution brings into question the actual existence of a far-field component among Classic Maya farmers since most areas containing arable soils also contained what appear to have been permanent residences; i.e., there was no vacant terrain on which to place far fields (see Turner and Sanders 1992:270). In fact, the variable-fallow, far-field component may have been a casualty of rising demographic levels and, in some areas, of political instability. In the region of Pulltrouser Swamp, for instance, residential units ringing the swamp seem to have had no adjacent uninhabited areas in which to place variable-fallow fields (McAnany 1992). The settlement of Nohmul abuts the swamp to the north and west (Pyburn 1989), with the settlement of San Estevan immediately to the south and east (Bullard 1965; Levi, pers. com. 1990). In some of the well-populated areas, an intensive near-residential component including swamp reclamation, orchards, and fields may have been all that spatial constraints of a Late Classic population permitted. Killion et al. (1991) extend this argument to the enclosed near-residential fields of the Petexbatún region.

At the opposite end of the continuum from the rain forest are the locales that remain in permanent cultivation: fields, gardens, and, most importantly, orchards (Figure 3.4). Numerous Spanish chroniclers noted the extensive groves of trees in southwestern Campeche, among the Cehache, in Belize, and to a lesser degree in the drier northern Yucatán.[3] At contact, orchards were located near residences if edaphic and rainfall conditions permitted, or, alternatively, at the closest suitable location where rights could be obtained or inherited. The spatial pattern of orchards ringing residences resulted in a dispersed settlement pattern such as existed in the Dzuluinicob province (north and central Belize) of the Colonial period—a pastiche of local and migrant groups from the North (Jones 1989). Apparently, Bishop Gregorio de Montalvo refused to institute a policy of *reducción* in this region precisely because it would lead to the abandonment of highly productive *cacao* orchards (Jones 1982:282). Northern Yucatán, on the other hand, was really too dry for *cacao,* and at contact most *cacao* was imported from wetter regions on the Caribbean side of the peninsula. Limestone-solution sinkholes (cenotes) that were collapsed or had filled with silt, however, did provide enough moisture and shade and were highly prized, individually named, and inherited regardless of their remoteness.[4] The soil and rainfall regime around Tah Itzá (Taya-

3.4   Orchards and fields in permanent cultivation in Veracruz, Mexico (photo by Thomas W. Killion).

sal), likewise, was poorly suited for growing *cacao*. According to the chroniclers of Hernán Cortés, who made an *entrada* through the heart of Itzá country in 1525, the lord of Tah Itzá, Can Ek, owned or controlled *cacao* orchards as far away as the base of the Maya Mountains (Jones 1983:73)—an extreme example of the noncontiguous land plots discussed above.

The sarcophagus of Pakal identifies some of the more common orchard species and also demonstrates rather elegantly that orchard species were used as a metaphor of royal inheritance and descent. Bordering the image of Pakal plunging into the afterlife are bas-relief carvings of his ancestors, each of whom is depicted as sprouting forth from an important orchard species (Figure 2.9): *cacao* for the mother of Pakal, Lady Zac-Kuk; *nance* for the father of Pakal, Kan Bahlum-Mo'; avocado for the maternal great grandmother of Pakal, Lady Kan-Ik (Figure 3.5), and also for a fifth-generation ascending ancestor, Kan-Xul; *guayaba* (guava) for the progenitors, Chaacal I and Pakal I; and finally, *chicozapote* for ancestral images of Chan-Bahlum I and his grandmother Kan-Ik (Robertson 1983:Figs. 174–177). Orchard species are valuable and inheritable resources just as is the institution of divine kingship. Planted by ascendant generations, orchard fruits are reaped by descen-

3.5   Lady Zac-Kuk (drawing by John Antoine Labadie after Figure 193 in Robertson 1983).

dants. In a similar fashion, Pakal inherited the throne, the political power, and the status accrued by his progenitors. Thus, Pakal documented his pedigree and his rights to the "fruits" of the throne through a metaphor conflating portraits of his ancestors with agrarian images of fruiting orchard species.

The species composition of this "ancestral orchard" seems to be grounded in principles of tropical arboreal ecology. One of the species noted by Gómez-Pompa, Salvador Flores, and Aliphat Fernández (1990) as growing alongside *cacao* (and providing necessary shade) in northern Yucatán today is depicted on the side of Pakal's sarcophagus—namely, *chicozapote*. The close relationship among orchards, descent, royalty, and inheritance is further suggested by a survey of tree species growing today in the archaeological zone of Cobá. Folan, Fletcher, and Kintz (1979) found that important orchard species are still concentrated toward the center of the site, where the bulk of elite residential architecture occurs. This pattern may indicate that the inter-platform areas of Maya cities were planted in economic tree species and that elite zones of settlement may have contained quantitatively more orchard species.

Both orchards and near-residential plots form the nucleus of the tropical farming system. They are landscapes that envelop the house and are so thoroughly managed and continuously cropped that the term "field" seems to be a misnomer. There were probably endless variations on the composition of these plots, with some planted in herbs, medicinal plants, flowering plants and shrubs, economic species such as *agave*, experimental crops, and tree crops—the *orchard-gardens* of which Turner (in Turner and Sanders 1992: 266) writes. In the same near-residential spaces, there were plots in which rows of staple grains such as maize were planted—analogous to the *calmil* of central Mexico (Evans 1992). An excellent example of the mix of orchard-gardens and field plots in a near-residential context comes from the archaeological site of Ceren in the Zapotitan Valley of El Salvador, where a catastrophic volcanic eruption around A.D. 590 created "Pompeii" conditions of archaeological preservation (Sheets 1992; Zier 1992). Within centimeters of the wall of a storage structure of a residential compound, a garden with plant casts of *macoyas* (small plants cultivated in clumps and used for medicinal purposes or for the production of fine fiber [P. Sheets, pers. com. 1993]) and bromeliads was found. A maize field complete with ridges, furrows, "sophisticated microtopographic slope management," and casts of maize stalks was located less than two meters south and west of the kitchen (Sheets 1992: 58–59; Zier 1992). The garden of another residence contained plant casts of manioc, while yet another yielded casts of *agave* (for making rope) and young *cacao* trees; Sheets (1992:120) suggests that "plants closer to the households were more valuable, were more closely tended, and were more productive than plants at greater distances." These phenomenal plant casts provide important evidence of a monocropped maize field right next to a residence and indicate a diversity in near-residence patterns of land use that includes more than herbal kitchen gardens.

The orchard species that provided shade, coolness, and privacy for the residence were the innermost armature of this variable biotic composition. Included also in this category of continuously cropped plots located relatively close to residences were those plots resulting from the reclamation of marginal lands—the wet and the steep—as per Farrington (1985). During the Classic period, such agricultural features might be located less than five hundred meters away from dwellings at places such as Pulltrouser Swamp.

Pyburn (1989), likewise, has documented structures near raised fields located on the north side of Nohmul. The terrace complexes of the Río Bec (Turner 1983), the Petexbatún (Killion et al. 1991), and the Belize River Valley (Fedick 1994) are also located near residences. The residence, then, is the nucleus of a tropical agricultural system that contained various ratios of near to far fields and intensively to extensively utilized areas. But even the extensively utilized far fields were not selected from a vast array of available lands in the manner of pioneer swidden; rather, they were repetitively cropped and inherited fixed plots.

Fixed-Plot Agriculture in the Maya Lowlands

Lowland tropical agriculture is best viewed as a multicomponent system of land use that crosscuts the biotic continuum from forest to field. Such a system is simplified excessively by use of the terms "swidden" or "slash-and-burn" to refer to Maya agriculture. These terms relate to only *one* type of land use at the "forest" end of the continuum and do not take into account the fact that field plots were fixed, that orchards as well as continually cultivated plots existed, and, most significantly, that settlement densities during the Classic period precluded swidden agriculture in many parts of the lowlands. The term *fixed-plot variable-fallow farming* (Killion 1987) is a more precise description of the manner in which many Maya used lands located away from their residence. Defined in this way, it is now possible not only to see that much of the "forest" is actually fallowed fixed-plot fields but also to contrast this type of farming with pioneer swidden, with which it is often confused due to the fact that "bush" is cut down and burned in both instances. Under pioneer swidden, fixed plots, of course, do not exist, and "new" lands are colonized every five to twenty years (Chagnon 1966: Tables 5 & 6;) as soil exhaustion, weeds, and insect invasion begin to preclude effective agriculture. Residential mobility is a continuous theme of pioneer swidden, and it may be several decades before an area is cultivated once again.[5]

Fields within a fixed-plot system may look similar to pioneer swidden gardens, but the resemblance is superficial and the length of fallow dramatically different. Under a fixed-plot system, individual fields are claimed by families or lineages. Fields tend to stay in the same family for many generations, since transgenerational mechanisms of inheritance, sanctioned through prior use by ancestors, facilitate a continuous (if often contested) chain of rights and privileges. Boundaries are carefully delimited, and the right to farm plots is inherited (in the Maya area generally, but not always, through the male line). In a system of fields with fixed boundaries, several noncontiguous plots may be in various stages of fallow, but even fallowed fields will be peppered with economic species and apiaries, indicating an ongoing productive effort regardless of their "fallow" state. The settlement accompanying this type of farming is one of residential stability rather than mobility. Dwellings are located at the center of the most intensive part of the farming system and are enveloped by orchards, fields, and "dooryard gardens." The dwelling itself anchors family and lineage to their land base and is emblematic of socially sanctioned rights. These resource rights are supported further through the interment of ancestors in the residence itself. The fixed-plot variable-fallow farming of the far lands is land demanding, however, since at any time multiple plots will be in various stages of regrowth and cultivation. The far-flung patchwork of field-holdings exerts a centrifugal force on settlement, as witnessed by the pattern of dispersed house lots throughout much of the lowlands. To some extent, this dispersion pattern favors kin-based power structures over the more centralized power base of divine kingship. Finally, because of dispersed and noncontiguous positioning, fixed-plot variable-fallow farming relies heavily on institutionalized boundary maintenance, a topic to which we return shortly.

Mechanisms of Risk Reduction in the Yucatán Peninsula

Contemporary accounts of tropical lowland agriculture indicate the importance of having multiple noncontiguous plots in variable edaphic locales as a means of minimizing risk (Wilk 1985, among others). When farmers around Laguna Petén Itzá are asked to scale risk factors such as soil fertility, soil erosion, and meteorological patterns, they inevitably scale variation in the amount of rainfall as the highest risk factor (Rice 1992). This risk is ameliorated somewhat by noncontiguous plots, since unpredictable and devastating meteorological events tend to have a patchy distribution. In the context of rainfall agriculture, dispersed holdings are an effective technique for "hedging one's bets" and avoiding starvation. Such a pattern has been suggested to explain the enclosed field spaces on Cozumel Island. Marcus (1982:257) calculated that, given average yields in northern Yucatán, a Maya family of five would have required thirty-five mecates (or 1.4 ha) of land to feed a family for a year; she notes that enclosed fields from Cozumel seldom reach this size. Either there was a patchwork of noncontiguous holdings, or more intensive agriculture was conducted on much less land than is the case today—probably a little of both.

Concern over insufficient water, too much water (floods), and violent meteorological events such as hailstorms and hurricanes is a leitmotif of both Spanish chronicles and earlier codices. Immediately after the first Spanish *entrada* into the Yucatán Peninsula (1535), a very bad drought occurred, during which people were reduced to eating bark of the KUMCHE tree (probably *Jacaratia mexicana D.C.*; Tozzer 1941:54). Because of the severity of the drought, the Xiu lineage and their entourage attempted to make the ill-fated journey through hostile Cocom territory (Sotuta) in order to offer a sacrifice at the sacred cenote of Chichén Itzá. Landa describes the severity of that drought (and locust infestation) by saying simply that "nothing green was left" (Tozzer 1941:55). After this natural catastrophe, there were several years of abundance (Tozzer 1941:56).

The resistance of the Yucatec Maya to the Spanish policy of *reducción* and nucleation of population can be viewed from the perspective of risk reduction. Specifically, this policy was envisioned by Gaspar Antonio Chi as *compounding* agricultural risk and *exacerbating* the effects of drought by nucleating the population (Jakeman 1945:105). One of the many reasons that the *reducción* was a bad policy was that the effects of catastrophic meteorological events tended to be localized. Dispersion of the population, in addition to the maintenance of noncontiguous plots, meant that famine did not affect all communities equally. Documentation of the localized nature of drought and famine comes from Landa (Tozzer 1941:148):

> This year, in which the character was Cauac and in which the Bacab Hosan Ek ruled, in addition to the predicted mortality, they regarded as unfortunate, since they said that the many ants and birds would devour the seeds, which they sowed. And as this would not happen everywhere, there would be food in some places, which they could get with a great deal of labor.

Jones (1989:197) likewise documents Colonial-period residential mobility in response to environmentally induced famine.

Hieroglyphic codices and later (and practically verbatim) passages written in Mayan with a European alphabet (specifically the books of Chilam Balam) give us insight into Maya efforts to reduce risk and predict weather patterns through ritual mechanisms. Here the emphasis is placed on the sacrifices and offerings that might avert or ameliorate natural disasters—primarily droughts, floods, and hailstorms. In the Codex Dresden, Maya scribes appear to be using the calendar in a predictive fashion to address the probability of severe meteorological events that might induce food shortages. Judging from the foregoing accounts, famines that ensued from such disasters were quite severe, and one wonders whether or not the role of the priest/scribe was affected in some way by their ability to read the auguries properly and warn the population of impending disaster. In relation to keepers of the calendar in ancient China, Feuchtwang (1974:103) notes that

> the "Shu Ching" records as history the legend that Hsi and Ho, ministers of Yao, were put to death for not regulating the calendar correctly. Everything depended upon it. A succession of natural calamities indicated a lack of merit in the Emperor, chief link of man with universe.

At any rate, the extant codices do inform us that Maya *literati* were chronicling and predicting cycles of natural disasters—a practice that sharply dismisses any myth of the Maya lowlands as an unchanging tropical paradise. One of the more vivid renderings (both in glyphic text and associated imagery) of these cycles of drought and abundance come from a portion of the Codex Dresden often referred to as the *Farmer's Almanac*. On four consecutive panels of this screen-fold book (42c–45c), the auguries of the four Year Bearers are set forth (Figures 3.6–3.9). As is commonplace in Maya language and art, space and time are expressed in complex and interlocking fashion, so that the vertical text of each panel corresponds for heuristic purposes to our notions of cardinal directions, while the sequence of four frames refers to successive years.[6] For instance, the first panel (Figure 3.6 [42c]) refers to a drought from the "south," while the image shows a Chak beating an eviscerated maize god over the head with a stone ax (in Yucatec Mayan ax = *baat*, which when spelled with a single "a" also means hail).[7] The two successive scenes (Figures 3.7 [43c] and 3.8 [44c]), associated with "east" and "north" respectively, both contain texts indicative of times of plenty and an abundance of maize. The texts are accompanied by compatible images, particularly that of a Chak paddling a canoe loaded with provisions being transported, perhaps as tribute or to the site of a ritual offering (Figure 3.7). In the fourth panel (Figure 3.9 [45c]), the Chak is brandishing two torches, and the predicted drought is foretold to be so severe as to cause the deer to die of dehydration and lack of food. Thus, glyphs for drought and death are included in the text on the left side of this final panel.

While it is true that the Codex Dresden most likely derives from one of the drier, northern Yucatec cities (as do the account of Landa and the books of Chilam Balam), rainfall is nevertheless highly variable from season to season and place to place throughout the Yucatán. Thus, the seemingly contradictory activities of the Chaks as both providers and withholders of rain (in both benign and malevolent form, e.g., as hail) were keenly observed and illustrated as in the lowest register of tripartite panels 33c–38c of the Codex

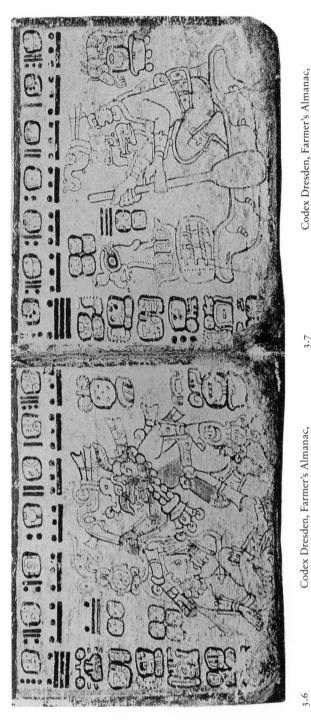

3.6   Codex Dresden, Farmer's Almanac,
       page 42c (Deckert 1989,
       courtesy Akademische Druck-u).

3.7   Codex Dresden, Farmer's Almanac,
       page 43c (Deckert 1989,
       courtesy Akademische Druck-u).

3.9   Codex Dresden, Farmer's Almanac, page 45c (Deckert 1989, courtesy Akademische Druck-u).

3.8   Codex Dresden, Farmer's Almanac, page 44c (Deckert 1989, courtesy Akademische Druck-u).

Dresden (Thompson 1972: 103–104). In Maya cosmology, cycles of drought and abundance were perceived as tied very closely to the Year Bearer. Certain types of weather were more likely when certain "supernaturals" were bearing the burden of the year, as Thompson (1972: 124–128) has discussed in great detail. Here, suffice it to say that the efforts of Maya scribes and priests to predict meteorological cycles display an anxious concern about the vagaries of rainfall patterns and thus make the Maya practice of fixed-plot, noncontiguous-parcel farming more understandable. Many far-flung fields reduce the risk of being wiped out by a single catastrophic event and thus also enhance the wealth and well-being of the polity in general.

Fixed-plot rainfall agriculture, common in many well-settled tropical zones, was built around three strategies of risk reduction: (1) noncontiguous plots, (2) dispersed settlement, and (3) meteorological predictions and appropriate propitiation. The notion that principles of land inheritance operated within all sectors of Maya society from the modest household to the splendid palace is fundamental to the efficacy of these types of risk reduction. The social practice of boundary demarcation and maintenance is one expression of land inheritance.

THE ROLE OF BOUNDARIES IN
TROPICAL LOWLAND FARMING

11 *Ahau* was the *katun* when they carried <burdens> on their backs. Then the land-surveyor came; this was *Ah Ppizte* who measured the leagues. Then there came the *chacte* shrub for marking the leagues with their walking sticks. Then he came <to> *Uachab-nal* to pull the weeds along the leagues, when *Mizcit Ahau* came to sweep clean the leagues, when the land-surveyor came. These were long leagues that he measured. (ROYS 1967: 65)

Passages such as this one were written in Mayan with a European script during Colonial times. They express the custom of measuring land and walking boundaries—actions that have been ascribed frequently to Spanish customs despite the linguistic evidence of a Yucatec Maya term, AH PPIZ K'AAN, for a specialist who measured fields (Marcus 1982: 254).[8] In this section, I build on the information presented previously regarding the multidimensional and fixed-plot nature of Maya agriculture to construct the argument that boundaries were present and critically important during pre-Columbian times. I will present evidence indicating that different types of land demarcation existed at different scales: between polities, between towns and cities within a polity, and within a settled place. Archaeological and epigraphic evidence suggests, specifically, that walking circuits (or surveying land), the quadripartite partitioning of land, and the definition of center and edges are deeply rooted in the Late Formative.

Much attention has been given to sophisticated Maya conceptions of time and calendrical reckoning, particularly as expressed in the long-count and calendar-round notational systems of the Classic period (Thompson 1978). But in Maya systems of thought, time and space are not separate dimensions (León-Portilla 1988:90; Bricker 1966:368–370; Gossen 1974:29–30; Tedlock 1982:178); rather, they are part of a complex interweave, a space-time continuum, which cannot be separated either in ritual or in everyday life. A few examples from the past and present serve to illustrate this point. Barbara Tedlock (1982:59) has documented how Quiché keepers of the calendar-round map their landscape through a complex association between place shrines and calendrical positionings. In effect, landscapes are given a historical texture through the strategic placement of ancestral shrines. The resulting landscape "map" provides a guide for the living as well as a testimony to the ancestors. Among the Tzotzil Maya, a ritual called K'in Krus plays a similar role (Vogt 1976). In larger cosmological terms, the quadripartite (or cross) motif is evocative of a partitioning of the universe in reference to solar cycles—another example of the conspicuous wedding of time and space (Coggins 1980). Ashmore (1991) has examined the manner in which the quadripartite pattern is manifest in Classic-period architecture of Tikal and Copán. For the Postclassic, Fox (1987) has suggested that the principle of quadripartition has a spatial reality and may, in fact, represent the distribution of lineage groupings at Utatlán, as it is said to have done at Mayapán (Proskouriakoff 1962:91–92). The antiquity of the quadripartite motif of space and time is suggested by its presence in Late Formative contexts in which it was painted on ceramic bowls, which were deposited as grave goods in a Formative ancestor shrine at K'axob, Belize (Figure 3.10).[9] In this example, the central axis is a fifth point, creating an *axis mundi* or center of rotation. Another Formative example is the Pomoná ear flare, in which the ends of the cross are marked by compound glyphs interpreted by Justeson, Norman, and Hammond (1988:143) to read "The holder of power is the Sun God; the Sun God casts corn to/for the sky god."

These examples illustrate a very simple but seldom perceived point. That is, Maya conceptions and calculations of space and territory were just as sophisticated and thorough as were their conceptions of time. To assert that Classic Maya employed a complex system of reckoning time and yet did

3.10   Close-up of cross motif on Late Formative bowl from K'axob
(photo by Mary L. Angelini).

not delimit and frame the space of their settlements, cities, fields, and orchards in an equally exacting fashion is to rend apart a tightly interwoven cosmology.

Edges of Lowland Polities

The importance of boundaries in the context of non-industrial states often has been dismissed, since large-scale political boundaries are asserted to have been a convention created by modern nation-states (Giddens 1981). Such assertions, however, suffer from the tendency to view early states as synonymous with a hyper-nucleated city in which a resident agrarian population departs daily from the city space to cultivate fields intensively on the outskirts of the city—such a pattern as would apply to Teotihuacán, for instance. In such a nucleated context, there is often a "gray area" between the agricultural holding of two adjacent cities or polities—a place in which very few people live, there is very little farming, and the vacuity of the territory is indicative of its status as a boundary zone. On the other hand, the relatively dispersed pattern of lowland Maya settlement, complemented by the expansive nature of the fixed-plot, variable-fallow farming system, means that we should think about whether or not such "gray areas" existed in the lowlands. If they did not, then boundaries, in the sense of demarcation of a landscape and the ritualized "framing activities" (Douglas 1966:63–64) that define these edges, would have been critically important to maintaining the integrity of political units as well as landholding lineage units. I suggest, in fact, that there is a tendency toward hyper-boundary maintenance among high-density tropical agriculturalists who are configured in dispersed settlement arrangements.[10]

A succinct description of the establishment of boundaries between political units comes from the Maní Land Treaty of 1557, which quelled a border dispute among the Xiu (Maní), Cocom (Sotuta), and Cupul lineages. Organized by the principal HALACH UINICOB after Spanish presence was a *fait accompli,* the treaty nevertheless seems to have been initiated by Maya elites to settle their own political boundary disputes. Technically speaking, the document is from the early Colonial period, but the ritualized manner in which the treaty proceedings were conducted and the accompanying feasting and gift-giving are totally pre-Hispanic in character. For instance, each BATAB and HALACH UINIC participating in the treaty was given the following traditional gifts counted in the pre-Hispanic vigesimal system: five bakal (four-hundred-piece lots) of *cacao,* five cotton mantles (four breadths each), a string of red beads as long as an arm, and one hunkal (unit of twenty) of green stone (jadeite). Apparently, a large quantity of wine (three *arrobas*) was also consumed during the negotiations (Morley 1941:159; Roys 1943:186).

The feasting and negotiation were followed by the actual demarcation of the agreed-upon boundaries with crosses and stone mounds, in a manner highly suggestive of the later K'in Krus lineage ritual among Tzotzil Maya (Vogt 1976:97–115), as well as the demarcation of individual plots (Collier 1975:90). Roys (1943:181) notes that the points listed along the borders of the treaty generally were not towns but rather consisted of natural features, particularly water sources (cenotes, wells, caves containing springs, ponds, and natural rock tanks). The subtext here suggests that rights to these critical resources were carefully safeguarded. Actual marking of the boundaries was achieved by walking a ritualized circuit. The HALACH UINIC of Maní, don Francisco de Montejo Xiu, traveled the boundary lines accompanied by BATABOB and *ah kuch kabob* from allied towns (Roys 1943:187). The Maya scribe documenting this historic event used the verb MANEBAL to describe this procession, a word with significantly broader meanings than simply "to walk over"; rather, it connotes a pleasurable passing through life "para pasar uno la vida, para gozar de algún dinero, comida o hacienda que tiene" (Barrera Vásquez 1980:497). In this way, the *ahaw* or HALACH UINIC himself participated in territorial demarcation or "framing activities" that established and maintained the edges between provinces. Tozzer (1941:43, n.216) describes

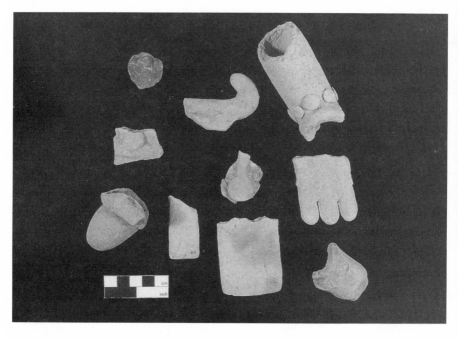

3.11   Postclassic incensario fragments from near the surface in front
of Structure 18 (photo by Mary L. Angelini).

a similar boundary circuit traversed by Nachi Cocom, *HALACH UINIC* of the
province of Sotuta, with a large entourage which included "*Ah Kins, Ah Ku-
lels, Holpops* and an *Ah Itzá Cocom*" and other Maya, possibly *ah kuch
kabob* who are described by Tozzer simply as "principal Indians."

Patterns of Postclassic deposits, particularly *incensarios* (Figure 3.11),
along the front face of Classic-period pyramids—ancient sacred locations—
may be the material remains of similar territorial processions, as Walker
(1990) has argued for Postclassic Cerros. This acute concern among the Postclassic Maya with demarcating edges has been interpreted as the result of the
collapse of strong Classic-period political institutions, such as divine kingship, and the concomitant rise of a more "balkanized" pattern of small competing polities. But if one casts one's gaze away from the large monumental
centers of the Classic period—Tikal, Palenque, or Copán—to note the variation in potential polity size across the lowlands, then one can see that very
small political units coexisted with large agglomerative ones throughout the
Classic period. Hypothesized boundaries of the large political units alone
(based on the assumption that emblem glyphs equal autonomy) cover thousands of kilometers (see Marcus 1993; Mathews 1991: Fig. 2-6), and if small
polities not participating in the tradition of hieroglyphic inscriptions (such as

many of those of Belize) are included, then this figure grows even larger. Thus, boundary disputes as a frequent cause of dissension and warfare such as mentioned in the *Relación de Dzonot* (RY 1983:85) may not be a characteristic solely of the Postclassic period. Roys (1943:178) has suggested that these border disputes resulted in part from the need to protect from encroachment the farming plots located at some distance from the residence.

Throughout the Maní Land Treaty there is frequent mention of guarded borders: for example,

> Ebtun, the border of the lands of the people of Maní, where a cross was set. Francisco Camal and Francisco Chi were the guardians of the forest [read variable-fallow fixed-plot] lands at the border of the lands of the people of Sotuta. These guardians of the borders of the forest [again, read variable-fallow fixed-plot] lands were Maní men. (ROYS 1943:188)

These guardians appear to have been appointed by *HALACH UINICOB* and placed at the borders in order to protect the outfields from encroachment by neighboring lineages. Along the border of Maní and Hocaba, they guarded against the incursion of slave-raiders from Hocaba who preyed upon the agrarian peoples living in dispersed settlements (Roys 1943:181).

A further example of boundary demarcation of political territories in a very precise manner comes from the *Chilam Balam of Chumayel*. Here, a priest/scribe recounts the fixing of political edges prior to the introduction of tribute to the rulers of Chichén Itzá:

> *Ah May hetun accunte u xukil u luumob, ah accunte u xukil; ah miz mizte u luumob, lay Mizcit Ahaue.*
> (ROYS 1967:18–19)
>
> Ah May it was who fixed the corners [play on words since *ahmay* = corner] of the land, he set the corners in their places; the sweeper who swept the land was Mizcit Ahau. (ROYS 1967:74)

A similar fixing of the boundaries may have taken place at the northern Puuc city of Sayil, where the eastern and southern extent of settlement is marked by rubble pyramids (Sabloff and Tourtellot 1991:15).

From earlier in the Classic period, hieroglyphic texts and toponyms suggest the antiquity of activities such as the royal circuit. Stuart and Houston (1994) have framed structural, syntactical, and linguistic arguments suggesting that many hieroglyphs following verbs such as *u-ti* ("it happened") specify a particular site, portion of a site, or building. Thus, specific place names are cited in texts as well as the politically overarching emblem glyphs. For instance, it is recorded on hieroglyphic Stairway 1 of Seibal that Ruler 4 of Dos Pilas performed a scattering rite at two different locations—once at Seibal and then two days later at Tamarindito; this text could be interpreted as one describing a circuit traversed by Ruler 4 who performed rituals at subordinate sites (Stuart and Houston 1994). Since war was initiated against Dos Pilas shortly thereafter, this text is indicative of the fact that, in this case, the scattering rite was not an effective means of quelling hostilities between polities.[11]

Demarcation within Polities

Political territorial boundaries are complemented by boundaries within polities—those that demarcated the farming lands of one city or village from those of another. Location and local geography, in fact, often form the cornerstone of community identity, as Wilson (1993:126) has documented among the Q'eqchi. For this highland Maya group, identity is vested in the local mountain spirit, Tzuultaq'a. In Yucatán during Postclassic and early Colonial times, these more localized territorial boundaries were managed by the governors of the cities and towns—the BATABOB. If rights to lands within a polity were contested, HALACH UINICOB apparently settled such disputes (Roys 1939:22).

Direct statements from the early Colonial period regarding land tenure and boundaries between villages are not numerous, and those that exist are contradictory.[12] Based on the extensive documentation of the 182-year dispute during the Colonial period over the Tontzimin tract as contained in the *Titles of Ebtun* (Roys 1939), a restrictive pattern of land tenure did exist. The Tontzimin dispute, furthermore, indicates the importance of local agricultural boundaries (within a system of nonadjacent tracts) to the Yucatec Maya. The deep historical documentation of the dispute itself indicates the speed with which Colonial Maya learned to use effectively the Spanish legal system. It is a strong indicator that there existed a deeply rooted pre-Columbian tradition of both recording and disputing resource rights and that Maya concern with land entitlements and boundaries was not created by inept Spanish domination during the Colonial period (Roys 1939:51).

In the recollections of a prominent Maya scribe of the contact period, Gaspar Antonio Chi, there were no boundaries between towns. In presenting and reviewing this testimonial, even Roys (1962:65–66), who did not think that the Maya had a particularly sophisticated system of agricultural land use or tenure, states that "it is hard to reconcile the statement that there were no landmarks showing the boundaries between the lands of different towns with the conditions that we find in very early colonial times. We read much about such landmarks in the Maní Land Treaty of 1557, only 15 years after the final conquest of that area. . . . This may have been a Spanish innovation but the Maya text of the treaty gives the impression that the practice was not new to the writer of the document." After translation of an impressive corpus of Yucatec Maya documents, Roys (1939:39) concludes that *caciques* probably always had rights to certain lands and that "each village or town had always possessed an area within which it did not suffer trespass." The Yucatec term, *kuchteel,* which can be translated as a small territorial unit (Barrera Vásquez 1980:345; Roys 1957:7), may refer to these inalienable lands of villages and cities. Thus, Gaspar Antonio Chi's remarks about the great land collectives of pre-Hispanic Yucatán may have been based upon the astute appraisal that Maya patterns of negotiating resource rights within the organizational context of a lineage structure were far more collective and inclusive than the Spanish approach to land entitlements, which favored primarily Spanish military conquerors and secondarily native nobility.

Lineage Lands and Boundaries within a Settled Place

As mentioned above, the sentiment that land was held in "communal holdings," as expressed by Gaspar Antonio Chi, could be interpreted as a reference to the role played by lineages in the distribution of resource rights as well as the organization of agrarian labor. The careful reckoning of the edges of space is integrally related to the maintenance of fixed-plot, inherited fields, which I suggest were administered by lineages (some royal and some not) during pre-Hispanic times. Our understanding of lineage-based organizational structures, as they existed during Colonial times and earlier, is very sketchy for the Maya lowlands. This lacuna is particularly obvious to scholars working with the contemporary Maya. Thus, Collier (1982:346) noted, "Equally important, though very difficult to achieve, is an approximation of how the Maya organized production at a level somewhere above the field and below the state and marketplace. . . . we have much to learn about such fundamentals for understanding Maya agriculture as property and the organization of labor." For the Classic and Formative periods, archaeological research foci have been directed simultaneously toward the large-scale political interaction of elites on the one hand and the composition of individual residential units or compounds on the other. The middle ground, the arena within which families coalesce as lineages with resource-holding rights, has seen little attention in the archaeology of the Classic period. The premise of this research is that lineage organization was a powerful force in structuring not only agriculture but also settlement and treatment of the dead—the latter two being common topics of archaeological inquiry in the Maya lowlands. In this section a case is made for the role of lineages and lineage heads in organizing land usage and in demarcating through ritualized framing activities the boundaries of lineage-controlled lands. Such social practices can be expected to play a determinative role and to structure the archaeological record of pre-Hispanic Yucatán.[13]

In contact-period documents, lineage heads or *ah kuch kabob* are referred to as council members or *regidores*—in other words, local leaders of their communities whose supporting vote, during Colonial times, was necessary for the town governor to rule successfully (Farriss 1984; Roys 1943; RY 1983:86). The term literally means, however, "he of the burden/obligation/authority of the land"; an expanded entry of this title in the *Diccionario Maya Cordemex* includes what I believe to have been an important role of *ah kuch kabob* in pre-Hispanic as well as post-Hispanic times: "jefes de linaje que formaban el consejo del pueblo . . . [y] colectaban los tributos y atendían otros asuntos municipales" (Barrera Vásquez 1980:344). An earlier entry in the *Diccionario de Motul* (compiled during the sixteenth century) is very similar: "indio principal que tiene cuidado de alguna parcialidad para recoger el tributo y para otras cosas de camunidad [sic]" (Ciudad Real 1984:80). The position of *ah kuch kab,* then, was one of lineage head and council member who had the responsibility of collecting tribute as well as attending to other municipal duties. Use of terms such as *municipios, parcialidad,* and *comunidad* indicates that the *ah kuch kabob* had strong links to places—that is, the lineages they headed were linked to lands and places. Defined in this way, the *ah kuch kab* and his respective lineage bear many organizational similarities to the *calpulli* of Central Mexico, described by Carrasco (1978:39) as a corporate unit with collective responsibility for the payment of tribute and communal administration of land.

Further support for the pivotal role of the *ah kuch kab* comes from the *Relaciones de Yucatán,* in which the heads of *barrios* or wards (gloss for lineage?) are described as being in "charge of organizing the tribute and public service at the proper times, and of assembling the people of their divisions both for banquets and festivals and for war" (translation by Roys 1939:40). Finally, in the *Códice de Calkini,* a series of documents from the province of Ah Canul (the pertinent texts of which bear the years 1579, 1582, and 1595), the official history of settlement in the area is compiled and signed by a group of BATABOB (Barrera Vásquez 1957:73–103) and, according to Farriss (1984:492), "aged *ahcuchcabs.*" Michael Coe (1965:104), moreover, suggests that the ubiquitous references to *principales* in the historical documentary record actually refer to *ah kuch kabob* or "rich men" who had access to wealth and community labor. In Bunzel's (1952:185–186) treatment of the leadership structure of Chichicastenango, however, the term *principales* refers to important men whose office is not hereditary, who are selected for their personal qualities of leadership and experience in judicial and administrative matters, and who hold the real political power of the town.

Clearly, the role of lineage leader refers to an important position of leadership both within the community and in external political connections and obligations such as tribute payments. If these leaders shouldered the responsibility of tribute payments, then is it not reasonable to assume that they did so because they also wielded authority over the distribution of lands and the disposition of labor? Although Maya lineages are not described as landholding units, the fact that the harvest portion destined to be sent as tribute to a local lord was collected by the *ah kuch kab* suggests that the most parsimonious explanation cedes coordination of production on these lands to lineage leaders.[14] In a small hamlet there may be only one lineage, and thus the lineage equates with community level of control over land (as it is expressed in many ethnohistoric documents). But in larger communities and cities, such as Mayapán, there were multiple lineages and thus the potential for adjacent plots of land to be claimed by different lineages. Demarcation of the edges of lineage lands within settled places represents a framing activity at another scale. Michael Coe (1965:112) has proposed a "community" model in which there is territorial integrity to lineages that, under ideal or idealized circumstances, are associated with one of four quadrants of a settlement. The head of lineage of each quadrant—*ah kuch kab*—rotates responsibility for the four principal Uayeb (New Year) ceremonies (so named after the four principal days in the 260-day count which begin the "vague" year). In this way, spatial territories are directly linked to calendrical ritual, another example of the link between space and time. Early chroniclers note this quadripartite type of intrasettlement territorial organization at Tah Itzá (with each quarter headed by a *BATAB*) and also at Acalan (Scholes and Roys 1968). These lineage holdings may correspond to the small territorial divisions described in Yucatec dictionaries, where *barrio* or the more political term, *parcialidad*, is translated as *tzucul, kuchteel,* or *kuchkabal* (Barrera Vásquez 1980:51; Ciudad Real 1984; M. Coe 1965:104). The spatial integrity of these lineage units is maintained by boundary-defining rituals that create and perpetuate social order. Circuits of lineage lands are still traversed by the Zinacanteco Maya of highland Chiapas in the form of the K'in Krus ritual which combines feasting and circuit-walking with shrine visitation. According to Vogt (1976:109), the ceremony "expresses the rights and obligations of its members to lands they have inherited." Propitiation of the ancestors from whom the land is inherited is done through prayer and offerings at the shrines located at strategic resource locales of the lineage lands.

In distinction to the more communal level of landholdings by lineages or, during the Colonial period, by their replacement, the municipality, Roys (1943:37) notes that there is also evidence of individual "ownership" very early in the Colonial period. He cites as evidence a 1561 document from the *Titles of Ebtun,* a portion of which is reproduced at the beginning of this chapter; from this document we know that lands were conveyed to the "principal men of the town here at Ebtun." Thus, although lands were held nominally by groups, in reality they were "occupied by individual families, among whom the right of occupancy was handed down from father to son" (Roys 1943:37). This introduces yet another level of boundary maintenance: that of individual families. Landholdings of families were centered on the residence, which, due to the highly maintained circumambient fields, gardens, and orchards, was considered private property in the sense of use rights rather than salability (Roys 1943:37). The private nature of the residence and surrounding fields and orchards was due in part to the fact that the lands were part of a totally managed cultural landscape in which rich (and probably fertilized) cultivated areas were intensively worked and long-term-investment tree-crops planted. Thus, labor investment in this zone superseded that of the far fields. Buried within the residential compound were the bones of ancestors who, by their presence, sanctified and legitimized the rights and holdings of the family. It is no surprise, therefore, that the residence was a focal point of inheritance among Yucatec Maya families. Glossing over considerable variation in actual patterns of inheritance, Roys (1943:28) tells us that sons (or a suitable male heir) inherited the "estate which consisted of personal effects, beehives, and improvements to the land, such as houses, fruit trees, and cacao groves."

Residences have been the focus of archaeological settlement research over the past three decades. In stone-impoverished areas of the Maya lowlands (such as northern Belize and parts of the Petén), boundaries of Classic-period residential compounds and circumambient lands were rarely demarcated by walls and can only be approximated by the overlay of idealized spatial constructs such as Thiessen polygons (Killion, Sabloff, and Tourtellot 1989). But where stone was plentiful or hill slopes so steep as to require terracing, then walls and embankments demarcating the limits of near-residential lands are very common, particularly in the drier and rockier northern Yucatán. Survey and mapping projects have detected such wall systems at Mayapán (Smith 1962: Fig. 1), on Cozumel Island (Freidel and Sabloff 1984:84–90 & Figs. 29–34), at Cobá (Folan, Kintz, and Fletcher 1983:103–119 & Map Sheet 6), and at Dzibilchaltún and Chunchucmil (Kurjack and Garza T. 1981:297). In hilly, stone-rich areas, terracing is often detected along with field walls. Such is the case in the Río Bec (Turner 1983) and in the Petexbatún (Killion et al. 1991). When such demarcated boundaries or "residential property walls" (Kurjack and Garza T. 1981:297) do exist, they frequently encompass multiple structures or structure complexes, as is apparent at the Late Classic site of Nim Li Naj in the Petexbatún (Killion et al. 1991: Fig. 35.13). These architectural groupings tend to be larger than that of a single extended family, a pattern particularly conspicuous at Dzibilchaltún (Kurjack 1974:80) and at Cobá, where Kintz (1983:179–190 & Fig. 12.1) has referred to them as "social clusters." Although variation in the size and elaboration of architectural units internal to these clusters is often viewed in dichotomous elite-versus-nonelite terms, cluster size and internal variation may in fact represent the multigenerational growth of an extended family or a segment of a lineage within which there are significant differences in wealth and rank, particularly among lineage heads (*ah kuch kabob*), household heads (*ah chun kahil*), and their constituent members—a topic to be pursued in greater detail in Chapter 4.

LINEAGE AS RESOURCE-HOLDING GROUP

Writing of the lineages of the "New Territories" of contemporary China, Freedman (1966:33) stresses the role of lineages as resource-holding groups: "Land was the most important material focus of any agnatically constituted groups. . . . The institution or augmentation of clan property was often regarded by successful men as the crowning achievement of their careers." Sahlins (1961:330) focused specifically on the strong link between lineage and intensified methods of subsistence: "Lineages . . . are typically found with a mode of production involving repetitive or periodic use of restricted, localized resources, as in secondary forest or irrigation agriculture and many forms of pastoralism." Among the Mae Enga, Johnson and Earle (1987:184) also have noted that lineages were linked to subsistence intensification. Regarding the resource exclusivity of lineages, Sahlins (1961:330) states that "a lineage is one social aspect of long-term use of the same resources, another aspect being the development of collective proprietary rights in these resources. The rule of descent creates a perpetual social group linked to perpetually valuable strategic property." These observations suggest that the link between lineage and land is not a common characteristic of groups employing extensive subsistence techniques such as long-fallow swidden horticulture—a type of agriculture that may have characterized the initial colonization of the Maya lowlands (see Hammond and Miksicek 1981).

Certainly by the Classic period, we can speculate (on the basis of settlement density and reclamation of marginal lands) that entrenched patterns of land tenure operating on the scale of family and lineage were the predominant pattern. References to the role of lineages in claiming lands and maintaining continuous chains of inheritance are scattered throughout the Yucatec Mayan prose of the early Colonial period. For instance, in the sixteenth century when the Canul lineage wished to legitimize their ancestral claims to the lands of Ah Canul, they invoked a history (recorded in the *Códice de Calkini*) through which their claim stretched back to the sacking of Mayapán: "Shown plainly were their lands and their forests, when the town of Mayapán was destroyed. We recall, we of their lineage, in case it is not known whence we come. This was the beginning [or cause?] of our seeking our land, our forests, we the descendants of the Ah Canul" (Barrera Vásquez 1957: 105–107; translation by Roys 1962:36). The statement also suggests the bloc movement of a lineage, a process hypothesized for the highland Quiché Maya (Fox 1987), a group for which the lineage has been described as the principal "owner" of land (Carmack 1981). Such *en masse* migrations of lineages are more directly mentioned in a later passage of the *Códice de Calkini*: "These roads were shown to us by our *batabs*, Ah Pa Canul, Ah Dzun Canul, of the lineage of Ah Itzam Canul, Ah Chuen Kauil" (Barrera Vásquez 1957:109; translation by Roys 1962:36). Jones (1982:291) has proposed that *en masse* movement of lineage groups may explain the rapid growth and shrinkage of Classic-period sites of the lowland Maya. Not only do lineages seem to have held land in common and to have migrated together, there is also evidence that factions within lineages coalesced into large agricultural work groups of twenty or more people such as those observed by Landa (Tozzer 1941:96).

Despite these documents, Roys (1939:40) opines that there is no direct evidence from the Colonial period that lineages controlled land; rather, he stipulates that the strength of data indicates that organizational structures of wards and villages controlled land distribution. I suggest that, due to the spatial clustering of lineages, there was a strong concordance between the *municipios* recognized by the Spaniards and the lineage organization recognized by the Maya and headed locally by *principales* or *ah kuch kabob*.

Principle of First Occupancy

We are reasonably confident that the pre-Hispanic Maya did not buy and sell land; regardless, there were several ways in which land rights were established and recognized. Land could be inherited from ancestors, land claimed by someone else could be encroached upon, or one could be the initial "occupant" or cultivator of land and thus lay claim to it in that way. This latter means, herein referred to as the principle of first occupancy, seems to have been a practice of the Yucatec Maya of both the twentieth century (Redfield and Villa Rojas 1962) and earlier. In the context of a discussion of land as common property, Landa tells us that "he who first occupies them [lands] becomes the possessor of them" (Tozzer 1941: 96–97). In Yucatec Mayan, the term YAX CHIBAL UAI TI LUM refers to the "first founding lineage of the land" (Roys 1939:40). Although the principle of first occupancy sounds fair and equal, given time and the expansion of lineages this custom sets in motion a chain of events that inevitably results in pronounced *inequality* in access to resources. Essentially, the best lands are claimed early in the colonization of an area. Families who arrive later or fission from established families must fight for land or cultivate plots of land that yield a harvest with considerably more expenditure of effort and sometimes require laborious reclamation projects such as ditching, field-raising, or terracing. Viewed in this way, the question as to whether there were set-aside dynastic lands worked for the benefit of the royal court during Classic times becomes moot, since those in such positions of power generally loudly proclaimed the genealogical depth of their lineage and would have either inherited some of the best lands of the kingdom or else would have attempted to co-opt lands claimed by weaker lineages.

FIRST OCCUPANCY AT K'AXOB. In many areas, this principle of first occupancy strongly affected the nature and composition of residential structure. For instance, at the Formative- and Classic-period settlement of K'axob, the platforms that attain the greatest size and elaboration during the Classic period are those with Preclassic cores. At one particular location (Structure 18; Figures 2.14 and 2.15), nearly two thousand years are represented by three meters of sequential floor and platform constructions (Figure 3.12). Successive Formative floor units are sealed by the Terminal Formative construction of an ancestor shrine. If we posit a link between the floor units of a Formative village such as K'axob and the overall process of establishing resource rights, then the residence can be viewed as an indicator of the entrenchment of patterns of resource inequality. Moreover, such inequalities are established early in the occupation of an area. Of course, I am not suggesting a static pattern in which the same family inhabited, inherited, refurbished, and enlarged the Structure 18 plaza group over a period of two thousand years. But I do assert that once these architectural features were established on the landscape they generally continued to grow and expand despite the fortunes of individual families and lineages. Thus, the residence itself, as the receptacle of the ancestors, assumes a quasi-legalistic character and stands as witness to the validity of the rights, privileges, and responsibility of its current occupants.

Archaeologists conducting test excavations in residential architecture in

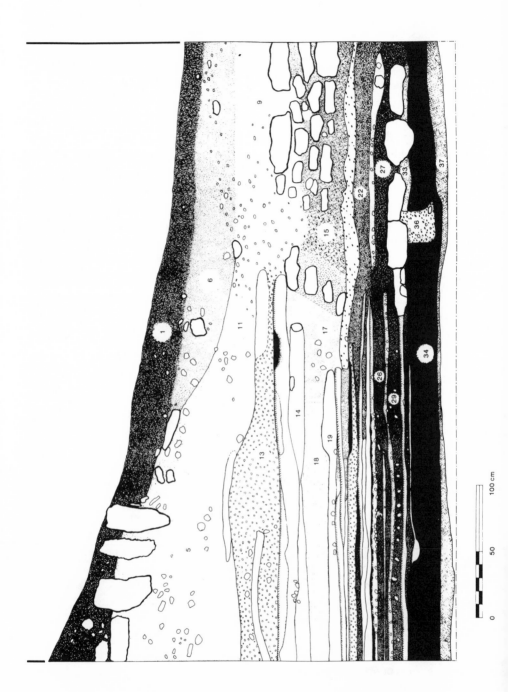

other parts of the Maya lowlands attest to similar long sequences of occupation (Haviland 1981 : 110, among others). Residential compounds, however, do not always contain features that may be called "ancestor shrines." Working with the settlement data from Tikal, Becker (1971 : 198–200) has documented the absence of shrines in small complexes conforming to Tikal Plaza Plans 3 and 5. This absence may be explained by reference to the developmental cycle of residential compounds, in which smaller compounds are linked by genealogy, ritual, and labor obligations to nearby larger complexes with ancestral shrine structures. In this way, position within a lineage and the principle of first occupancy together form a crucible of social inequality (see Chapter 4).

Instruments of Inheritance

In A.D. 1588, an agreement on the boundaries between the lands of Ticul and Ppustunich was reached and recorded in the following way: "These are the limits [of their fields, the people of Ticul] also said, and they said that no one should [say anything to the contrary, nor shall] our sons in time to come" (Roys 1943 : 190). The sons of the leaders of Ticul, the inheritors of the land, would also inherit the agreement signed by their predecessors. This document suggests that not only were the house, the near fields, the orchards, and rights to salt beds inherited (Roys 1943 : 28), but use rights to the far fields—the areas of contested and constantly encroached-upon lands—were also inherited.

The practice of inheritance emphasizes genealogy, since demonstrating established linkages to ancestors is the means by which resource rights are inherited. Among the Tzotzil, Collier (1975) has demonstrated the close linkage between descent-based kinship and inherited land. Among Classic Maya royalty, the careful construction (in hieroglyphic texts and explicit pictorial compositions) of genealogies has been well documented; not as amply documented, however, is the "text-free" (Freidel 1993) documentation of nonelite genealogies through the building of burial crypts and ancestor shrines and the recurrent refurbishing events that accompanied the transmission of power, authority, and responsibility between generations. (See Haviland [1988 : 125] for a description of the sequence of construction at Group 2G-1, Tikal, as it relates to burial patterns.) In effect, residences express a *genealogy of place* (de Certeau 1984 : 122) that is only less explicit than the hieroglyphic texts because we lack methods to link these refurbishments to specific named individuals. But in a very real sense they are the material residue of the intergenerational transmission of resource entitlements.

A clue to the critical importance of inheritance is revealed by Landa in reference to the value placed on the inheritance of icons of the ancestors

(Tozzer 1941:111). As discussed earlier, these "idols" were sometimes hollowed out and filled with the ashes of prominent ancestors. Thus, the material stuff of inheritance is inseparable from its source, the ancestors. The two together provide a strong, if conservative, charter for the distribution of resource rights, privileges, and social obligations.

WHERE THE ANCESTORS "SLEPT"

Among the highland Maya Quiché lineages, the *warabal ja* were the "sleeping houses" for the ancestors (Carmack 1981:161), the sacred spots on lineage lands where altars were built and ancestors were venerated. We do not know whether the lowland Maya also built *warabal ja* on their lineage lands; the archaeological record of the lowlands does indicate that, in a literal sense, the "sleeping place" of the ancestors was the residence itself. Unlike the Chinese lineages studied by Freedman (1966, 1970), in which the material remains of the ancestors were distributed throughout the agrarian landscape and by virtue of their placement served to anchor claims to vital resources (Figure 1.2), lowland Maya preferred to keep the physical remains of their ancestors nearby—creating a kind of domestic mausoleum in the residential complex itself (see also Coe 1973:7, 1988:234). With the successive interment of ancestors in the domicile, the architectural features of this locale began to encode a genealogy of place. Through the plaza resurfacings and the platform enlargements that often closely followed burial events, we can begin to read not just the construction history of a locale but also the progressive empowerment and sacralization that resulted from repeated interment of ancestors.

The conflation of the ancestral shrine with the physical remains of ancestors within the residence may be partly a result of the importance of near-residential fields and orchards in lowland tropical areas. Ancestors were placed proximate to the resources that they are often perceived as safeguarding.[15] As Bunzel (1952:18) notes, the conception of land rights among the Quiché was linked inextricably to the ancestors: "Land is conceived of as belonging to the ancestors; one lives upon it by their grace. One does not own land, it is merely loaned to one as a lodging (Sp. *posada*) in the world, and for it one must continually make payment in the form of candles, incense and roses to the ancestors, who are the real owners." Although Quiché no longer bury their ancestors within their houses, the link between progenitors and the residence is very strong, and ancestors are perceived as maintaining order in their past/present homes (Bunzel 1952:270). The place of residence, thus, is given preeminence and viewed as a primary link between ancestors and land entitlements. Certainly there exists a considerable bulk of documentary data suggesting that the residential complex was central to Maya existence and that it was considered a place of sacrifice, feasting, and ritual observance as well as the place where production was organized.

Enveloping the Ancestors

The structural mass of the residential compound, as well as the surrounding orchards and fields, provides a kind of envelope or container within which the ancestors were interred. The orchard as an inherited resource had such a strong association with the ancestors that Pakal the Great conflated the two images on his sarcophagus. Orchards were the locale of ritual activities: in 1562 an event occurred in a *cacao* grove that so incensed Bishop Diego de Landa that some cite it as one of the primary events that led to the Inquisition trials. Specifically, Francisco Uc, a *cacique* of Chuhuhub, alleged that Juan Xiu of Hunacti had sacrificed a Maya Indian in his *cacao* grove during the previous year (Morley 1941:192; Scholes and Adams 1938:1:166). Elsewhere, Jones (1989:151) notes that during the 1619 visit of friars Fuensalida and Orbita to Tah Itzá a ritual of major significance (which resulted in the expulsion of Fuensalida and Orbita from Tah Itzá) took place in the orchard of Can Ek. These events serve to identify the orchard as a ritual space in addition to a place of economic species that reflect long-term, intergenerational investment of labor and resources.

Several scholars working with Postclassic- and Colonial-period material have noted that orchards are indicative of the "private" nature of the household compound (Freidel 1983:55; Jones 1982:288; Roys 1939:40). On Cozumel Island in particular, the well-documented and regular network of field walls becomes distorted within communities—a skewing that Freidel (1983:55) has ascribed to the private, inheritable, and probably improved resources of the houselot compound. The orchards, then, are indicative of the wealth of a family at the same time that their biomass, if placed strategically around a residence, can conceal the wealth of a residential group. Since the very trees of the orchard were planted by ancestors, the inheritance of an orchard is, in a very direct way, a gift from the ancestors. Thus, it is not surprising that these locales were places of ritual.

The archaeology of circumambient fields and orchards is in its early stages of development in the Maya lowlands. Few researchers expect to replicate the spectacular discoveries that Payson Sheets and associates have made at the "Pompeii of the Americas" (the archaeological site of Ceren), where casts of *cacao* trees and maize plants have been discovered in the spaces between residential structures (Sheets 1992; Zier 1992). Increased attention to "vacant" architectural spaces, however, has yielded evidence of cultivated plots both through chemical phosphate analyses and artifact distribution patterns (Ball and Kelsay 1992; Dunning, Rue, and Beach 1991; Killion, Sabloff, and Tourtellot 1989; McAnany 1992). Moreover, macrobotanical remains retrieved from Formative- and Classic-period residential middens through water flotation generally show a high proportion of burned charcoal from economic tree species such as avocado, guayaba, chicozapote, nance, and *cacao* at the expense of primary and even secondary rain forest species (Cliff and Crane 1989; Hammond and Miksicek 1981; Miksicek 1983, n.d.). This evidence suggests that orchards located next to or near residences are a very ancient pattern in the Maya region.

By far, the bulk of archaeological settlement mapping and excavation has focused on platforms with detectable surface elevation—that is, architectural units that can be spotted in a contemporary rain forest, field, or pasture due to their elevation above ground level. No doubt many complexes lacked such height, and the recognition of low-profile residential locales through testing programs and serendipitous discovery is a major topic within Maya archaeology today (Johnston, Moscoso Moller, and Schmitt 1992; McQuarie n.d.; Pyburn 1990). Those structures detectable by surface survey represent the subset of domestic units where (1) sufficient construction labor was amassed to build a rubble or earthen platform cumulatively greater in height than around 20–30 centimeters, and (2) subsequent natural processes of erosion or aggradation, or cultural processes of destruction, did not erase such a construction from the sight of an archaeological surveyor. Indeed, the available sample is a biased subset, but from the formal characteristics of known residential complexes we can glean very specific archaeological insights regarding the manner in which a genealogy of place was encoded architecturally:

(1) Many residences are composed of multiple structures arranged around an interior plaza. In the structures ringing Pulltrouser Swamp, for example, over half of the platforms (supporting structures for a perishable building) occur in groups (Figure 3.13), and often they are placed around the edges of a large basal platform, creating an interior space, a configuration that Ashmore (1981) has noted elsewhere. This expansive arrangement suggests very large residential groupings, an inference supported by ethnohistoric data discussed below. Size, elaboration, and cardinal orientation tend to vary within a grouped set of structures. Sometimes an ancestral shrine structure occupies one side of the group, often the eastern or northern side, and burials within such structures tend to be axially oriented and better furnished than subfloor burials (Haviland 1981; Welsh 1988).

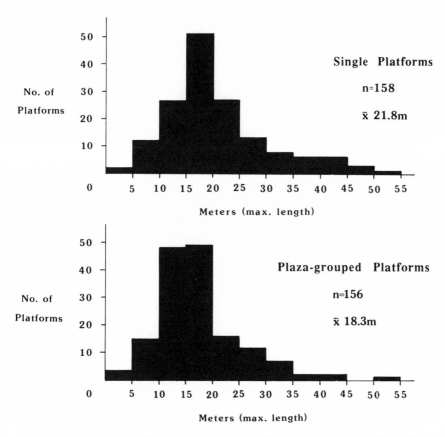

Pulltrouser Swamp

Single Platforms

n=158

x̄ 21.8m

No. of Platforms

Meters (max. length)

Plaza-grouped Platforms

n=156

x̄ 18.3m

No. of Platforms

Meters (max. length)

3.13   Histograms of number and size of platforms surrounding Pulltrouser Swamp, showing propensity toward plaza-grouped
platforms.

(2) Within structure groupings, there often are demarcated areas of burial
with pronounced differentiation in burial placement, orientation, preparation of a receptacle, and furnishings. Diamanti (1991:219) has commented
on the close association between burials and architecture in the elite residential zone of Copán; at Tikal, Haviland (1988:125) has noted that the burial
of adults is associated with sequential refurbishing and expansion of structures, Group 2G-1 being a typical example. Burials in eastern-position ora-
tories, such as in Tikal Group 7F-1, also are associated with "significant
construction activity" (Haviland 1981:94). In Tikal Group 2G-1, structures

that are older, larger, and more complex architecturally tend to contain more burials (Haviland 1988:123).

(3) Clusters of platform groupings often occur in a pattern that suggests a large "alpha" residence, possibly that of a lineage head, surrounded by smaller satellite residences that may lack some of the shrine features of the larger residence, as indicated on the map of southern K'axob (Figure 2.14). The latter may house lesser members of a lineage. This pattern of "building clusters" has also been discussed by Kurjack and Garza T. (1981:298–300; in reference to Dzibilchaltún), by Kintz (1983:179–190; for Cobá), and by Haviland (1968:109), who noted the presence of macroclusters of seventeen to thirty-three structures at Tikal. In this way, the lineage may be physically constituted on the ground in a way that can be detected by archaeological survey. Osteological (and, in the future, DNA) analysis of skeletal remains will be the critical key to demonstrating familial relations within and between platform groups. Differentiation in architectural units of the living and place-ment and elaboration of the dead suggests differentiation in status, role, and access to resources within a lineage. From this perspective, such variation can be ascribed to asymmetrical social and economic relations among members of a lineage (see Chapter 4).

(4) Maya proclivity toward constant remodeling of places has been re-marked upon by several scholars in relation to monumental architecture (e.g., Coe 1956; Haviland 1981). But the pattern can be extended to the residence as well (e.g., Haviland 1981:110). In both contexts (monumental and residential), the refurbishing such as mentioned above is often accom-panied by dedicatory and commemorative rituals of both new and old struc-tures respectively (Freidel and Schele 1989, among others). For instance, at K'axob shortly before the Late Formative ancestor shrine was built, a cache was deposited that consisted of four vessels arranged in a quadripartite pat-tern (Jackson 1992; Masson 1993; Figure 3.14). The small bowls contained seasonally sensitive (calendrically associated?) faunal remains, and the quin-cunx pattern of bowl arrangement confirms the centrality of this location. Later, and upon final burial of the shrine and its associated plaza, a Terminal Formative cache composed of ceramic vessels (one of which contained an assortment of delicate jade and shell carvings) and seven pecked limestone spheres was deposited in the fill of an overlying construction unit (White 1990; Figure 2.19). It is postulated here that these events, both constructional and ritual, are linked to the passage of power between the generations. The study of the material residue of the transmission of rights, obligations, and duties is, essentially, the archaeology of inheritance. Places with long chains of transmission will also have long sequences of construction events punctu-

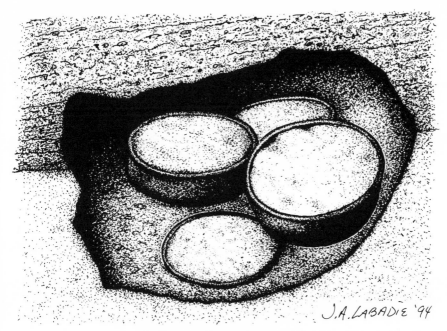

J.A.LABADIE '94

3.14   Dedicatory cache vessels arranged in quincunx pattern (drawing by John Antoine Labadie).

ated by dedicatory and commemorative cache deposits as well as actual ancestor interments—in other words, the construction of genealogies of place.

Inhabitants of Maya Households

As ancestors "slept" beneath the surface, the overlying domestic context was alive with activity. It is hard to appreciate the extent to which the domestic locale was a nexus of many different types of activity—political, social, economic, and, of course, ritual. In our urban society of Western postindustrialization, the residence has been reduced to a passive locale where inhabitants sleep, dress, and eat. Except for the symbolic display of wealth, the residence largely has been stripped of its power and authority, and those in attendance at the residence—formerly a maternal female—have also been stripped of status and authority. But in an agrarian society in which much of the activity is kin-organized, the residence is the place from which power and authority emanate. This fact has implications for gender roles, discussed further in Chapters 4 and 5.

Farriss (1984:133) observes that Maya extended family structure is rarely mentioned in modern or colonial accounts although property-holding documents in colonial records indicate that it was quite common. She describes a

Maya extended family as four or five patrilineally related males plus wives and unmarried daughters, all functioning as a cooperative economic unit with a residential base. Ideally such a unit spanned three generations and was important for communal aspects of farming, tool-sharing, shared stores of food, and child-care.

The large size and sprawling physical plan of many Classic Maya residential compounds suggest the earlier presence of multiple-family households with complex networks of asymmetrical social, political, and economic relations operating among its members. There is ample documentary evidence from Postclassic and Colonial times that, indeed, residential groupings included large numbers of related and unrelated individuals. After reviewing documentary texts for the post-Hispanic period, Scholes and Roys (1968:54) venture this opinion:

> Contemporary sources tell us that multiple-family houses were common among the Yucatecan Maya, the Chol Lacandón, the Manche Chol, and the Itzá on Lake Petén. In 1582 small settlements containing large multiple-family houses were also reported some distance east of Tixchel and north of the Candelaria drainage. . . . The Tixchel matrícula of 1569 records *nine* [emphasis added] married couples in the house of the cacique [lineage head?].

Similar patterns of multiple-family residences are apparent from a 1570 census on Cozumel Island and from the reports of early chroniclers such as Bienvenida.[16] In all cases, household size appears to have been related to the wealth and political power of the occupants.

A revealing part of the early census data from Cozumel Island—a place where the *encomendero* was particularly lackadaisical in his efforts to christianize Maya inhabitants and discourage multiple-family residential units—is the proportion of related to unrelated couples who resided together. The information, reproduced here from Roys, Scholes, and Adams (1940:15) as Table 3.1, comes from the villages of San Miguel and Santa María. At San Miguel, sixty-two couples were counted in only seventeen households. While twenty-three are associated by name with the household head or his wife, fully twenty-two couples are completely unassociated by name. As is clear from Table 3.1, the unrelated couples tend to be more prevalent in the largest household grouping (Nos. 1, 3, 11, 13, and 16), all of which have from four to six couples in residence; Spearman's Rank-order Correlation Coefficient of 0.528 (alpha = .05) indicates a positive relationship of moderate strength between the number of couples residing at a household and the number of unrelated couples. At Santa María, a total of eighty-one couples were counted; thirty-three were noted as associated by name while twenty-six were unrelated to the head of household or his wife. Once again, the presence of unrelated couples is more prevalent in households with four or more couples (Nos. 4, 6, 7, and 9), although large households with very few unrelated couples also exist (Nos. 1, 3, 11, and 16); for the households of Santa María, Spearman's Rank-order Correlation Coefficient reveals a stronger directional relationship (r = 0.74 with an alpha value of .01). Two *matrículas*, one from Tixchel compiled in 1569 and one from Ppencuyut in 1584, reveal a similar pattern.[17] Ironically, the large residential compounds—which in the archaeological record of the Classic period are more likely to contain ancestor shrines—are more likely, on the basis of ethnohistoric data, to contain inhabitants who are not related genealogically to the head of the household, such as servants, laborers, or in-laws. Large households, thus, tended to absorb unrelated persons who must have been critical to production activities organized at the domestic compound (McAnany 1993). In Chapter 4, the inequality of these production relationships is investigated.

Lowland Maya groups are often described as patrilineal and patrilocal despite the known flexibility of kinship structures. In this regard, the census data from Cozumel are pertinent since they reveal a strong tendency for men with the same name as the household head to reside together (most likely sons or brothers; Table 3.1). Households of the pre-Hispanic period also grew through the practice of polygyny among the wealthy. Apparently, it was not uncommon for male heads of household to take a wife of similar social standing followed by a series of "slave concubines" (Roys 1943:27).[18] Although the children of the concubines bore the patronymic of the household head, they were vulnerable upon the death of the head and could be chosen as the object of human sacrifice or sold into slavery (Roys 1943:27).

Regarding the contemporary Tzotzil who organize farming production within localized descent groups, Collier (1982:347) discusses the measures that are taken by heads of household to maintain large household size: "This is how Tzotzil farmers build up efficient field and kitchen operations. Withholding inheritance of the means of production (e.g., land, pack animals, and tools) . . . counteracts fission of the family in the domestic cycle. As a result, family groups endure as localized multigenerational units of production and consumption." Bunzel (1952:25) also comments on the intergenerational antagonisms produced by the withholding of inheritance. Tozzer (1941:101, n.459) stresses the contribution of widespread bride service (in which a

TABLE 3.1. MULTIPLE-FAMILY HOUSEHOLDS ON COZUMEL ISLAND, 1570 CENSUS
(after Table 1 in Roys, Scholes, and Adams 1940).

San Miguel

List Number of House	Married Couples in House (Including Head)	Same Name as Head		Same Name as Head's Wife		Couples Associated by Name with Head or Wife	
		Men	Women	Men	Women	Yes	No
1	6	1	0	0	1	2	3
2	2	0	0	0	0	0	1
3	4	0	0	0	1	1	2
4	4	1	0	1	0	2	1
5	3	1	0	0	0	1	1
6	2	0	0	0	0	0	1
7	3	1	1	0	0	2	0
8	4	1	1	1	1	3	0
9	2	0	0	0	0	0	1
10	3	1	0	0	0	1	1
11	7	1	1	1	0	3	3
12	2	0	0	1	0	1	0
13	4	0	0	0	0	0	3
14	4	0	3	0	0	3	0
15	2	0	0	0	0	0	1
16	6	2	1	0	0	2	3
17	4	1	0	1	0	2	1
Total	62	10	7	5	3	23	22

Santa Maria

List Number of House	Married Couples in House (Including Head)	Same Name as Head		Same Name as Head's Wife		Couples Associated by Name with Head or Wife	
		Men	Women	Men	Women	Yes	No
1	6	1	1	0	1	4	1
2	3	0	0	0	0	0	2
3	5	2	1	1	1	3	1
4	6	1	0	0	0	1	4
5	2	1	0	0	0	1	0
6	4	0	0	0	0	0	3

TABLE 3.1. *continued*

List Number of House	Married Couples in House (Including Head)	Same Name as Head		Same Name as Head's Wife		Couples Associated by Name with Head or Wife	
		Men	Women	Men	Women	Yes	No
7	5	0	0	0	1	1	3
8	2	0	1	1	0	1	0
9	4	0	0	0	0	0	3
10	3	0	1	0	1	2	0
11	8	4	0	1	2	5	2
12	2	0	1	1	0	1	0
13	3	0	0	1	0	1	1
14	3	0	0	0	0	0	2
15	2	0	1	0	0	1	0
16	5	2	0	1	0	3	1
17	2	0	1	0	0	1	0
18	4	1	0	0	0	1	2
19	3	0	2	0	0	2	0
20	2	0	0	0	1	1	0
21	4	0	0	0	2	2	1
22	3	1	1	0	0	2	0
Total	81	13	10	6	9	33	26

newly married daughter and her husband live and work at the compound of her father for five to six years) to the large extended-family households of the Postclassic and Colonial periods. In short, labor demands of agrarian production select for large household size. Pertinent ethnohistoric data from highland Morelos (Carrasco 1976) indicate that the participation of households in a larger political economy with tribute, taxation, and labor drafts also favors larger household size.

ANCESTORS AS GUARDIANS OF THE FIELDS

To recapitulate the thread of the argument of this chapter, here I will touch upon the main points covered. First of all, from the Late Formative on, an increasingly small component of Maya agriculture was conducted as long- or short-fallow swidden, and this land-extensive component may have ceased altogether in many parts of the lowlands by the Late Classic.

The term *swidden* itself is really not an effective descriptor of Maya agriculture for several reasons: (1) it minimizes the importance of tenure and systems of inheritance indicated in the ethnohistoric record, (2) it does not encompass the orchards and near-residential plots that were continuously cultivated, and (3) it is a consequence of a temperate-based classification system that cannot stretch to accommodate the variability within and between tropical agricultural systems. In the Yucatán, the mistranslation of the term *k'ax* throws some light on this conceptual problem. I suggest that the phrase *fixed-plot, variable-fallow farming,* though not an elegant term, certainly comes closer to describing the way in which many Maya used their agricultural landscape.

In our society, land claims and inheritance are handled through recourse to the legal system. In many traditional societies, however, these issues are handled in the context of death rituals, burial rites, and continued interaction with the dead through ancestor veneration. It follows, therefore, that when we detect archaeologically the selective social practice of creating ancestors, this indicates that proprietary resource rights have crystallized, generally at the level of a macrofamily grouping such as a lineage. When this more restrictive pattern of use-rights emerges (that is, when ancestors become the guardians of the fields), the place where the ancestors "sleep" can become a strategic locale in reference to social identity and economic rights. The sequential interment of ancestors establishes a genealogy of place in the same sense that hieroglyphic texts give credence to the genealogical constructs of rulers. By 400 B.C., many Maya residences were assuming the characteristics of a domestic mausoleum. In effect, ancestors come to symbolize the coalescence of lineage and locale.

FOUR

Lineage as a Crucible of Inequality

In a definitional sense, the residence is the primary place where ancestral genealogy is encoded both ritualistically and corporally. Relationally, however, the ancestors, through the structure of the lineage, serve to underwrite and reinforce social and economic inequality, particularly in large, expansive households. Many current anthropological theories of social inequality stress the emergence of class structure and warfare as primary factors of inequality. Lineage organization is more frequently analyzed from the perspective of group inclusiveness rather than as a crucible of inequality. Yet among groups such as the Mae Enga of highland New Guinea who are generally not classified as societies with class stratification or hereditary leadership positions, there is, in fact, clearly a tremendous amount of social and economic inequality (Meggitt 1965). This type of inequality, which emerges from the spirit of the ancestors and resides in the heart of kin groupings, is the subject of this chapter. This approach is distinct from studies of inequities which examine the consequences of the crystallization of hereditary positions of authority and political centralization. In many respects, this is an analysis of inequality at a very personal level— within the residential compound, within the lineage, and between lineages. The goal is not to contrast chiefdoms with states or ranked with stratified societies—that is, to artificially or heuristically constrain the study of inequality to evolutionary pigeonholes. In fact, what I am attempting to do here is to move our perception of Maya society away from simple dichotomies of inequality, as between the elites and nonelites, and to examine the specific social contexts in which asymmetrical relationships develop and consequently imbue further social interaction with the quality of inequality. It is in this regard that the lineage is viewed as a crucible of inequality.

As discussed below, asymmetry pervaded many aspects of Maya life. Even today, it is evident from the linguistic analysis of Yucatec Maya practices in relating to other members of large households (Hanks 1990); in the past, the extensive use of the concept of "burden" or *kuch* in reference to kings, lineage heads, and even Year Bearers (Thompson 1972) can be interpreted as a social mechanism by which inequality was socially glossed or masked. An examination of the contexts and mechanisms of such inequality starts with the predatory relationship between lineage and land.

VORACIOUS APPETITE OF LINEAGES FOR LAND

The fact that lineages generally are territorially based and residentially stable (at least across several generations) has been stated repetitively by ethnographers who have examined lineal descent groups in Africa, Asia, and the Americas.[1] In effect, lineage organization can be seen as a basic vehicle for the organization of demographic superiority and economic advantage at the suprafamily level. A result of this predatory aspect of lineage organization (Sahlins 1961) is the emergence of inequality, not as the outcome of an individual family pulling itself up by its bootstraps or one village conquering another through warfare, but as a consequence of the demographic and economic success of a lineage, which can effectively monopolize the resources of a region at the expense of another group. This process yields unequal access to resources not unlike that discussed by Fried (1967). This type of inequality, however, is highly unstable and is more easily torn asunder than the class-based inequality such as existed between elite and nonelite sectors of the Maya population by A.D. 250.

Due to their demographic and economic advantage, strong lineages potentially can dominate the best land, as Smith (1959) has demonstrated for rural Tokugawa-period Japan. Along a similar vein, Freedman (1966:36) has described the expansionist nature of local Chinese lineages:

> Once all the good land was taken up, a new local
> lineage could not normally expect to expand to great
> size, and the general picture in the contemporary
> New Territories suggests how *date of first settlement,*
> *agricultural advantage, and size* of local lineage are
> connected in such a manner as to distribute the great
> Punti local lineages on the rice plains and the smaller
> local lineages, both Punti and Hakka, by and large on
> poorer land [emphasis added].

In Chapter 3, the principle of first occupancy was discussed as a rationale for a transgenerational system of land tenure; the "downside" of such landholding systems is the inevitable codification of differential access to resources both between and within lineages. Goody (1962:269) expresses succinctly the causal connection between lineage resource control and inequality among the African LoDagaa: "[T]he creation of perpetual tenure was also a way of legitimizing the process of alienation"—an observation echoed in a cross-cultural study of social transformation by Johnson and Earle (1987:190).

Insofar as the archaeological record provides the only means at our disposal to test the applicability of these ideas to the Formative lowland Maya, one can postulate that the emergence of lineages with proprietary resource rights (which is archaeologically invisible) may be diagnosed by reference to corollary changes in archaeologically visible domains such as land use, architecture, and burial practices. Lineage membership is generally predicated upon the demonstration of inclusion within a particular kin group, and it is here that ancestors play a vital role in establishing the criteria of group membership and, conversely, exclusion from membership.

THE CONCEPT OF DESCENT IN MAYA SOCIETY

The role played by specific ancestors in the formation of lineal descent groups is critical. For it is by reference to an ascending multigenerational chain of progenitors that individuals establish their social identity as well as their rights, privileges, and authority over others. The ancestors generally are invoked to legitimize, sanctify, and bring order to everyday existence. For the Quiché Maya, Bunzel (1952:269) has noted that "The powers whose influence on human affairs is continuous and unremitting are the ancestors, who represent the great moral force of the universe. . . . As former owners of the house and land, the ancestors, along with the idols, enforce social order within the house." Ancestors also serve to maintain the social cohesion within descent groups, as Feuchtwang (1974:212) shows in his contrastive analysis of the institutions of Chinese ancestor veneration and *feng-shui*. The former is oriented toward the past achievements of the group (particularly as expressed in rituals conducted in the ancestor halls), while the latter is concerned with the siting and placement of individual ancestral graves and, as such, expresses the anticipated future success of a family. *Feng-shui* rituals surrounding the interment of an ancestor in reality constitute a break with the past and a look to the future (Feuchtwang 1974:214; see also Watson 1988:204), much as did structure renovations following the interment of ancestors at many Maya sites. In this way, architecture expresses the concept of descent through the continuous use with modification of a structure.

What was the size of these kin groups? Estimates vary considerably. For the Classic Maya of Tikal, Haviland (1968:110) has proposed the conservative figure of three to nineteen extended families per "clan" (a term more or less analogous with lineage). Based upon ethnohistoric sources, Carmack (1981:105, 162) has suggested a population of about fifty thousand for the Quiché capital of Utatlán at which fifty-one lineages resided; this yields a significantly higher average estimate of lineage size at around a thousand individuals per lineage, and no doubt there was significant variability in lineage size. Notwithstanding variation in size, membership in a specific kin group was critically important, and gaining an understanding of the emergence of such social distinctions is essential to our understanding of Formative Maya society. Elite Classic and Postclassic Maya society has been shown to have been organized according to principles of lineal descent, but, significantly, few have investigated the formative roots of these social conventions. Examination of an archaeological case study of the genesis of lineage groups and ancestor veneration will illustrate the kinds of data that may be brought to bear on this issue.

Genealogy without Texts: An Example from K'axob

Recent excavations in the ancestral portion of K'axob suggest that the Maya custom of creating ancestors who served as the ritual focus of lineal descent groups is rooted in the Formative. By the later part of the Late Formative, or around 200 B.C., the creation of ancestors (as opposed to the interment of deceased family members) was an active social practice at K'axob. Upon death, the remains of certain individuals were enshrined under a low platform in a small, central plaza (Figure 2.18). A wide variety of grave goods was interred with these individuals (Figure 2.16), but the most significant accouterments by epigraphic standards were a series of ceramic vessels emblazoned with a cross or quadripartite motif (Figures 2.17 and 3.10). This motif is common in Maya iconography and, as discussed in Chapter 3, is symbolic of a partitioning of the universe in reference to solar cycles and places on the landscape evocative of ancestors. It is a motif integral to the agrarian, solar calendar—a basic armature of Maya cosmology (Hunt 1977: 248). Among Quiché day-keepers, Barbara Tedlock (1982:59) has documented an intricate linkage between the calendar-round and lineage shrines placed strategically on the landscape. Coeval with the use of the cross motif at K'axob are two cache deposits from Cerros and Nohmul in which several images were arranged in a quadripartite pattern (Justeson, Norman, and Hammond 1988). These occurrences suggest a deep history to the genealogies of the sixteenth century in which there are generally four founding ancestors. The repetitive use of the cross motif in the ancestor shrine of K'axob indicates the centrality of this burial locale to the Late Formative inhabitants of K'axob (Headrick 1993) and the ancestor status of the individuals interred at this place.

Emerging inequality that is a corollary of ancestor-focused lineal descent groups is expressed in the differential treatment of the dead. Other individuals, perhaps not destined to become revered ancestors, were interred under the floors of nearby satellite residences in a variety of grave types ranging from bell-shaped pits to interment directly into construction fill (McCormack, Henderson, and Estrada-Belli 1993). In comparison with the shrine burials, other Late Formative burials had rather spartan grave goods, many with only a single ceramic vessel (none painted with the cross motif). Rather than the imported marine shell jewelry, many individuals were buried with a cache of *Pomacea* shells—a swamp mollusc available within fifty meters of the place of burial.

Throughout the Formative and through a series of floor and platform constructions and renovations, most of the structures at K'axob took on the characteristics of domestic mausolea. The Structure 18 area, however, accrued a special significance as the ritual and physical focus of a high-status kin group; repeated renovation of the shrine and, in particular, of its underlying burial pit indicates that succeeding generations of ancestors were interred at this location. The increasingly ritualized and differentiated character of the burial deposits culminate in the construction of a pyramid over this ancestral locale during the Early Classic period (Figure 2.15). This progressive sacralization of place, i.e., the trajectory from domestic space to a ritual locale, is an architectural expression of a genealogy of place that has been documented elsewhere (see Andrews and Fash [1992] on Copán, Group 10L-29).

Ceramics associated with field-raising and canalization in Pulltrouser Swamp, located just five hundred meters to the west of Structure 18, include Late Formative types. This synchronicity in the construction of an ancestor shrine, the establishment of a genealogy of place, and reclamation of nearby swampland is particularly interesting in light of the fact that repetitive and intensive patterns of land use are highly correlated with the presence of proprietary use rights and lineage organization (Blaikie and Brookfield 1986; Johnson and Earle 1987:184; Sahlins 1961:330). Collier (1975) in particular has demonstrated that when there is a shortage of land, kinship structures emphasizing descent gain prominence.[2] At K'axob there is no textual record of descent-based kinship structures or named ancestors; rather, burial patterns, architectural changes, and intensification of land-use practices together suggest that by the end of the Late Formative lineage groups organized around ancestor veneration were well established.

Apparently, the principle of first occupancy not only served to legitimize unequal distribution of resources, it also provided a cornerstone for the ranking of lineages. In reference to the founding of Mayapán, Landa tells us that each lineage was ranked by the antiquity of its pedigree and that resources were allotted accordingly: "In this enclosure [within the walls of Mayapán] they built houses for the lords only, dividing all the land among them, giving towns to each one, according to the antiquity of his lineage and his personal value" (Tozzer 1941:25). This observation reflects a widely held notion—that the descent line of noble families is deeper and more venerable than that of commoners and therefore deserving of access to more and better resources—that is the final outcome of the politicization of lineage hierarchy through the establishment of permanent leadership positions not accessible to all. In the Calotmul Document (a version of the Maní Land Treaty) the same sentiment is expressed: "Herewith we declare our true testimony of how this land is not slave which we leave to them, in order that the nobles may sustain themselves, in order that they may farm it in time to come" (Roys 1943:192). In this passage, "slave" may refer to the fact that the lands were not captured from another group or that they are the lands of a free people; the Maya word used here is *PPENTAC*, literally "a slave." Although this reference to the ability of nobles to sustain themselves suggests more of a class distinction than one based upon lineage membership, in reality class distinctions among the Maya crosscut lineage membership, so that many lineages were composed of both elites and commoners (Roys 1943:35). In specific detail, Morley (1941:444–446) has documented both the *hidalgo* or elite line of the Xiu family and the non-*hidalgo*. Even within the *hidalgo* line, the limited resource base available to the Yucatec Maya during the Colonial period resulted in the eighteenth- and nineteenth-century diaspora of junior branches of the *hidalgo* line of the Xiu family (Morley 1941). This example indicates clearly that there was pronounced hierarchy and preferential access to resources within lineages. This hierarchical structure was probably not exclusive to lineages that were composed of a mixture of elites and commoners. In reference to Aztec *calpulli* composition, Carrasco (1978:37) has noted that even *calpulli* of the lower social segments would have had *jefes* (leaders) and commoners. The antiquity of this hierarchical pattern certainly reaches back into the Classic and even Formative periods. If structural mass and elaboration, as well as the differential frequency of burial goods, is a key to the archaeological recognition of these hierarchical relationships within lineages, then the residential settlement of southern K'axob, with its single large "alpha" plaza group surrounded by smaller patio configurations (Figure 2.14)—all with a Formative core overlain by Classic-period platform expansions—suggests a Formative basis for this pattern of inequality. The scale of this pattern—at the lineage level rather than the individual household level—also illustrates the need to move beyond studies of "household archaeology" and examine the larger groupings of which single structures are but a part.

The Burden of Authority

A key to the decipherment of ancient Maya hieroglyphic script has been the acceptance of its phonetic structure and the corresponding use of Yucatec and Cholan Mayan languages to decipher the script; by extension, and within reason, living Mayan languages may be used to inform us about past political and economic relationships. A word with implications for understanding the social perception of lineage authority is the Yucatec Mayan term *kuch*. With numerous shades of meaning, *kuch* can refer to a "burden," such as one that is carried on a tumpline against one's back, a burden of conscience, a responsibility, an obligation, or the authority of an office (Barrera Vásquez 1980: 343–344).

For the purpose of examining authority and inequality within the lineage, however, the most pertinent use of the term *kuch* in Yucatec Mayan is in regard to a position of leadership known from Postclassic times and one that probably existed during earlier times as well: the role of *ah kuch kab* ("he of the burden of the land"). As introduced in Chapter 3, this term can refer to a lineage head and member of a community council who also attended to other municipal duties. In positions of authority within their respective lineages, *ah kuch kabob* also had the responsibility or real burden of amassing tribute for the *ahau* or HALACH UINIC.

During the 1500s, the BATABOB (and later the Spanish-appointed governors) were ultimately responsible for the transfer of tribute goods from the households to the provincial head or Crown coffers, but it was the lineage heads (*ah kuch kabob*), in consultation with the heads of households (*ah chun kahil* as expressed in Yucatec Mayan [Barrera Vásquez 1980: 116]), who actually engineered, supervised, and bore the economic burden of producing the surplus tribute goods, termed *hol* by the Yucatec Maya. Following M. Coe (1965), I suggest that the office of *ah kuch kab* is deeply rooted in the pre-Columbian past; furthermore, it represents one of the earliest institutionalized structures of inequality to pervade the lowlands.

For the Colonial portion of the Yucatec sequence, Farriss (1984) has argued convincingly that the survival of Yucatec Maya society was due in large part to the fact that the small Spanish colonial population did not disassemble the fabric of Maya society, particularly the rights and privileges of Maya leaders, both elite and nonelite. Rather, the Spaniards co-opted the existing structure to meet their needs and tribute demands. However, Morley (1941), in a detailed study of the genealogy of the elite Xiu family, has pointed out that while the Crown continued to acknowledge the rights and privileges of noble families, they did chip away systematically at their political power base just as Classic-period kings must have tried to chip away at the power base of lineage leaders.

During the Postclassic and probably earlier times, the lineage heads (*ah kuch kabob*) and the household heads (*ah chun kahil*) organized and supervised agrarian and commodity production on the local level. Some portion of that production was consumed locally or used in exchange transactions to procure nonlocal products, but another portion of production was transformed into a type of political "currency" and used to "pay" taxes and tribute to political heads, plus to sponsor local events such as banquets and feasts which increased the collective power and status of the lineage. The labor demands of the BATAB and the "in-kind" tribute demands of the HALACH UINIC or *ahaw* represent only the most formalized portion of the political economy in Maya society. As discussed in Chapter 2, a parallel prestation economy (of which feasting was of great importance) coexisted with the political economy. In many respects, the prestation economy was even more formalized in the sense that we have written accounts of pre-Hispanic calendrical cycles of ritual feasts although we lack similar accounts of pre-Hispanic tribute lists. Landa chronicled an extremely full calendar of feasts and rituals celebrated or observed on a local level (Tozzer 1941). Many of these feasts were a celebration of the ancestors, and most of them resulted in the consumption of large quantities of luxury foods, particularly *cacao* and meat (fowl or venison) and beverages such as *balche,* and frequently the distribution of manufactured items, such as cotton cloth and ceramic vessels. This custom has continued, in one form or another, as the *cargo* system documented by Vogt (1969) and others in highland Chiapas.[3] With this consideration of the burden of production, we shift focus away from the larger structure of the lineage and consider the structures of inequality in the most atomistic unit of production in Maya society: the household unit.

INEQUALITY AND ASYMMETRY AT THE NEXUS
OF PRODUCTION

It is within residential relations that we see social inequality on a very personal level. Also at this scale, ancestors play a significant role in structuring asymmetrical relations between coresidential individuals, particularly in regard to what Nash (1970:97) has called the "age-ordered hierarchies." The sociological term "extended-family compound" is often used as a cover term for large multistructure residential complexes, intimating a multigenerational context in which all family members share in the resources of the family or lineage. The imputed equality of this unit, however, is contradicted by linguistic and ethnohistoric data which suggest that asymmetry is an essential part of residential relations and is inextricably linked to the organization of production. For Maya society and Mesoamerican societies, information from sixteenth-century documents suggests in general that the social structure and composition of a residence is strongly influenced by the larger political economy within which this atomistic unit is situated. In other words, the household, as a unit of archaeological, ethnohistoric, or ethnographic analysis, must be analyzed in terms of its connections to a larger political milieu.

In Chapter 3, evidence of extended and multifamily households was presented. The different sources of information all point to the same conclusion: in the past, many Maya preferred to live in large and sprawling residential compounds, and in fact many continue to do so today. Seeking to inflate the number of tributaries on their tax lists and disapproving of the close physical proximity between a young woman and her affines (father-in-law in particular), sixteenth-century Spanish officials and missionaries tried, with varying success, to break up these large households. But the existing residential pattern seems to have been based upon a long-standing and successful strategy employed particularly in wealthy households. For decades now, field archaeologists have been mapping Late Formative— and Classic-period multiplatform residential complexes. Haviland (1968:106–107), in particular, has noted the Formative roots for extended family groupings at Tikal, e.g., Group 6E-1, which is composed of two contemporary structures dating to about 25 B.C.; see also Ringle and Andrews (1988) on multiplatform complexes at Komchen. Haviland sees the formation of extended families as a response to the development of unilocal postmarital residence patterns. I suggest, on the contrary, that large extended-family residences are a consequence of political centralization and the imposition of revenue-raising strategies upon the household.

A hint of the fundamental asymmetry of relations within large residential groupings is suggested by linguistic research among contemporary Yucatec Maya. By reference to specific expressions, Hanks (1990:115–119) analyzes the "asymmetric genre" that is encoded linguistically among household co-residents on the basis of age, gender, and wealth. He suggests that "the Maya household as a social organization embodies principles of segmentation, reciprocity, and asymmetry that are the basis of communicative patterns, particularly those which involve reference to or interaction in domestic space"

(Hanks 1990:95). The actual social and familial composition of households, as well as the economic roles of subsidiary males and females who reside alongside the household head (*ah chun kah*) and his immediate family, was (and is) extremely variable and subject to situational contingencies. Nonetheless, knowing the Maya proclivity toward patrilocal residence and inheritance patterns, several possible combinations (not mutually exclusive) of social and production relations could explain the supranuclear composition of many Maya residential complexes:

(1) Sons of the *ah chun kah*, with their own wives and children, remain at home to increase their chances of being the prime inheritor of the family resources much as Wilk (1988:140) has documented among the Kekchi Maya of today. The father-son relationship is vitally intertwined with land and inheritance and fraught with continual conflict as well as cooperation. The transmission of land rights from father to son lies at the nexus of this asymmetrical relationship, which is discussed in detail by Collier (1975: 79–108) and expressed eloquently by Bunzel (1952:24–25) for the Quiché Maya: "Land is something which a man receives from his father and withholds from his son; it is the material symbol of continuity between generations. . . . [L]and . . . is the focus of the bitter and suppressed antagonism between father and son, and the still more bitter rivalry of brothers for their father's favor." The tyranny of the household head over succeeding generations is not unique to Maya society; parricide—the killing of one's father, grandfather, father's brother, and their wives—is the most heinous offense recorded in the Imperial Ch'ing dynasty penal code. Impiety toward one's elders is the second most heinous offense (Feuchtwang 1974:213). The asymmetry of the father-son "bond is upheld in [Chinese] ancestor worship" (Feuchtwang 1974:213) much in the same way that it must have been reinforced by ancestor veneration among the Maya.

(2) Since the sixteenth century, many Maya have followed the practice of so-called bride-service, in which the daughter and son-in-law of a household head reside temporarily in the household of the head for a variable amount of time, often from two to five years. The antiquity of this practice is not clear, although it is certain that the son-in-law is obliged to assist the head in production activities during this time, thus increasing the size of the labor force under the authority of the head. Tozzer (1941:101), for one, thought that this practice alone might explain the Maya tendency toward multistructure residences.

(3) At some point in the cycle of household development, elders must yield their authority to younger generations even though they may continue to survive. In this way, ascending generations contributed to the heterogeneity of the residential compounds.

(4) By definition, a multifamily compound contains extra families or single individuals, either related or not, who are coresident with the family of the household head. Ethnographic and ethnohistoric descriptions of this arrangement from the Maya region and elsewhere indicate that these individuals often are without their own resource base and live with the main family of the household as "helpers" in domestic and field labor. Using a less euphemistic term, we could refer to these individuals as servants or tenant farmers, and the asymmetry of their relation to the head of the household is painfully obvious. The presence of coresident tenant farmers has been documented by Roys (1943:34) for post-contact Yucatán and is referred to by Landa (Tozzer 1941) in the context of unrelated orphans who were adopted into households and took the family patronymic. In the highlands of Morelos, Carrasco (1976) has noted a similar residential pattern which he terms the "stem family." Dependent household members were called *tequinanamique* or "those who help with tribute" (Carrasco 1976:55)—an example of the manner in which household composition is not independent of larger political context.

At Classic-period sites, programs of large-scale excavations generally yield evidence of extremely simple and modest residential structures spatially juxtaposed with elaborate architecture. Haviland (1981), for example, interprets the less elaborate structures of Tikal Group 7F-35 and 36 as those of poor relatives living in a dependent relationship with a wealthy family; further examples of simple pole-and-thatch structures built on masonry platforms in proximity to the monumental architecture of Tikal include Structures 5D-6 to 5D-9 (west of West Plaza group), 7F-35 to 7F-36 (off a plaza with two range structures and two temples), and 6B-41 to 6B-44, which is near a large group that also includes Structures 6B-34, 6B-30, and 6B-33 (Haviland 1968:112). From the area of Río Azul also, Eaton (1987) has documented a large, diverse residential compound with stone buildings as well as low platforms, the latter interpreted as housing for servants. Andrews and Fash (1992:83) also note a large area of servant and craftsperson housing just to the west of the large elite plaza Group 10L-2 of Copán.

(5) During the Postclassic the taking of slaves through warfare and raiding was extremely common in northern Yucatán. Reasons for human enslavement seem to have been multiple and to have included the humiliation of enemy warriors, the desire to bolster the size of a household labor force (and to have on hand individuals for immolation), the punishment of local theft, and the reality that enslaved persons represented tradable "merchandise" in the large dendritic trading network operated by Maya and Aztec traders. Men, women, and children who became slaves as a result of these unfortunate circumstances were bound in an asymmetric relationship of dependency

and resided at or near the household compound of their captor or owner. The Spaniard Aguilar, shipwrecked off the coast of Yucatán in the early 1500s, was subsequently captured, enslaved, and required to haul wood and water and to transport foodstuffs, such as fish (Cervantes de Salazar, in Tozzer 1941:237). This popular account is probably representative of an important function of slaves in Maya society, i.e., as human beasts of burden. The large market for slaves during the Postclassic, coupled with the fact that slave-taking was a crucial part of Postclassic interpolity rivalry in Yucatán (Roys 1957), suggests that additional household labor—particularly for production, trade, and tribute-related transport needs (not considering sacrificial victims for the moment)—was highly desired. Although we lack concrete examples of enslavement from the Classic period, the iconography of warfare shows plainly that the taking and sacrifice of captives was an accepted hazard of war. Thus, the overall situation regarding enslavement was probably not appreciably different during the Classic period, particularly in light of the archaeological evidence of large, multistructure residential compounds at which captive labor would be useful and easily supervised.

If only a few of these possible permutations of residential composition existed at the multistructure compounds of the Late Formative and Classic periods, then such compounds would have been extremely heterogeneous, both socially and economically. Common ground shared by household members, other than a focal conjugal unit, was primarily that of being in an asymmetric relationship with the household head. A continuum of inequality can be envisioned from the partially power-engendered senior sons to the totally dominated slaves and orphans whose very lives were dependent on the whim of the *ah chun kahil*. A head of household, for instance, could decide that the sacrifice of a human life would benefit the household more than the continued productive labor of a slave or an orphan. From an archaeological perspective, it is clear that the larger the compound the more internally heterogeneous. To gloss over this heterogeneity for the sake of classification is tantamount to disregarding the lives of servants, slaves, and other individuals who undoubtedly contributed substantially to the productive capabilities of the household.[4] If we wish to write a social history of the Maya rather than create elite-focused scenarios, then (as I have proposed elsewhere [McAnany 1993]) we need to conceptualize and implement more sophisticated and inclusive methods of analysis that will give voice to those who lived in relationships of dependency and not just to those wielding power.

This look at inequality among members of the same "house" reveals that there are many arrangements of social and economic inequality that are not actually class-based but rather are situationally defined by factors such as age, capture through warfare, loss of productive lands, or loss of parents.

Should we add gender to this list of circumstances engendering inequality at the residence? The data are ambiguous in this regard. Clearly, Maya society of Postclassic and possibly earlier times exhibited a tendency toward patrilineality in genealogy and inheritance; on the other hand, some of the best-known genealogies of elite Classic rulers, such as Pakal the Great of Palenque, are based on matrilineal inheritance. Bilateral descent patterns, furthermore, seem to have been operative among the Maya nobility of the Classic period (Marcus 1983:470). Patrilocality in residence patterns of the common Maya, however, would have resulted in the dislocation of a female from her ancestral hearth, and this could have resulted in a lessening of the power and influence of females. If this was the case, then the lesser status of females might result in a tendency to omit females as recognized ancestors and thus to accord them very simple burials with few grave goods in contrast to male burials. In a survey of published burial data from the Maya lowlands (actually a small fraction of the total number of excavated burials), Welsh (1988: 146) found that males and females were accorded nearly equal status (in terms of grave goods) at the time of burial. For Copán, Webster (1989:14) estimates that four to five hundred individuals were buried at elite Group 9N-8; of the two hundred and fifty burials recovered, two-thirds of the skeletons identifiable as to sex are female, an overrepresentation of females in a specialized elite context. On the other hand, Tourtellot (1990) has noted the low incidence of female burials from excavations conducted at Seibal (mostly in elite contexts), and elite rulers buried under pyramids do tend to be males. The pattern emerging is a complex one with significant variation by period, site, and archaeological context. What we can say right now is that the Maya tendency toward patrilineality and patrilocality did not translate into male hegemony in the realm of ancestral veneration.

On the Emergence of Multifamily Compounds

Maya society was a tapestry of power relations that were negotiated at many different levels from the polity to the lineage and the residence. The lineage, as the crucible of inequality, is given temporal priority for two reasons. First, because of its emphasis on lineal descent, it is an institution engendering exclusion and alienation from resources as well as inclusion and resource accessibility. Second, it is a macrofamily organization in which leadership roles are institutionalized although not necessarily hereditary. Inequality within the large multistructure residential compounds, on the other hand, may have been a response to the emergence of political centralization and an extractive political economy during the Late Formative—a time when labor and production demands on the household would have increased substantially. In this regard, the Cerros pattern is particularly interesting in that there is a shift in residence type between 400 and 200 B.C. from a nucleated village of single dwellings to dispersed, multiple-dwelling compounds (Cliff and Crane 1989; Robertson and Freidel 1986). A similar change occurs coevally at K'axob and takes the form of a shift from very thin ground-level house floors found only in one locality (Operation I) to the construction of large building platforms at multiple locales. At the multiple-dwelling residential compounds, social and economic inequality existed on an individual-to-individual level, and the largest compounds undoubtedly harbored the most complex and diverse array of asymmetrical relationships involving the productive labor of men, women, and children.

FIVE

Kin Groups
and Divine Kingship
in Lowland Maya Society

"There is a blind spot in the [documentary] sources on ancient Mesoamerican life, covering the crucial region between the kinship terminology and political structure" (M. Coe 1965:98). This observation reflects the fact that sixteenth-century conquerors/chroniclers of the Americas approached the "other" from two perspectives: (1) with an eye to gaining military supremacy and political dominance, which required an understanding and conquest of the governing structures of the elite, and (2) with a desire to garner resources, enslave productive labor, and capture the "souls" of indigenous inhabitants. The latter necessitated population tallies and some knowledge of the familial residence and scale of production. As a consequence of this agenda, rarely did chroniclers of the past (or archaeologists of today, for that matter) speak of that middle ground in which kin groups coalesced to form factions which, in turn, played a powerful role in defining and changing the nature of pre-Hispanic political authority. This chapter addresses the interaction and the relationships, often conflictive, between these two realms of authority—that of kin groups and divine kingship. It is an investigation of the imposition of power by a centralized authority upon the more diffuse power network of the lineage; it is also about the myriad ways in which such an imposition is thwarted, resisted, and accommodated through the formation and mobilization of factions. To glimpse at these past dynamics, I refer to material from archaeological, ethnohistoric, and Maya prose sources. First, I examine how, by the end of the Formative, the ethic of "living with the ancestors" was transformed by the emergent elite segment of Maya society. Specifically, I refer to the elite subversion of ancestral veneration from a practice that linked family and lineage to landholdings to one that validated the semidivinity of the royal lines, legitimized systems of taxation and tribute, and in general sanctioned kingly prerogative—characteristics of divine kingship also noted among such institutions in Africa (Feeley-Harnik 1985:282, 297). With this overt politicization of ancestor veneration, the practice began to serve different ends. These "different ends" stem from the centralized authority structures of Classic Maya kings, contrasted with the older, "deeper" structure of the lineage in which authority and power were dispersed widely across the landscape. Finally, from various sources I glean information regarding the conflictive relationship between kinship and kingship and, in doing so, address the nature of factions (Brumfiel 1993) during Classic and Postclassic times. Too often conflict, if discussed at all in relation to the Classic Maya, is perceived as either class strife (between elites and nonelites) or interpolity conflict (such as is recorded in stone on stelae, lintels, and stairways of many Classic-period cities; see Pohl and Pohl 1993). I will focus on intrapolity factions and the conflict and accommodation that occurred among such groups as opposed to conflict between polities over territorial hegemony.

POLITICAL MANIPULATION OF
ANCESTOR VENERATION

In reference to South America, Clastres (1977:171) argued that political transformations are more significant than technological changes even though the latter are often accorded primacy in our postindustrial models of social change. More significant, he argued, are transformations in the actual bases and social perceptions of power and authority. Pertinent to this issue is the transformation of the practices and perceptions of ancestor veneration between the Formative and Classic periods. Ancestor veneration of the Formative tends to be revealed more subtly in the archaeological record of differential burial location and interment of grave goods, as discussed in relation to Formative K'axob in earlier chapters. In this context, the archaeologist recreates, in effect, a genealogy of place by "reading" the record of burial interments and structure modification. Classic-period elite ancestor veneration, on the other hand, is already writ large in texts and monumental architecture. Ancient genealogies were constructed through hieroglyphic texts and explicit iconography in which dynastic lines and ancestral connections are literally spelled out using words and imagery, as discussed in Chapter 2. The explicitness of Classic-period ancestor imagery has misled some investigators to conclude that ancestor veneration was a creation of Classic elites, and others to assert that commoners probably did not reckon descent from an apical ancestor nor engage in extended ritual commemoration of their ancestors (e.g., Carlson 1981; Coggins 1988; Holland 1964; Schele and Miller 1986). Ironically, contemporary scholars have "weighed in" on a political discourse discussed by Morris (1991:56) in which the dead are manipulated to resolve social conflicts that define the groups having access to political power and production resources. That is, by asserting that nonelites did not practice ancestor veneration, contemporary scholars have, *de facto,* defined nonelites as lacking political power and access to production resources.

The thesis presented here is that, on the contrary, ancestor veneration was not created by Classic-period elites; rather, it was appropriated from a larger social milieu, politicized, and used as a means to sanction elite power and authority. This appropriation is reflected in the fact that the iconography of royal ancestor veneration is replete with agrarian images of regenerative life and inheritance, such as the example discussed in Chapters 2 and 3 in which several orchard species were "borrowed" by Pakal to anchor his royal genealogy. The connection between ancestors and agricultural territories, so clearly seen in ethnographic accounts, is not developed in Classic-period iconography and hieroglyphic texts. This absence is due to the fact that in the latter case we are dealing with a highly derived elite version of ancestor veneration that was distilled and disembodied from a Formative, agrarian base. Unlike the Zapotec region, where Marcus and Flannery (1994) have examined the Formative roots of ancestor veneration, the origins of this practice have not been researched widely in the Maya region, and when this topic is approached, a seamless continuum from the Formative through the Classic is often envisioned. By "seamless continuum" I refer to the fact that transformation of power relations within which a practice such as ancestor veneration is seated are seldom factored into descriptive scenarios of the genesis of such practices. It is precisely the dynamics of these power relations which define the transformation of Maya society from kin-dominated to king-dominated.

Ancestral Apotheosis as an Instrument of Domination

Focusing on the royal component of Maya society, Schele and Miller (1986) have suggested that ancestor veneration was a basic element of the institution of kingship (*ahaw*)—argued by some to have developed during the Late Formative (Freidel and Schele 1988). Certainly, Classic Maya script and iconography, now coming under increasingly intensive study, are replete with references to semidivine ancestors—the sarcophagus lid of Pakal and other texts at Palenque providing perhaps the most vivid examples of the semidivinity of the ruling lineage and the extreme importance of genealogy among Classic Maya elites (Lounsbury 1974; Schele 1981; Schele and Miller 1986). Through a practice that Marcus (1992:301) has termed "euhemerism," dead kings became heroes and, ultimately, deities: "By linking himself with heaven and its denizens, the living ruler partook of the attributes of supernatural beings and powerful natural forces."

This type of genealogical reckoning—that which asserted the divinity of a descent line—separated society vertically into upper and lower strata rather than into roughly equivalent and competing groups. So socially conflictive and foreign is the institution of divine kingship that the transformation of a person into a king is often perceived as the creation of a stranger or foreigner (Feeley-Harnik 1985; Freidel 1985; Sahlins 1985). The ideology of kingship created what is referred to in the *Book of Chilam Balam of Chumayel* as rightful rulers: "But those who are of the lineage shall come forth before their lord on bended knees in order that their wisdom may be made known. Then their mat is delivered to them and their throne as well" (translation by Roys 1967:92). These metaphors of kingship are the same as those used during the Classic period: the mat as a symbol of authority and the throne as a seat of authority. The ancestors lend authority to the political office of king, and the apotheosis of a progenitor is more a function of the purity of the bloodline than it is of lifetime achievement. A great political leader is recognized by virtue of his or her bloodline first ("those who are of the lineage") and by superior qualities of leadership second.

It is no wonder that the Maya elite of the Classic and Postclassic reckoned descent through both matriline and patriline, for it allowed one to raise one's royalty and semidivinity to the second power. Also, this practice left room for flexibility in that an individual could vie for power even if only one side on the family genealogy displayed an impressive pedigree. The bilaterality of the Yucatec term for noble (*almehen*) indicates the strategic role of elite women in Maya society. The Yucatec Maya apparently also used two terms for lineage: *ch'ibal*, descent through the father, and DZACAB, descent from the mother (Tozzer 1941:98, n.441).

THE POWER OF LITERACY. As discussed in Chapter 2, elite ancestor veneration was expressed in myriad ways: in the pyramidal architecture of monumental funerary shrines (as opposed to shrines in domestic contexts), in complex iconography, in depiction of deceased rulers, and in genealogies written in hieroglyphic script. Of the latter, Thompson (1978:23) has speculated that "like the peoples of central Mexico, the Maya had also hieroglyphic documents covering distribution and ownership of land, tribute lists, dynasties, and mythology." Although none of the surviving codices addresses dynastic genealogies, Classic-period inscriptions preserved in stone do attest to the central role of hieroglyphic texts in the politicization of the ancestors. In fact, the content of a large percentage of known texts is genealogical. Insofar as politics is a branch of religion (cf. Feeley-Harnik 1985), hieroglyphic texts such as the panels from the Group of the Cross at Palenque—in which the royal line is linked genealogically with mythic creator supernaturals—are a demonstration of the process of ancestor politicization, where the primary role of the ancestor is to legitimize an offspring's right to rule. Other sources also indicate that the information conveyed in writing represented zealously guarded information that was manipulated for political reasons and used as an instrument of domination. Quoting from the *relaciones*, Roys (1943:87) notes that, according to Gaspar Antonio Chi, literacy (specifically, the ability to write) existed only among elites: "And they did not teach these [their letters] to any except noble persons; and for this reason all the priests, who were those most concerned with them, were persons of rank."[1]

From a nineteenth-century unilineal evolutionary perspective, the invention of a logo/syllabic script was one of the crowning achievements of Classic Maya society since it made them more like classical civilizations of Greece and Rome. While not disputing this achievement, here I emphasize the literal power of the written word (Leventhal 1990) in terms of its ability to "stabilize memory" (Houston 1994) in accord with the perspective of an upper stratum of society—the *literati*. Based upon the fact that scribes were drawn from the elite population exclusively (and often were the younger siblings of rulers), the capacity to express one's pedigree in the medium of hieroglyphic script was not an option open to all members of Maya society. The portable screen-fold codices, regardless of content, also were part of the material accouterments of elite power and kingly authority. Relevant here is Landa's discussion of the dismantling of the centralized power structure of the Postclassic city of Mayapán: "The most important possession that the nobles who abandoned Mayapán took away to their own country was the *books of their sciences;* for they were always very submissive to the counsels of their priests [read *scribes*], and it is for this reason that there are so many temples in those provinces" (Tozzer 1941:39; emphasis added). So we see that the notion of being "elite" in ancient Maya society was bound up in preferential access to the written medium.

Recently, scholars have grappled with the depth of literacy in Classic and Postclassic Maya society (e.g., Coe 1992; Brown 1991; Houston 1994; Marcus 1992; Schele and Freidel 1990). Houston (1994) has pointed out that reading and writing, while considered a complementary pair in our society, may have been somewhat more separate spheres of activity in the past and should be envisioned as orthogonal axes of skill. He suggests that some general rudimentary ability to read Maya hieroglyphs is indicated by the fact that this writing system possesses and retains a considerable pictorial component (such as the use of a profile of an elite male as a variant hieroglyphic expression of the Maya word for king, *ahaw*). The public, plaza location of many of the inscriptions suggests that many members of Maya society could "read" rudimentary features of the texts (birth and death dates, exploits of leaders) even if they could not form the calligraphic elements themselves. The mixed iconographic/hieroglyphic content of stelae, lintels, wall murals, and polychrome vessels facilitated perception of the message. Certainly, the intended meanings of vivid depictions that accompanied texts, such as those of humiliated and bound captives or of the "handing off" of the accouterments of the "throne," were not lost on a nonliterate audience.

Elite prerogative, then, resided in restricted access to the production of a written record and also to the sidereal-based prophecies, almanacs, and astronomical calculations of the screen-fold, bark-paper books. The latter are written in a style that is not a narrative but rather is a series of mnemonic devices and arithmetic calculations. From such a "crib sheet," a scribe or priest undoubtedly extemporized for ritual orations regarding forthcoming happenings such as calendar-regulated festivals, anticipated times of great agricultural risk or abundance, dangerous periods of eclipse, or auspicious times for waging war. This type of literacy is what Houston (1994) refers to as *recitation literacy*—a characteristic of many early writing systems. In short, the position of Maya elites as producers and storers of information considered crucial to the continuation of society represents a kind of appropriation of the collective memory. In this way the written record becomes an effective mechanism of domination (Giddens 1981:35) much as Roman law and rhetoric was an effective weapon of the upper class in Classical Roman society (Morris 1991:161).

Formal education in and of itself played a role in maintaining distance between rulers and ruled as well as "shoring up" the exclusionary basis of dynastic lineage structure, thereby underwriting what Weber (1968:1:43) referred to as the *principle of exclusionary closure*. Judging from the wide distribution of a mutually intelligible hieroglyphic script across the Maya lowlands, formal education was an important part of the maintenance of this uniformity. Harrison (1970) has suggested that parts of the Central Acropolis of Tikal may have been devoted to the housing and schooling of young elites. Apparently, elite children were taught not only "sciences" such as calligraphy, astronomy, and astrology but, in the Postclassic at least, also learned the answers to Confucianlike riddles. A well-known example of the pedagogical ethic of exclusion comes from the *Book of Chilam Balam of Chumayel* in a section entitled "The Interrogation of the Chiefs" (Roys 1967: 88–98). Composed of a series of riddles to which only a person educated as an elite would know the answers, this text was a test (in the "Language of Zuyua") of literacy, learnedness, and royal pedigree and apparently was used to "weed out" would-be elites and potential competitors to political offices.[2] In this way knowledge and power were inextricably linked, with the former perceived "as a scarce resource" (Feeley-Harnik 1985:292). The Yoruban

Ijesha have a specific word—*olaju* or enlightenment—for this concatenation of knowledge and power which is embodied in divine kingship (Feeley-Harnik 1985:292).

CONTRASTING KINGSHIP WITH THE *LONGUE DURÉE* OF KINSHIP

Due to the small scale of many Maya polities, some scholars have suggested that the institution of kingship (and the governance of Maya polities) was organized simply as a lineage or household writ large (i.e., Ball and Tascheck 1991; Sanders and Webster 1988)—specifically, that the differences are quantitative rather than qualitative.[3] Partly, this assertion reflects confusion between the source—that of kinship—from which kingly power arises and the subsequent and sharply divergent trajectory of kingly power. Upon closer inspection of the organization of kinship, it is clear that significant, qualitative differences exist between the organization of familial-based lineages and that of kingly domains. In this section, kingship and lineage are contrasted on five points: (1) centralization of authority structures, (2) strategies of revenue raising, (3) labor drafts, (4) gender and production roles, and (5) institutionalized domination. Examination of these points of contrast engenders further discussion of the conflict between these two structures of authority and serves to highlight the rather episodic nature of divine kingship in contrast to the *longue durée* of kinship structures.

Centralization of Authority Structures

Kingship is an unstable and centralizing force in society. In a historical analysis of the Thai monarchy, Tambiah (1976) has emphasized the instability of kingship by employing the term "galactic polity," which he perceived as pulsating between centralization and dispersion—"the summary of cooperation and opposition involved in relations between ruler and ruled at every level" (Feeley-Harnik 1985:304–305; see also Demarest 1992). The palace residence, governmental structures, and abodes of the royal entourage are metaphorically a planetary sun which pulls in labor, goods, and population. The hierarchy of kingly authority structures, with so much authority concentrated at the top, emphasizes the centralizing goals of divine kingship. Lineage authority, on the other hand, tends to be dispersed, with more individuals participating in decisions and in the production of a livelihood that supports the group. Although it is clear from ethnohistoric and modern sources that a powerful lineage head can in a sense "rule," nevertheless such rule is based upon powers of persuasion rather than a divine charter; furthermore, the productive capacity upon which a lineage leader draws is highly circumscribed. The *ah kuch kabob* or lineage leaders of Postclassic Yucatán exemplify the manner in which lineage authority within a single polity was vested in several individuals who could coalesce into a powerful bloc in support of or against the centralized authority structure of the king (see Scholes and Roys [1968] on the structure of government at Acalan).

Divine kingship in the Maya lowlands resulted not only in the centralization of political power but also in greater centralization of settlement and of the labor force of family and lineage. Specifically, through the Classic period and into the Postclassic, there is greater overall centralization of population around areas of core monumental architecture and a shift from a pattern of single-family dwellings of the Middle Formative to a predominance of large multifamily residences with considerable investment in settlement agriculture between residences. Although Classic-period populations are generally described as "dispersed" in contrast to the hypernucleation of the Mexican highlands, there nevertheless were considerable centripetal forces (political and otherwise) acting upon these populations. The adverse effects of centralization on food production and provisioning in a tropical lowland environment are evident in the words of Gaspar Antonio Chi in reference to the Spanish policy of settlement congregation: "And from this [centralization] has resulted another misfortune, which is that famines have befallen, because the people who are now together in one town were accustomed to be divided in six and eight, and as they were spread in all the land and had it all occupied, no rain fell which did not fall on cultivated lands, which was the cause of their having in that time great abundance of provisions" (Jakeman 1945: 105). Undoubtedly, this sentiment reflects partially the desire of a Maya noble for a return to a pre-Hispanic world, but the underlying sentiment that population centralization enhances agricultural risk applies equally to pre-Hispanic times. In this regard, Chase, Chase, and Haviland (1990:500) note that

> Around A.D. 600, many houses located on prime upland terrain in the countryside around Tikal were abandoned; at the same time, the city population swelled to its maximum size. We have evidence for a substantial relocation of population from the countryside to the city, a shift that must have required political coercion.

The centripetal effect of the Spanish Colonial congregation policy represents the most recent (and most devastating) of a series of strategies to centralize Maya populations; earlier instances associated temporally with the local florescence of kingships are coming to light as spatial and temporal controls on archaeological settlement data are refined.

In reference to the Postclassic Quiché, Fox (1987:170) suggests that political centralization is expressed in the monumentality of architecture, arguing that the introduction of sumptuous "palace" structures at Utatlán bespeaks the transformation of segmentary lineage organization into a more unitary state controlled by relatively few royal lineages. While pyramidal structures express the politicization of ancestor veneration, palaces connote the centralization of power which leads to the diminution of the autonomous power base of all but a few lineages. There is a great contrast, therefore, between kinship and kingship, with the latter resulting in the centralization of power, of roles of authority, and of the population itself. These forces of centralization, rather than simply amplifying the structure of family and lineage, are actually in competition with them since the object of centralization—restricted access to positions of authority—co-opts the older authority structure of lineage.

Extractive Tendencies—Those "Who Ate from Our Land"

A fundamental distinction between kinship and kingship is the extractive relationship of the latter to the productive bases of society. Rulers of states need to raise revenue to support a royal household and its entourage and artisans, and to wage war, demonstrate reciprocity and largesse through lavish banquets, repay favors, and otherwise place others into their debt. Many of these activities (feasting, supporting a household, and repaying favors) are also conducted at the lineage and family levels; however, within lineages, members who contribute to the accumulation of surplus are generally also the beneficiaries of the distribution of largesse. Kingly revenue-raising, on the other hand, represents an extraction of productive resources from one component of society and a corresponding allocation often to an entirely different component—thus the sentiment expressed by the creators of the highland Mexican narrative of exodus and migration, the *Historia Tolteca-Chichimeca,* that the ruler Totomochtzin "ate from our land in Zoltepec Tlaxocopan for three years" (Leibsohn 1993: par. 412, F.48v, ms. 54–58). Be it taxation-in-kind, labor obligation, or tribute, no centralized political authority can exist without a method of extraction, and the Classic Maya were no exception.

Scenes suggestive of tribute are often painted onto Classic-period polychrome vases. Figure 5.1, for example, is a vivid representation, from the elite perspective, of the homage and obeisance due to a "natural" lord. An individual is shown kneeling and offering a symbolic platter of food to a ruler who sits on a throne. Cloaked in the body language of hierarchy, this palace

5.1b

Late Classic Maya vase with offering scene: (a) photo of vessel showing dominant ruler figure seated on raised platform, (b) painted rendering of full roll-out scene on vessel showing kneeling and seated figures in secondary relation to ruler (courtesy of Dumbarton Oaks Research Library and Collections, Washington, D.C.).

5.1a

scene represents the secondary participants as more diminutive than the central figure. Shown seated or kneeling, subordinate figures maintain a lower profile than the regal protagonist. In similar scenes on other vessels bundles are also shown and accompanying texts mention tribute offerings.

During the Postclassic, it was the *ah kuch kab* or lineage head who bore responsibility for the burden of tribute and taxation, and there is no reason to suppose that such leaders did not exist during the Classic period; in fact, there are many partially deciphered and poorly understood glyphic titles. Certainly, during the Colonial period it was the *ah kuch kab* who acknowledged Spanish decrees legitimizing the continuation of the rights and privileges of the "native" nobility and who agreed to abide by Crown decrees and mobilize necessary labor and goods (Roys 1941).

Through closer examination of documents from Colonial Yucatán, we begin to glimpse the rather substantial labor demands that were placed not only on the lineage heads themselves but also on the heads of individual compounds. While this information certainly cannot be directly applied to the Classic period, nevertheless it does inform us of the lineage and household response to the extractive demands of centralized authority. Furthermore, scholars of the Colonial period generally agree that two salient characteristics of Spanish occupation of the Yucatán Peninsula are (1) the limited degree to which the Spaniards attempted to restructure the indigenous hierarchical organization of production (i.e., they simply co-opted the existing structure), and (2) the comparatively small size of the Spanish Colonial force (Farriss 1984; Roys, Scholes, and Adams 1940:8). Finally, it must be kept in mind that this late period is one in which household production was scaled back from the preceding Postclassic and Classic periods due to sharply decreased participation in extended trading networks (see Jones 1989), profound social upheaval and continuous desertion of Colonial-controlled villages for politically open areas in the southern part of the Yucatán (Jones 1989), and the lower productive capacity of a shrinking post-contact population coping with a catastrophic morbidity rate.

Despite, or perhaps because of, the ravages of Spanish Colonialism, considerable quantities of tribute were funneled from Maya households to regional centers of the Spanish Crown from the mid-1500s to the 1800s. A 1549 list of tributaries indicates that from the Yucatec province of Maní alone, the following items (and their approximate quantities) were transported to Mérida on the backs of the people of Maní: over seven thousand cotton *mantas*, more than seven thousand turkey hens, approximately eleven thousand pounds of wax (for Spanish candles), and thirty-six hundred *fanegas* of corn (5,688 bushels).[4] Descriptions of pre-Hispanic tribute, such as that transported to Mayapán from the surrounding provinces, differ little in kind from the Spanish tribute list with the exception of the deletion of wax and the addition of honey, salt, fish, or game (Tozzer 1941:26). These tribute lists come from the drier northern part of the Yucatán Peninsula, an area excellent for turkey-raising (Pohl and Feldman 1982) and reasonably good for the cultivation of cotton. There was regional variation in tribute goods with a corresponding adjustment in the structure of production; for instance, in parts of the wetter southern lowlands, such as Belize, where *cacao* thrived and turkeys did not, there was more emphasis on producing *cacao* (Jones 1982, 1983) and less on turkeys. It is difficult to evaluate whether the quanities listed in the 1549 list were greatly inflated from pre-Hispanic times or whether Spanish Colonials in the Yucatán established quantities based upon existing systems of HALACH UINIC–based tribute obligations. Tribute documents such as the Codex Mendoza (Berdan and Anawalt 1992) suggest a measure of concordance between pre- and post-Hispanic imperial extraction systems in the Mexican highlands. If such was the case for the Yucatán, then quantities such as those listed in the 1549 tributary list may be close to pre-Hispanic obligations.

For communities owing allegiance to a distant *ahaw* or HALACH UINIC, demands on the household would have been considerable during pre-Hispanic times. These extractive demands of a political economy, would have been exacerbated by a parallel set of production demands associated with a local-level prestation economy, which coexisted with the regional political economy and included not only in-kind contributions but labor drafts as well (Morley 1941; Tozzer 1941). The lineage leaders were the intermediaries between the rulers (*BATABOB* or *HALACH UINICOB* of the Postclassic period, Spanish Crown of the Colonial period) and the households. In order to participate in both the political and prestation economies of the Classic and Postclassic periods, a successful household head needed to draw upon the productive labors of a large dependent group of related and unrelated individuals—all the better if they resided "under one roof." The range of productive tasks was large: house-building, roof-mending, bee-keeping, stock-raising, farming, food storage and preparation, and the spinning, weaving, and embroidery of cotton cloth. These activities were honored, extolled, and calendrically celebrated in the written records kept by Maya scribes. The Codex Madrid, in particular, indicates the keen interest of Maya elites in the continued and successful enactment of these tasks that, while basic to society, were even more essential to the continued maintenance of the hierarchical infrastructure of Maya society.[5]

Labor Drafts

Given the Maya proclivity for expressing authority and power through the construction of monumental architecture, labor obligations (construction, maintenance, and provisioning) must have been a regular feature of Maya living near the large cities. Commencing in Late Formative times when pyramids decorated with stucco masks were constructed at places such as Cerros, Uaxactún, Nakbe, and El Mirador, labor drafts continued through Colonial times when politically subjugated Maya were ordered to tear down pyramids and reuse the stone for the construction of Catholic churches. Traveling through the Yucatán today, one cannot fail to notice that the large Colonial churches in towns such as Muna are built with finely hewn veneer-stones taken from pre-Hispanic Puuc structures of this sierra region. Farriss (1984:166), in fact, observes that Spaniards immediately recognized the extraordinary construction and masonry skills of Maya artisans and that the primary artisanship to survive through Colonial times is stonemasonry, particularly in the village of Oxkutzkab.[6]

Labor drafts do not represent a simple geometric amplification of the large collective work groups organized at the lineage level; rather, they are an exercise of social control by centralized powers that can be linked with punitive actions for noncompliance. Equally important within the context of divine kingship, however, is the ideological link forged between labor and ritual. Specifically, there often is no clear distinction between royal work and royal ritual, particularly when labor obligations involve the construction and maintenance of royal funerary shrines (Feeley-Harnik 1985:293). Alternatively, royal work can be couched ingeniously within an ethic of kinship-based reciprocity much in the way that Inka imperial structure co-opted the ethic of reciprocity from *ayllu* organization (Murra 1980).

Based upon ethnohistoric records, labor drafts seem to be a form of appropriation sanctioned in a wider context of power relations than was the appropriation of goods. The BATABOB (local nobles) of the Postclassic apparently had no authority to exact contributions-in-kind from their constituencies (Roys 1943); however, we know from the seventeenth- and eighteenth-century *probanzas* (royal petitions) of the Xiu family that local nobility and BATABOB were accustomed to the following labor services from their communities: (1) seeding, cultivating, harvesting, and storage of produce from a "corn" field of approximately sixty *mecates;* (2) a male and a female household servant drawn from the community each week; and (3) construction and maintenance of homes of the noble family (Morley 1941:235–236; Roys 1941:666). Labor drafts, then, seem to have been common in a wide range of hierarchical relationships, whereas in-kind contributions seem to have been the prerogative of more remote and kingly authorities, or perhaps as Freidel (1983:55) has suggested, were a "matter of political and perhaps military dominance." The two forms of extraction, however, go hand in hand as exemplified by the cooperation during the early Colonial period (specifically around 1564) between don Diego de Quijada, alcalde mayor of Yucatán, and don Francisco de Montejo Xiu, Maya noble and ruler of the district of Maní. Specifically, the latter agreed to mobilize a labor force of three hundred Maya for three months in order to build a road from Maní to Mérida. Such a road facilitated the centripetal flow of tribute-in-kind by reducing the traversed distance from fifteen to nine leagues (Scholes and Adams 1938: 144–145).

The ethic that labor drafts were the special right and privilege of nobility persisted into the Colonial period as attested by the following testimony given by Diego Tzut of Yaxakumche as late as May 13, 1641, in response to the petition for continued recognition of the status of nobility (*hidalgo*) of don Juan Xiu:

> And this witness saw that for don Alonso Xiu, father of the said don Juan Xiu and his sister, while he lived[,] the community cultivated his cornfield and provided service for his house every week. And when a new house was needed, the community constructed it, and they always respected him as a natural lord. And so for these reasons his children, as descendants of natural lords, should enjoy what their fathers, grandfathers and ancestors enjoyed, not paying tribute nor rendering personal services like the other plebeian Indians. (ROYS 1941:649)

Apparently, the system of weekly rotation of villagers who performed domestic services for the Xiu family was not quite as voluntary as it may seem and, at times, verged on indentured servitude or slavery. Morley (1941:236–243) records a complaint by villagers that the Xiu family held individuals in the lock of personal servitude for the better part of a year. Likewise, those obliged to render labor services apparently seized upon opportunities to renege on those services whenever the obligation became ambiguous due to the death of a leader, as is apparent from the 1632 petition lodged by Catalina Cemé, wife of deceased don Alonso Xiu, who complained that after her husband's early death the town had become lax in fulfilling their labor obligations to her (Morley 1941:243).

The ubiquity and prevalence of labor drafts and their effects on the structure of Maya households are often overlooked because of the preoccupation by Mayanists with the production of elite things by elites. This small and highly biased sample of elite sumptuary materials that have been preserved from Classic and Postclassic times attests to the presence of skilled specialists: surveyors, architects, building engineers, sculptors, painters, scribes, jewelers, and flint knappers capable of making exquisite "eccentrics." Even in classes of material that are totally perishable—such as feathers, wood, and most of all cloth—the pictorial details of stone sculpture and screen-fold paper-bark codices indicate the high degree of skill and artistry necessary for their production. These sumptuary goods are often thought to represent the quintessence of Maya society, yet only a small fraction of the labor of a small group, probably of elites, was ever involved in their production. The bulk of society was involved in the labor that produced and transported tribute goods, grew and harvested corn fields for local elites such as don Francisco de Montejo Xiu, ground maize and prepared tamales for elite families, and built and repaired the palatial houses and ancestral pyramids of the nobility. It is these tasks and their products that are the quintessence of Maya society—a preponderance of jobs to be done by a culturally capable labor force. As the burden of providing labor fell on the heads of households, so the strategy for meeting those demands evolved into an expansive network of asymmetrical production relationships (discussed in Chapter 4) materially expressed in large residential compounds. Thus, over time the role of lineage head is transformed from that of political negotiator and organizer of production to that of political intermediary or social broker (Fox 1977:86) attempting to navigate the metaphorical straits of Scylla and Charybdis with the rapacious extractive demands of the king on one side and the productive limits of the extended-family household on the other.

Gender and Production Roles

Segregation of production tasks by gender is an old and familiar condition of human society. In all but the most generalized hunting and gathering societies, men and women tend to focus on different tasks. Recently, however, scholars have begun to investigate the power differentials associated with these tasks, particularly in the context of ranked or state-organized societies (Brumfiel 1991; Gailey 1987; Gero and Conkey 1991; Silverblatt 1987, 1988). In the case of Maya society, production roles undertaken by women included lengthy food-production tasks such as preparation of tamales or the reconstitution and grinding of dried maize. Other more specialized tasks included weaving and stock-raising. Working at or near the household, women produced items that went directly into the political and prestation economies—such as finely woven *mantas* (Tozzer 1941:127)—or raised turkeys and other animals consumed during ritual feasts (Pohl and Feldman 1982). The importance of cloth in the tribute economy of the Yucatec Maya is attested by the fact that many of the entries for the term "tribute" or *patan* in the *Diccionario Maya Cordemex* (and its predecessor the *Diccionario de Motul*) include explicit reference to tribute *mantas*. The verb *pak* (to count) refers specifically to a count of tribute *mantas*. These bolts of cloth represented a substantial labor investment. During the Colonial period, the standard *manta* was thirteen meters in length by sixty-three centimeters in width and was woven of such fine thread that Spaniards used the term *hilo* (linen) in reference to them (Barrera Vásquez 1980:633; Morley 1941:155).

Thus, the labor of women produced key items within the tributary and prestation economy. Demands on the productive labor of females, particularly nonelite females, must have increased substantially as kin groups were drawn under the political umbrella of kingship; Brumfiel (1991) has discussed the change in the status and labor of women in reference to the Aztec-period Basin of Mexico, and Gailey (1987) has done the same for historic-period Tonga. It is paradoxical that while the productive labor and social identity of Maya women were centered in the residence, the fruits of their labor provided valuable fuel that ran the supradomestic economies. Places such as the *acllawasi* of the Inka (structures where young women resided and devoted their labor to weaving cloth for the greater glory of the Inka) have not been documented (either archaeologically or ethnohistorically) among the Maya, yet the obvious importance of cloth to lowland Maya society suggests that the large residential compounds served to physically aggregate and manage the labor of daughters, female affines, servants, orphans, and slaves. Even Landa, who had only limited understanding of the role of women in Maya society, noted the tendency for women to spin and weave in large work groups (Tozzer 1941:127).

Institutionalized Domination

The Postclassic Maya *ah kuch kabob* held positions that while nonhereditary were nevertheless powerful and influential. They lacked the credentials, however, to dominate their constituencies with the same impunity of a BATAB or HALACH UINIC. This distinction, which I refer to as institutionalized domination, is not a unique characteristic of the Postclassic but rather is another fundamental way in which the authority structures of the lineage and the state differ.

Kingly power and domination were expressed in several different ways, perhaps the most conspicuous being the attempted monopoly on the use of force as expressed in the royal prerogative to draft men for military service. In this regard, Roys (1957:6) notes that a HALACH UINIC could summon the whole male population for military service. Depending on the rapacity of the kingly appetite for land, captives, and tribute (Orellana 1984:57; RY 1983:2:85), these military drafts could be quite frequent. The *Book of Chilam Balam of Chumayel* makes it clear that a warlike leader was viewed with ambivalence by his constituents, who were perfectly capable of seeing the inevitable consequences of incessant warfare: famine and strife at home. One passage from a section that Roys has titled "The Creation of the World" states this sentiment quite elegantly: "This was the reason for mourning his power, at that time there was too much vigor . . . sad is the general havoc" (Roys 1967:103). This lament leads to a discussion of the types of famine foods people were forced to eat as a result of the aggressive nature of their leader: *ramón* nut (nutritious but not tasty), *jícama cimarrona* (a bland, watery root crop), *ix-batun* (an unidentified plant), and *chimchim-chay* (a cabbagelike plant). Faction-based resistance to the excessive abuses of kingly power is also indicated. The fall of Mayapán, for instance, may have been linked to the fact that the Cocom family allegedly attempted to sell people from villages under their hegemony into slavery in the lucrative market of Laguna de los Términos (Freidel 1983:53).

It is now becoming increasingly apparent that these conflictive relationships of the Postclassic period also must have been a subplot of Classic and much earlier times. More evidence of interpolity strife, conquest, and elite captive-taking is coming to the fore in the form of explicit "conquest iconography" and texts on monumental architecture, walled cites, and enclosed agricultural spaces (Demarest et al. 1991). If we could recapture the conversations of Classic-period lineage heads who lived within the polity of an unusually aggressive *ahaw* such as Ruler 3 of Dos Pilas (Houston 1993; Houston and Mathews 1985; Mathews and Willey 1991:56), we probably would find expressions such as "at that time there was too much vigor" or "sad is the general havoc" to have been very common. How dissatisfaction with abuses of kingly power may have been mobilized into actions designed to curb such abuses will be addressed shortly.

The kingly appetite for land and the alienation of land from other sectors of society is another consequence of institutionalized domination. Sahlins (1985:94–95) discusses the means taken by members of Fijian society to protect their landholdings from usurpation by a newly installed ruler: "at the rituals of the installation, the chief is invested with the 'rule' or 'authority' (*lewa*) over the land, but the land itself is not conveyed to him. The soil (*qele*) is specifically identified with the indigenous 'owners' (*i taukei*), a bond that cannot be abrogated." For common people, ancestors provided a compelling social sanction for resource rights, but the influence of those ancestors was effete against sanctioned appropriation by nobility whose pedigree lent them a claim to semidivinity. While much of the time these kingly leaders probably maintained a "hands-off" posture in regard to the land rights of the commoners, being content to "accept gifts" offered from harvests (much as is pictured in Figure 5.1), nevertheless elites generally came to control the lion's share of valuable land and resources through warfare, conquest, or peacetime appropriation. The predatory inclination of rulers is aptly summarized by an old Hawaiian proverb recorded by Handy and Pukui (1972:199) and quoted by Sahlins (1985:79): "A chief is a shark that travels on land." Inequality in resource control is evident in the following observations on the state of affairs during the Postclassic and Colonial times.

In the drier part of the Yucatán, areas suitable for *cacao* and fruit trees were restricted to collapsed limestone sinkholes and other microenvironments which retained moisture better than the surrounding semiarid northern plain (Gallareta Negrón, Andrews, and Cobos Palma 1989; Gómez-Pompa, Salvador Flores, and Aliphat Fernández 1990; Pérez Romero 1988)—in other words, orchard areas were a scarce resource. Retelling the story of the sacking of Mayapán from the Xiu (or Gaspar Antonio Chi) perspective, Landa describes the punitive actions taken by the Xius: "And this they did, killing at the same time all his [Cocom] sons, except one who was absent [on a trading expedition in Ulua]. They sacked his house and *took away the lands which he had in cacao and other fruits*" (Tozzer 1941:36; emphasis added). So we see that the metaphor used by Pakal, that of an ancestral orchard, might have been an equally appropriate convention for the Cocoms, even in the dry northern Yucatán. Complementary research by Farriss (1984:180) on the distribution of land and resources throughout the Colonial period indicates that, although the Spanish invasion of the Yucatán was devastating to the power structure of Maya elites, nevertheless elites did manage to hold onto the better lands with a measure of control more akin to ownership as opposed to usufruct rights. Furthermore, Farriss (1984:180) finds that the lands of elites often contained cenotes or *aguadas* of great value for small orchards of citrus and *cacao*. Roys (1943:37) concurs, noting that although the land tenure system is unclear for Postclassic Yucatán, the ruling class seems to have enjoyed a preferential position.

Freidel (1983:54), following Roys (1943:34), asserts that during the Postclassic some elites had the equivalent of private estates that were worked by slaves. It is not clear how these estates came into existence—possibly through military conquest with subsequent distribution of land among elites as spoils of war. Some of the original population may have been alienated from their own land and reduced to the status of serfs or slaves. This tactic was used commonly by the Triple Alliance during the Postclassic (Carrasco 1978), and given the high level of interpolity strife during the same time period in northern Yucatán and during earlier times in the Petén, a conquest-and-reappropriation-of-land tactic may well have been used in the Maya region as well.

The keen interest of Postclassic kings in land, resources, and the edges of their domains is also indicated by the Maní Land Treaty and other documents in which HALACH UINICOB such as Nachi Cocom and Francisco de Montejo

Xiu actually traverse the boundaries of their *kuchkabal* or jurisdiction. Nachi Cocom, for instance, apparently surveyed the boundaries of his province with a full entourage of *hol pop, ah kuch kab,* and others. Clearly a predecessor to the K'in Krus ritual circuit of land conducted by the Tzotzil Maya of Zinacantán, the group apparently paused frequently to "talk" with ancestors (Tozzer 1941:43, n.216), suggesting a role for apotheosized ancestors in the appropriation of land and the negotiation of boundaries. As mentioned in Chapter 3, these ritual circuits were probably also part of the behavioral repertoire of Classic-period elites, as suggested by the sequence of toponyms and dates recently translated from hieroglyphic texts on stone monuments (Stuart and Houston 1994).

Is Divine Kingship Lineage Writ Large?

In a reference to the fact that the charter of divine kingship is often predicated upon tales of heroic and horrific social exploits, Sahlins (1985:79) contrasts kinship with divine kingship: "Power [through divine kingship] reveals and defines itself as the rupture of the people's own moral order, precisely as the greatest of crimes *against kinship* [emphasis added]: fratricide, parricide, the union of mother and son, father and daughter, or brother and sister." Far from an amplification of kinship, the institution of divine kingship assaults the conventions of kinship with impunity and, by doing so, seeks to establish hegemony over kinship. The many and varied exploits of the hero twins Hunahpu and Xbalanque of the Maya epic of the *Popol Vuh* (Kerr 1992; Tedlock 1985) are no exception to this pattern. Moreover, divine kings have the sole prerogative to impersonate deities and in this transformational quality are decisively distinct from lineage leaders.

From another perspective, in order to argue that the organization of Maya polities of the Classic and Postclassic periods was simply that of a household writ large and not that of a state-organized kingdom, one must show that the organizational differences between kin groups and divine kingship are purely quantitative rather than qualitative. In this section, I have shown that kingship and kinship in fact are highly contrasting forms of human organization in terms of the centralization of authority structures, the strategies of revenue-raising, the ability to conduct labor drafts, the transformation of gender and production roles, and the institutionalization of domination. Chase, Chase, and Haviland (1990:501) have argued a similar point in regard to Classic Maya central places at which "over-vigorous" kings thrived, to wit: "Urban Caracol can in no way be construed as simply an elite household writ large." With a purported population of between thirty-four and sixty thousand people who, around A.D. 700, lived within a three- to four-kilometer radius of the epicenter (Chase, Chase, and Haviland 1990:502),

Caracol was governed by more than the persuasive powers of kin leadership. Years ago, Carneiro (1970b) demonstrated a simple and predictable relationship between population size and centralized structure of political authority. Now that sufficient surveys have been conducted in the Maya region to empirically demonstrate high population levels (Culbert and Rice 1990), we must face up to the fact that Classic Maya states were not organized as many "big families" but rather were complex polities riddled with internal fractures and factional conflict.

CONFLICT AND AUTONOMY IN THE
MAYA LOWLANDS

Asserting that the power of kings is qualitatively different from that of kin leaders is not equivalent to stating that all Maya society everywhere from the Late Formative through the Postclassic was in the grip of aggressive kings. Herein may lie the confusion among Mayanists and the reason why the literature on Maya political structure seems to vacillate between assertions of hierarchical, state-organized polities (Chase, Chase, and Haviland 1990; Marcus 1993) and those of revved-up chiefdoms residing in regal-ritual centers (Ball and Tascheck 1991; Sanders and Webster 1988). As Marcus (1993) notes, there is tremendous variability through time and across space in the presence, size, organization, and monumental expression of centralized authority—a variation not well captured by static typologies. Throughout the lowlands, especially outside of the Petén heartland of kings, there were areas in which kin leaders continued to operate "households writ large" in a semiautonomous fashion throughout the Classic period. In addition to variability across this spatial frame, there is variability along a temporal axis that results from the cyclic expansion and contraction of kingdoms and the associated loss and gain of local autonomy. We certainly know this to be the case for Postclassic northern Yucatán, and the settlement data, the distribution of palatial and monumental architecture, and the limited spatial extent of hieroglyphic texts point either to the presence of kingdoms that lacked the recognizable accouterments of kingship (doubtful in a highly competitive elite peer-polity context [Freidel 1986a; Renfrew and Cherry 1986; Sabloff 1986]) or to the coexistence of variable forms of less centralized political organization alongside more centralized ones. Archaeologists have traditionally analyzed these less centralized regions, such as northern Belize, from a Petén-centric and world-systems perspective (Wallerstein 1974), seeing them as quasi-rural peripheral resource zones to be exploited by the center. While it is true, and somewhat ironic, that these peripheral zones do tend to contain richer agricultural soils and more stable hydrological regimes than the central Petén (for instance, much of Belize is an area of rich alluvial soils and ample rainfall—an ideal environment for *cacao* production), there is no evidence that the settlements of this area were far-flung colonies established by more centralized polities of the Petén. In fact, the early settlement of the Belize region at sites such as Cuello (Hammond 1991), Cahal Pech (Awe 1992; Awe et al. 1990), Colha (Potter et al. 1984), K'axob, and other places indicates a vigorous and autochthonous occupational history. What, therefore, does the absence of written texts and other accouterments of a king mean? Are these areas in which "peoples without history" (in the sense of Clastres [1977] and Wolf [1982]) struggled against the imposition of a state, or are they independent areas that thrived on a lively trade with the central Petén—a trade fueled by the insatiable demand for status and sumptuary goods? If we invert our Classic-period perspective and view the Petén as the strange and anomalous land, then we see the lands and people outside this area as being in a situation both advantageous and precarious: advantageous because of the political alliances and trading opportunities afforded by proximity to heavily populated kingdoms run by highly competitive elites, but precarious because of the constant danger of being absorbed into this centralized and extractive system of governance. This view gives priority to the broad spatial variation in systems of governance. On a much smaller scale, important consideration should be given to the dynamic relationship between structures of kinship and kingship within royal realms.

Dynamics of Factional Conflict

Traditional analyses of conflict in state-organized societies focus on two arenas of conflict: interpolity hostilities and class conflict within polities. J. Eric Thompson (1954:266–267), for example, was particularly vested in the notion that conflict between the aloof "astrologer-kings" and an undifferentiated peasant mass brought about the downfall of Classic Maya society. More recently, warfare and captive-taking among Maya polities have been a focus of research (Culbert 1991; Webster 1993). Among some researchers, this type of conflict has assumed "prime-mover" causality in the societal transformations of the epi-Classic period. In a starkly contrastive fashion, then, significant power dynamics are seen to exist either between polities or between classes within a polity. Now, a third and very significant dimension of conflict, that between factions, is under consideration. Factions represent organizational structures that exist within polities and often cross class lines; factions may be synonymous with kinship structures such as the lineage or they may be ad hoc structures constituted in response to a compelling and divisive political situation. Brumfiel (1993) suggests that factions be envisioned as similar groups that are in competition for resources, political power, and prestige. In this sense factional conflict can be orthogonal to class conflict in that it does not refer to a dynamic of domination and resistance but to one of nearly equal opposing forces. Class conflict, after all, is but one of many fissures along which a larger group is likely to split apart. The significance of the concept of factional conflict for this research lies in the fact that it highlights an organizational structure—primarily kinship based—that is overlooked and understudied in the general anthropological approach to state-organized society.

In reference to the interplay between factional and class conflict, Brumfiel (1993) identifies the suppression of commoner mobility as a prerequisite for the emergence of class structure in agrarian contexts. In other words, for class conflict to assume dominance over factional conflict, commoner populations must be "tethered in place" or else they will simply move from an area (taking actual or symbolic remains of their ancestors with them) when their landholdings, political autonomy, or general well-being is endangered, this mobility being a form of resistance or rebellion. As Jones (1982:291) has noted, this very pattern is repeated over and over again in the lowlands; emigration due to political instability and general decline in the agricultural effectiveness of the Petén probably had a lot to do with the perceived demographic collapse of the ninth century. Throughout Classic and Postclassic times, there are innumerable instances of sudden and geometric population expansion (even on an archaeological timescale) that cannot be explained by autochthonous growth rates. This fluidity of population movement suggests that the "social circumscription" described by Carneiro (1970a) may have never crystallized into a rigid class structure over the entire Maya region, precisely because political unification, which results "in uniform conditions of exploitation for the commoner class" (Brumfiel 1993), was a mercurial condition in the Maya lowlands. Powerful factions in the form of competing lineage groups were seldom effectively dismantled in the lowlands, except perhaps in the core areas of divine kingship—the central Petén.

Discussions of factional schisms within larger groupings have existed in the ethnographic and ethnohistoric literature for many decades, despite the fact that archaeological inquiry into the nature of complex political entities has tended to focus on the systemic "glue" that binds together so-called unitary polities. Instead, we should be grappling with the more complex schisms, conflicts, and relational tensions that, in reality, shape these political organizations and consequently determine their material expression which we, as students of the past, attempt to decode using archaeological methods. Based on African examples, Southall (1957) originally proposed a type of state organization called the segmentary state, more notable for its internal schisms than for its unitary structure. Richard Fox (1977) wedded this notion to a variant form of urbanism which he called the regal-ritual center (a city type thought by some to be applicable to the Maya lowlands—e.g., Sanders and Webster [1988] and Ball and Taschek [1991]). Sahlins (1961) examined the predatory nature of segmentary lineages in reference to the Nuer and the Tiv; Carmack (1981) and John Fox (1987) combined the work of Sahlins and Southall to develop a model of the Postclassic highland Quiché Maya as a predatory, segmentary, lineage-organized state entity. More recently, Houston (1993) has applied the segmentary state model to the Classic-period polities of the Petexbatún region.

The ethnohistoric and archaeological work of Carmack and Fox on the Quiché lineages indicates the degree to which factional groupings can result in differential access to resources and ultimately be transformed into institutionalized differences between vassal and royal lineages—the transformation from kinship to kingship. Among the Quiché Maya, the vassal lineages were apparently tied to the major lineages through vertical obligations of taxation and corvée labor. Carmack (1981:161) asserts, nevertheless, that the vassal lineages were independent lineages, even though they lacked the "big houses" of the royal lineages. The Postclassic Maya highland countryside, therefore, was not organized into a simple two-class system composed of a royal dynasty and a homogeneous rural peasantry such as that imagined by Thompson (1954) for the lowlands. In fact, this feudal-like structure probably never existed anywhere in the Maya highlands or lowlands. The lesson to be learned from Carmack's ethnohistoric research among the Quiché is that the "commoner" population was composed not of an undifferentiated mass but rather of many distinct factions and lineages which were in and of themselves highly structured and internally differentiated. It is very unlikely that this richly textured, internally diverse, and nonroyal segment of society ever operated as a class-based bloc—an observation that Smith (1990:20) and Wilson (1993:131–133) would extend to twentieth-century highland Guatemala Maya.

Even among the principal lines of the Quiché, there was an acute concern for maintaining and expressing autonomy. Carmack (1981:192–193) tells us that in the major lineage houses (*nim ja*), a fire burned continuously to symbolize the autonomy of the faction. Furthermore, famous and just rulers were buried in the *nim ja* under the spot where they had exercised power (Fox 1987:25). In the Postclassic of northern Yucatán, factions and internal schisms are well documented ethnohistorically. Relying on accounts from the

Relaciones de Yucatán, Roys (1957:114), for instance, writes of internecine warfare in the Cupul province between lineage members ruling Ekbalam and Nabalam—warfare that culminated in the capture and enslavement or sacrifice of prisoners. In reference to the *Book of Chilam Balam of Tizimin,* Edmondson (1982) refers to the calendrical rituals of the *tun* and *baktun* as integrative forces within a political milieu that was both fractious and competitive; J. Fox (1987) applies this interpretation to the highland Quiché as well.

In the deeper history of the lowland Maya Classic, information on factions within royal realms is now being teased from the architectural, textual, and iconographic sources which superficially dwell on the divinity and legitimacy of the primary ruling line. At Copán, for instance, textual evidence strongly supports not only the presence of factions but the fact that they represented a power bloc that could not be ignored by the paramount ruler of Copán. Specifically, during the Late Classic reign of Yax-Pac, nonroyal elites began to erect textual monuments within their own residential compounds (e.g., Structures CV-43 A, 9N-82, and Altars T and U of Group 9; see Fash 1991: 160–165). Some of these texts describe the presence of the king at ceremonies dedicating local lineage structures. These actions have been interpreted as indicative of a strategy of power-sharing by Yax-Pac in an effort to keep fractious lineages from cleaving off and organizing a force in opposition to the paramount ruler (Fash 1991). Is this pattern unique to Copán, located as it is in a frontier locale, or does it reflect a tension that existed throughout the lowlands? On the basis of clustered architectural units, Kurjack and Garza T. (1981:30) suggest that competing kin groups played an important role in the political milieu of Dzibilchaltún. Thus, we see factions operating on different planes—between groups and between lineage and lord.

Kingship: Dissenting Voices

Much of the history of society, it has been argued, is the struggle against the centralizing and hierarchical forces of the state (Clastres 1977:185) and the power abuses that result from such social control. Hero twins Hunahpu and Xbalanque wage battle against exactly such social malaise—self-magnification and excesses of greed and power—in Part 4 of the Maya epic *Popol Vuh.* They emerge victorious from their defeat of Seven Macaw and his two sons, Zipacna and Earthquake (Tedlock 1985: 90–101).[7] Despite such vivid narratives, the topic of resistance has seldom been the focus of archaeological discourse in the Maya region, perhaps because direct evidence of it is seldom identified archaeologically. Yet our models direct our field research, and methods are often created to address new questions; that is, data exist in the context of research issues. Throughout the Colonial period, ample evidence of Maya resistance to centralized authority is recorded in the *Book of Chilam Balam of Chumayel*. Herein a Maya scribe and priest speaks eloquently of this conflictive relationship:

> If you do not submit, you shall be moved from where your feet are rooted. If you do not submit, you shall gnaw the trunks of trees and herbs. If you do not submit, it shall be as when the deer die, so that they go forth from your settlement. Then <even> when the ruler <himself> goes forth, he shall return within your settlement bearing nothing. (ROYS 1967:122)

In a series of footnotes, Roys interprets this quote strictly in terms of Colonial-period oppression, but given the deep historical roots of this genre, there is no reason to think that such sentiments are not rooted in pre-Colonial contexts of political conflict between kin groups and the centralizing forces of kings. As Jones (1989:126) has noted in relation to Colonial-period resistance to Spanish rule, political action and commentary often are couched within the prophecies of the *katun* cycles—a tradition with strong pre-Hispanic precedent (Love 1992). The prophecy of the fourth *katun* (Katun 5 Ahau), specifically, suggests a wariness toward those who would be king and recognition of the abuses of such power, in a passage that I believe has deep pre-Hispanic roots, as does the majority of this text:

> [T]he opossum chieftain, the fox chieftain, the *ah-pic* chieftain, the <blood-> sucking chieftain, the avaricious ones of the town. He is set up perchance . . . the two-day occupant of the throne, the two-day occupant of the mat. They deceive the town, the two town officials, the chieftain opossum and he who lies in wait on all fours. They bring the pestilence. . . . The kinkajou claws the back of the jaguar amid the affliction of the katun, amid the affliction of the year; they are greedy for dominion. (ROYS 1967:153)

This passage refers to a "pretender to the throne" whose rule lasts only two days. His brief occupancy of "the mat" is a direct reference to kingship and the weave design often used to signify the authority and power of this royal office holder. Rather than embodying the fierce courage and kingly qualities of the jaguar, the pretender to the throne is cast as a kinkajou or opossum—both of which are arboreal animals. Thus, even among the scribal priests who were the authors of these texts and who certainly were linked to the elite power structure, there is a display of wariness and a circumspect attitude toward divine kingship which is suggestive of active factional conflict.

Quelling the Dissent

An effective means of quelling dissent to centralized rule is to dismantle the organizational nexus of that dissent—the kinship structure—and thereby reduce factional conflict to simple class conflict, which yields a more easily controllable playing field since conflict is resolved in favor of those who have the power to resolve it. The strategies employed by state entities to dismantle or discredit kinship structures is an understudied topic but one worthy of intense scrutiny, for the success of these strategies is one measure of the centralization of power. One widely recognized strategy is to sever the link between a kin group and their ancestors. In imperial China, for example, Feuchtwang (1974:219, following Duke [1912]) notes that "when a rebellion breaks, the first act of the authorities is not to raise troops but to send messengers to spoil the *feng-shui* of the rebel leaders by despoiling their ancestral tombs." In many kin-organized societies, the link between a group and their ancestors is such a fundamental part of social identity and economic rights that tampering with that linkage is an extremely effective means of social control. Prehistoric looting of royal tombs may be purposeful neutralizing of the power of the ancestors of vanquished lineages.

Among the Classic lowland Maya, Haviland (1968:112) interprets the settlement and architectural record of Late Classic Tikal as indicative of the breakup of lineage organizations among the nonelite population; specifically, at Tikal during the Late Classic only elite compounds retain ancestral shrine structures. Apparently, limited evidence for lineage organization does exist in "modest" complexes where intensive nonagrarian production took place, but "households occupied by farmers do not appear to be organized according to lineage. Cross-culturally, one of the most common functions of lineages is to act as landholding corporations, but at Tikal they may have lost this function to the ruling elite" (Chase, Chase, and Haviland 1990:500–501). Although it is not known whether this inference is generalizable to other large cities of the Petén, the premise that control of production is critical to the maintenance of extrafamily kinship structures is valid in many different cultural contexts (Haviland 1968). Specifically, when production becomes vested in nonkin groups, descent groups lose their economic (and power) basis and tend to disintegrate. Thus, an appropriation of land by the ruling elite—perhaps the establishment of estates for the nobility—is an effective means of dismantling the structure of kinship and was probably far more common in the central Petén than it was in areas such as northern Belize where the power of kings was weaker and the prophecy of the fourth *katun* a sad but remote horror rather than an imminent and grim reality.

Adjudicating the Conflictive Basis of Kingship

Within Maya polities, there would have existed two prominent types of factional competition: that between corporate groups for resources, titles, and privileges and that between corporate group heads and their paramount ruler over the centralization of resources and power. Brumfiel (1993) suggests that overarching competition among polity rulers (which we know to have been the case during the Classic and Postclassic periods) mitigates the exploitation of commoners. In effect, acute competition among kings diverts attention away from the establishment of more effective means of social control; in such contexts, a high level of intrapolity factional conflict may be sustained. Above, I discussed factional conflict; in this section some institutional mechanisms by which such conflict can be mediated and negotiated are explored.

There are strong indications from ethnohistoric texts that most Maya kings, at least of the Postclassic period, were not autocrats. That is, they did not hold absolute power, despite their claims and titles to semidivinity (such claims perhaps indicating limitations to their power). At Acalan and Xicalango, for instance, Scholes and Roys (1968:35) cite early chroniclers who note that the ruler was dependent upon the decisions of councillors and could do nothing "without the counsel and advice of the principal men [*ah kuch kabob*], who came every day to his house or assembled on the square to discuss whatever came up." This type of power-sharing is also indicated in the *Relación de Dzonot* for northern Yucatán (Roys 1943:86); Farriss (1984) too has observed that the king had no power without the vote of the *ah kuch kabob*. These accounts indicate the widespread distribution of council houses during the Postclassic. This architectural and organizational form is now being postulated for the Terminal Classic (Freidel [1986b] for the Puuc region; Lincoln [1991] for Chichén Itzá) and Late Classic periods (Fash [1991] and others for Copán) as well.

Some scholars have attempted to link the network of power relations among royal, elite, and nonelite sectors of Maya society to a particular quadripartite spatial configuration of power at Maya central places. For Acalan, Scholes and Roys (1968:56) suggest on the basis of a 1550 chronicle (in which the burning of "idols" is described) that "the god of the head chief was housed in the principal temple and that each of the patron deities of the four quarters had its own sanctuary. This was the case at Tenochtitlan, where each of the four quarters had a special temple and was a religious as well as a military and administrative subdivision of the city." As discussed in Chapter 3, M. Coe (1965:105) has attempted to link this quadripartite structure with the rotational nature of the Uayeb ceremony by suggesting that the office of the *hol pop* was also rotational—a position held briefly by an important and wealthy *ah kuch kab* who organized the Uayeb ceremony. Whether the *hol pop* was a rotating post held successively by important lineage heads or an office held permanently by certain individuals, various passages from the *Relaciones de Yucatán* indicate the key role played by the *hol pop* as mediator between the king and the *ah kuch kab:* "They were governed in former times by their *caciques,* whom they called *holpop,* who were like *mandones* ('overseers'?); and these consulted with the lord about matters and embassies from outside; others [did] not" (Roys 1957:94; see M. Coe 1965:105; Roys 1941:40). Ambiguity surrounding the role of the *hol pop* is corroborated by Roys (1939:44). It is clear, however, that during Postclassic times the *ah kuch kab* interacted with the BATAB (who had a judiciary role, among others; Tozzer 1941:87) and the HALACH UINIC, and that they (*ah kuch kabob*) are listed in the *relaciones* as the second person in the government. Roys (1939:430) variously describes them as important local headmen, perhaps heads of minor lineages or *parcialidades,* who totaled two or three to a town and who apparently had a vote. Several lower-ranked political positions are also described by Roys (1939), such as AH KULELES (apparently arbitrators, mediators, and advocates between any two groups of people) and AH TUPILIL (a sort of constable). What is not clear from Roys' description, however, is the position of individuals in the intersecting mazes of kinship and kingly structures. AH KULELES may have been political appointees (much as the BATABOB themselves sometimes were; Roys 1957:41), since BATABOB are described as generally accompanied by two or three AH KULELES. On the other hand, AH KULELES might be designated representatives of the lineages appointed by an *ah kuch kab* rather than a BATAB or HALACH UINIC in order to adjudicate conflicts among the lineages or between the lineages and the king. Support for this latter point of view comes from an observation made by Freidel (1983:54) that the Maya facility for making use of "the Spanish legal system following the conquest may be due to established tradition on the peninsula." In other words, Yucatec Maya were accustomed to political mechanisms by which they might assert their land claims, defend counterclaims, and generally adjudicate matters.

Representation of the interests of those other than the king is not a topic often discussed in terms of Classic-period Maya archaeology. Within each small polity, a unitary perspective—from the top down—tends to dominate our approach to Maya political structure, perhaps because of the powerful and sophisticated visual imagery (iconographic, architectural, and hieroglyphic) used by Classic Maya elites to foster exactly this notion of supreme and total rule. Recently, however, recognition of places and positions analogous to the *hol pop* and *ah kuch kab* of the Postclassic period have been discovered at Copán. Specifically, Structure 10L-22A may have functioned as a council house to which the Copán paramount (the so-called Smoke Shell) invited lineage heads from all over the Copán polity in order to confer with them (Fash 1991:134). In fact, from independent studies of many different places across the lowlands the previously invisible leaders of factions and lineages who interacted with divine kings are now being identified through the deciphering of hieroglyphic texts containing names and a diverse array of subordinate titles. Currently unknown, however, is the meaning of these political titles: whether they were hereditary or nonhereditary, whether the social status of such individuals was elite or nonelite, and the degree of political dependency or autonomy of these named individuals (see Fash [1991: 178] for notation of this current research). Regardless of the unknowns, these new discoveries do suggest that the well-titled nature of Maya lords may be masking the fact that when it came to the business of negotiations and the power-brokering necessary to hold a polity together, royal and nonroyal leaders rubbed shoulders.

The inherent power differential between a paramount ruler and those of lesser status, such as lineage heads, is a leitmotif of Maya political iconography. However, the inequality of this arrangement may have been mitigated by practices such as ritual circuits/visits and feasting that were undertaken by royal rulers and that likely facilitated the forging of consensus during the Classic period. Also relevant here is the Maya concept of *kuch* or "burden-bearing." Some Yucatec titles of authority were constructed verbally on the base root of the word *kuch,* such as *ah kuch kab,* and many words indicating a political territory or jurisdictional realm are compound words based on *kuch.* For example, immediately after the final Spanish incursion into the Yucatán Peninsula, don Francisco de Montejo Xiu signed the Maní Land Treaty with, among others, his mortal enemies, the Cocom family; he referred to the province over which he had political and economic hegemony as *kuch-kabal* (literally "burden/authority of the land"; Roys 1941:623). Likewise, the Yucatecan term for a small independent unit is *kuchteel. Kuch,* then, is a term for power but also for the *burden* or *responsibility* that comes with such power; perhaps it meant "power with accountability."

The concept of *kuch* or burden occurs also in Maya hieroglyphic texts, including the surviving painted codices. Early on, Thompson (1978) deciphered the glyph for *kuch* which occurs repeatedly on pages 25–28 of the Codex Dresden, a section about prognostications for the New Year (Thompson 1972, 1978:59, 125). In this context, the Year Bearers shoulder the burden or responsibility for carrying society through periods of drought, famine, abundance, flood, or disease. All members of society, even cosmological entities, were envisioned as bearing *cargo* either literally or figuratively. So prevalent was this image during the Classic period that when *ahaw* "18-Rabbit" (or "18-Jog") of Copán filled the central plaza with stelae depicting himself in his various royal guises, he used full-figural glyphs to record dates on the back of the stelae so that he could represent the Year Bearers as porters with tumplines pressing into their foreheads. When even cosmological entities bore a burden, how could one distinguish a lowly porter from a mighty lord?

Living outside the Web of Kingship

In Maya society of the Classic, Postclassic, and certainly the Formative periods, there were many villages and towns at which inhabitants lived outside of the net of kingship. For the Postclassic period, Roys (1957:6) notes variation in the degree of political centralization throughout the Yucatán. Some districts were headed by a *HALACH UINIC* while others were loose federations headed by multiple *BATABOB*. The Yucatec province of Cupul, for instance, had no *HALACH UINIC;* rather, members of the Cupul lineage governed about half of the thirty-six towns of the province (Roys 1957:113). Neither were towns that were not directly ruled by a *HALACH UINIC* or a *BATAB* necessarily absorbed into a larger political net of tribute and taxation. A hint of such coexistence can be found in the *Relaciones de Yucatán*, in which *encomendero* Juan de Urrutia is quoted as follows: "Chancenote [was] the capital (*cabecera*) of the Province of Tases, where the other towns of the said province recognized the lords of the said capital as superiors, and this not by way of vassalage [a tributary relationship?] but by confederation and friendship" (Roys 1957:109). Clearly, then, during the Postclassic period there was a good deal of variation in political and economic arrangements across the Yucatán, while at the same time central places and small villages joined together for defensive purposes and to celebrate certain rituals such as the festival of Pacum Chac in the month of Pax, during which "the lords and priests of the lesser villages joined those of the more important towns" (Tozzer 1941:164). In the ceremony described, the *NACOM* (military leader) played a very important role, and this ritual may have been linked to building solidarity in defense.

If the Postclassic, a period generally associated with political balkanization, is characterized by such a complex tapestry of local and far-flung power relationships as well as economic interdependencies, then what of the Classic period? Was the range of variation at the small, autonomous-community end of the political spectrum restricted during Classic times, while at the same time it was expanded at the opposite, hierarchically structured end? Settlement data suggest, in fact, that a much wider continuum of political arrangements may have existed during the Classic period with small, semiautonomous units persisting from the Formative period, particularly in the Belizean portion of the eastern lowlands. In this area at places such as K'axob, there is a long continuous sequence of settlement from about 800 B.C. to A.D. 900 with the construction of monumental architecture through the Late Classic period and a general absence of hieroglyphic material. This pattern suggests that there were places that persisted throughout the Classic period with some semblance of autonomy. In the competitive milieu of peer-polity interaction across the lowlands, there were small communities "in which there [was] characteristically only a short distance in the time-space 'meshing' of interaction" (Giddens 1981 : 39). That is, in contrast to places such as Naranjo, Tikal, Caracol, Dos Pilas, and Copán, where kingship was constituted through intermarriage with royal bloodlines from other places, the people of K'axob, for instance, probably thought of their world in a more spatially circumscribed way. The larger places of Nohmul to the northwest and San Estevan to the southeast framed the regional picture from the perspective of the place we now call K'axob, which had its own Classic-period pyramid complex and another large plaza group that was the ancestral focus of settlement.

Fascination with the history of Maya occupation in the region of Belize (particularly the northern part) lies in the fact that while this area contains some of the richest soils in the lowlands, has demonstrable early settlement, and becomes very populous during the Classic period, this region (by and large) exhibits monumental architecture of modest proportions and very few hieroglyphic texts and long-count dates. In other words, many places in this Maya subregion do not seem to have participated fully in elite Maya geopolitics and the iconography of "power legitimation" that was so prevalent elsewhere during the Classic period. Were these populous settlements subordinate to Caracol, Naranjo, Lamanai, and Nohmul, or were they independent, unaligned settlements?

Judging from the resource base of this area and the materials excavated from archaeological sites such as K'axob, Cuello, or Colha, this region was not impoverished in an economic sense. However this area was constituted politically, one thing is certain about its socioeconomic structure: it was *not* an area occupied by a "middle class" as some authors have suggested; rather, it represented a "pocket" in which the class concept itself was much less established than it was in other parts of the lowlands, such as the central Petén. These places may represent areas of what Schele and Freidel (1990 : 87) have characterized as "allied nonelite lineages" and may have retained a "fair degree of autonomy" (Marcus 1989 : 206).

Places such as K'axob indicate that the emergence of kingship in the lowlands was an uneven process that proceeded in a leapfrog fashion across the Yucatán Peninsula centralizing some but *not all* areas, achieving maximum but not total centralization during the Late Classic period. This organizational variation across space suggests that the dynamic conflict between kinship and divine kingship was never resolved absolutely in favor of divine kingship in the Maya region, and in some areas reference to the over-zealous king was the stuff of good stories rather than the cause of daily toil.

SIX

Ancestors and the
Archaeology of Place

Godelier (1986) has referred to the false dichotomy between the mental and the material—between the "superstructure" and the "infrastructure." To my mind, a similar and false polarization has characterized ancient Maya studies. More than a matter of scholarly perspectives, however, these "polar" entities have been linked to social segments; the mental—the ideological—has been linked with the study of all things "elite," and the material with all things construed to have been "nonelite." This construct is not only inaccurate, it is denigrating. The dawn of the twenty-first century (in the Gregorian calendar) and the imminent end of a long-count cycle (A.D. 2012) in the Maya calendar provide an auspicious opportunity to move beyond the ecological/ideological dichotomy to a new fusion of settlement and epigraphic research; this study is one effort at such a new kind of synthesis.

In current ethnographic research, many investigators have abandoned the "voice" of authority as we know it from traditional ethnographies and attempt to present their research giving full voice to interviewed participants. I suggest a similar course for Maya studies—an abandonment of the unitary "top-down" approach and a concomitant broadening of the "playing field" to include nonstatist organizational structures in our models of Maya political power and economic organization.

Ostensibly, this book is about Maya society and the historical processes that shaped this society. Rather than introduce more complexity into a book that is already unusually concept-laden for this area of study, I refrain from expanding my frame of reference to general Mesoamerica. Readers familiar with Mesoamerica west of the isthmus or south of the Sula River, however, will recognize the wide reach of issues discussed in this book—lineage, land, the domestic focus of ancestor veneration, inequality, and the oppositional nature of kinship and kingship. There is a historical specificity here that is distinctly Maya, but the broad issues can be broached for many parts of Mesoamerica.

LINEAGE AND THE FALLACY OF THE
TWO-TIER MODEL

This research is the product of a discordance between observed archaeological patterns and traditional modes of interpretation based upon ethnographic and ethnohistoric analogy and traditional, yet untested, assumptions about ancient Maya society outside the courts of divine kings. The most grievous of these assumptions asserts that Maya society was nothing more than a simple two-class or two-tier society with a literate elite class that monopolized the governing structures of society and a more or less undifferentiated mass of agricultural producers. As I discuss at the beginning of Chapter 5, this two-tier model can be traced to European chroniclers who classified Maya society in terms of their own social backgrounds and their situational goals: i.e., political conquest, tribute extraction, and evangelism. The failure of later Mayanists to grapple with the politics of history has resulted in an uncritical use of ethnohistoric and ethnographic sources, and the sixteenth-century construct—one that was elegantly simple but grossly inaccurate—has lived on. Meanwhile, settlement surveys over the past thirty years have yielded evidence of significant variability in structure size and elaboration outside city epicenters, a pattern not congruent with a homogeneous underclass of toiling peasants. The concomitant model of concentric settlement structure that stipulates a clinal distribution in wealth, status, and other urban characteristics has been called into question repeatedly (Arnold and Ford 1980; Chase and Chase 1992). Yet on a synthetic level, the two-tier model persists to this day, probably due to its simplicity. Ironically, the shift of attention in settlement archaeology to the most atomistic of residential structures—the household—only served to exacerbate the situation, and attention to the "trees" obscured the "forest." At this point in time, there is no adequate model of ancient Maya society that incorporates empirically observed settlement patterns.

The variability in residential structure, to my mind, is a function of several variables, but predominant among them is the fact that architecture is expressive of social structure. In this case, the hierarchy of the lineage is indicated by structure arrangements such as exist at southern K'axob (Figure 2.14), and, in fact, such architectural groups are ubiquitous throughout the Maya lowlands and many parts of lowland Mesoamerica. To suggest that this pattern is indicative of lineage structure is to bring into play a host of considerations not often acknowledged in Maya settlement studies. If we acknowledge that lineages existed outside of the royal dynasties, then we must contend with these organizational structures in terms of their political and economic roles. The macrofamily groupings of lineages, and other ad hoc corporate structures, represent a powerful force within society; production and land are generally controlled within this matrix of power—unless, that is, such control is wrested from the dispersed lineages by the centralizing forces of divine kingship. In noncapitalist agrarian societies, "households" seldom exist as atomistic units of production; thus, our household studies must be contextualized within the larger realm of macrofamily political and economic groupings. Such organizational forms crosscut social strata, and a model of Maya society that accommodates this formation is more richly textured than a two-tier strata model, lending itself less readily to simple generalizations and more readily to incisive analyses.

LINEAGE AND LAND

The failure to incorporate macrofamily kinship structures into current models of extraelite Maya society has resulted in an impoverished notion of agricultural organization and land tenure in this lowland tropical environment. Anthropological studies from Africa, Asia, and the Americas (see Chapters 1 and 3) have documented the interlacing of lineage organization and land tenure systems; in the Maya lowlands, the neglect of the former organizational structure has led logically to ignoring the presence of the latter. In their most fossilized form, simplistic models of ancient Maya society impute that individual farmers of the Classic period practiced the equivalent of pioneer slash-and-burn agriculture! Considering that over thirty years of settlement survey have yielded a population profile indicating that the Yucatán Peninsula was one of the most densely populated lowland tropical locales of the first millennium A.D., this model of Maya farming is ludicrous!

In Chapter 3, I scrutinized the historical and linguistic roots of the notion that Maya agriculture was based upon a single-component *milpa* system on communal land plots. Partly, this ill-conceived assumption is a result of early mistranslations of Yucatec Mayan terms such as *k'ax*—a term for fallow fields—which was translated simply as *forest*. In the temperate-zone lexicons of Spanish and English, there is no suitable term for a temporarily fallow field that is covered with trees fifteen feet in height. Such translations helped to form an image of Maya agriculture as one of shifting slash-and-burn farming despite the fact that seventeenth-century testimonies from Maya witnesses indicate a tradition of inheritance of fixed plots. Likewise, descriptions by early chroniclers and more recent scholars of multigenerational orchards and continually cultivated plots near residences failed to dislodge this entrenched model. The complexity of land use in lowland tropical environs—

with differing suites of cultigens (with different harvesting cycles) grown on plots at varying distances from the residence—by and large was lost on early Maya scholars, and the notion that a patch of "forest" could be an inherited field plot was incomprehensible. Besides, when coupled with the sophistication of Maya hieroglyphic script and calendrical systems, the imputed simplicity and primitive nature of agriculture made for just another great "riddle" of the "inscrutable" Maya.

How can we scholars assert that a land tenure system which included inheritance of fixed plots was absent from a society in which a great premium was placed on the close observation of events along an intermeshed space-time continuum? The traditional retort to such questions has been that such observations and techniques of time-space calculation were the prerogative of Classic-period elites and did not extend to the extraelite segment of society. However, excavation in Formative contexts at K'axob, Cerros, Nohmul, and other sites throughout the lowlands is beginning to reveal the specious character of the unitary, elite-based model of Maya society. Specifically, deposits relevant to calendrical notation, such as the use of the quadripartite motif, indicate the antiquity of practices and ritual relating to an understanding of the space-time continuum. For instance, mortuary rituals and dedicatory cache deposits from the small Formative village of K'axob, Belize, indicate a widespread understanding and incorporation of Maya calendrical cosmology *before* the emergence of the institution of divine kingship. What has been previously asserted to have been the creation and prerogative of elites turns out to be a suite of Formative agrarian practices that were appropriated and elaborated by Classic-period elites.

ANCESTORS AS PLACE-MARKERS

Twenty-five years ago, Saxe (1970) suggested that burial practices were indicative of a developing linkage between people and places. Subsequent research (Brown 1981; Chapman, Kinnes, and Randsborg 1981; Goldstein 1981; Renfrew 1983) pursued this line of thought. Morris (1991) has contributed a reflexive revision to this theoretical premise, stressing the political uses to which ancestors are put. Oddly enough, this research has had virtually no impact on Maya mortuary studies, in which attention to ancestors is often viewed as the prerogative of the elite (as expressed in funerary pyramids), with deceased relatives of nonelites being simply buried under the floors of their houses or, worse yet, in domestic middens. Frequently, these interments are perceived as simply burials of the "hoi polloi" with less jade and fewer pots, to be analyzed for age, sex, and nutritional status so as to be disadvantageously compared to richly adorned elite burials. One could scarcely use the term "ancestor" in reference to these relatively modest interments!

On the contrary, I suggest that ancestors are exactly who these individuals were. Not ancestors in the generic sense of all deceased relatives, but ancestors as a select subgroup of a population who were venerated by name because particular resource rights and obligations were inherited through them by their descendants. This is precisely why ancestors "slept" within the construction mass of residential compounds—to insure the chain of continuity in resources as transmitted between the generations. These contexts are, in effect, domestic mausolea. Subfloor and shrine burials represent vital links in the chain of inheritance; thus, the placement of individuals in these residential contexts involved elaborate ritual, much of which is not preserved archaeologically. It is no wonder that Becker (1992) questioned the conceptual discreteness of Tikal contextual terms such as "burial" and "cache." At K'axob, careful excavation has revealed that Formative "burials" are so temporally and contextually connected with construction of a new structure that often they reside stratigraphically in a place betwixt an old and a new building. Burial of ancestors often marks the termination of the use of an older structure and the commencement of the construction of a new one. Over time, these places of the ancestors often become sacralized locales at which ritual structures such as temples or shrines completely replace domestic structures. I have cited one such sequence from K'axob, but the pattern is ubiquitous throughout the lowlands of Mesoamerica.

In the past, Quiché Maya of Chichicastenango expressed the sentiment that their land and home belonged to their ancestors and that they themselves were but temporary lodgers in a protracted chain of inheritance (Bunzel 1952). In the Andean area, Salomon (1991:20) has noted the active role played by ancestors in establishing a sacred geography linking "territorial places to ancestral time." To my mind, these sentiments capture the manner in which attention to ancestors is linked most often to concerns with land and inheritance: ancestors as markers of places. It follows, therefore, that the emergence of the practice of creating ancestors can be symptomatic of the entrenchment of a pattern of land tenure in which inheritance of fixed plots and orchards plays a primary role. In this regard, it is most interesting that ancestor veneration appears to be solidly rooted in the Formative period and, in some places, may be present at the onset of Middle Formative settlement, although at K'axob it appears during the Late Formative.

As markers of places and rights, sequential ancestral interments in ancient Maya residences create a kind of text-free genealogy that is more subtle and difficult to interpret than genealogies written in hieroglyphic texts. The "decipherment" of these "genealogies" is a critical area of study if we are to recreate a social history of Maya society giving full voice to the agrarian strategies and practices of ancestor veneration of all sectors of Maya society, elite and nonelite alike.

The practice of ancestor veneration ultimately is not about the dead, but about how the living make use of the dead. The title of this study—*Living with the Ancestors*—stresses the vibrant and proactive nature of this social practice. Maya ancestor veneration is not a "cultic" practice engaged in by a group sharing an obsessive or esoteric interest in the dead, and neither is it a mindless worship of "idols"; rather, it is a type of active discourse with the past and the future, embodying what Carlsen and Prechtel (1991:35) have described as the centrality of Maya understanding of death and rebirth—called *jaloj-k'exoj* in the cosmology of the Tzutujil Maya.

INEQUALITY IN LINEAGE AND RESIDENCE

Traditional ethnographies of contemporary Maya have hinted at the basic egalitarianism of these societies. Less frequently mentioned is the fact that many modern Mayan speakers, particularly those in Guatemala, live under the subordination of what is essentially a conquest state. Employing an ill-advised ethnographic analogy, Mayanists of earlier times imputed a structural similarity between contemporary Maya and nonelite Maya of deep history. In Chapter 4, I have tried to show how Maya society outside the web of kingship was anything but egalitarian. On the contrary, from a very early point in time inequality in social, political, and economic relations permeated the kinship structure. Ancestor veneration in particular is not a practice that promotes social equality; rather, it promotes and perpetuates inequality and alienation from resources within the household as well as the polity. The principle of first occupancy gave preferential access to land to certain lineages and within lineages to certain families. Lineage organization itself can be viewed as either a mechanism for cementing land claims or for alienating certain segments of society from such claims. Inequality in political power between lineages, within lineages, and particularly within the multifamily residential compounds that emerged in the Maya lowlands during the Late Formative must have been particularly acute, the conflict between household heads and their heirs being the stuff of legends, laws, and vivid ethnographic description. Conceptualization of multifamily compounds as socially heterogeneous (as they are tabulated in an early census of the Yucatán; Table 3.1) leads to the realization of the ubiquity of multifarious asymmetrical production relations between residents and the household head. Even in the absence of a divine king, inequality permeated Maya society, although I have taken great pains to clarify the critical differences between kinship and kingship (Chapter 5).

FORCES OF DIVINE KINGSHIP

In this volume, I present a view of ancient Maya society in which kinship is cast in dynamic tension with the forces of divine kingship. Since I am suggesting an investiture of lineage organization into our model of Maya society and also inferring that these units of kinship were active players in the geopolitics of the Classic period, I realize that I run the risk of overly creative re-creation. Nevertheless, both settlement and epigraphic research are beginning to show that conflict between kinship and kingship was a significant political dynamic of Classic times, and this dynamic has already been documented for the Postclassic. The tension is between factions rather than classes—between two organizational forms in which the centripetal forces of divine kingship vie against the centrifugal forces of kinship. As divine kings gained control of labor, land, and exchange processes, so the power of traditional lineage leaders waned, particularly in the Petén heartland of kings. On the other hand, there were areas where lineages remained vital organizational forces throughout the Classic period, either coexisting with kings or living outside of the web of kingship. This is the case particularly in Belize, where mapping and excavation programs have shown time and again significant local variability in architectural elaboration and burial furnishings—indicators, I suggest, of the vitality of kinship structures and the role of lineage headship rather than of a "middle class" (cf. Chase 1992).

The waxing and waning of the power of kings and lineage leaders (*ah kuch kabob*) is captured in episodic "snapshot" fashion in sixteenth-century chronicles of northern Yucatán. Perhaps these accounts do not reflect an anomalous period of political balkanization. Rather, these chronicles, for all their inherent biases in original observation and later translation, give a reasonably accurate picture of the full range of variation in leadership positions and political dependencies—a range of institutional arrangements that certainly existed during the Classic period as well, even though the scholarship of this earlier period has given preferential attention to polities organized along the more centralized end of the political array.

Few would dispute that divine kingship in the Maya lowlands emerged from the agrarian matrix of Formative society. If the construction of tombs for the interment of deceased rulers can be used as a rough indicator of the emergence of this institution, then it is the first century B.C. before the first kings ruled Tikal (Haviland and Moholy-Nagy 1992:58). Few have acknowledged, on the other hand, that one of the most salient features of divine kingship, that of ancestor veneration, also emerged from the identical matrix. As Fortes (1976:3) has noted, ancestor veneration is located primarily in the familial domain of social life. It is about the perpetuation of links between descendants and the land and rights of their forebears. Thus, in the Maya region, as in China and Egypt, emergent elites appropriated the practice of ancestor veneration and converted it to an institution that cemented the transmission of political power rather than agrarian rights. It is this right to rule according to precedent set by ancestors that led Hocart to declare that "the first kings must have been dead kings" (Needham 1970).

In the Maya region, the politicization of ancestor veneration included the wholesale incorporation of the agrarian imagery of a lowland tropical environment—thus giving Maya kingship cosmology its distinctive "organic flavor." This imagery was born of fields, orchards, and swamps, and plants such as maize, avocados, and water lilies provided strong visual metaphors for kingly larger-than-life themes of life, death, inheritance, and continuity. The "ancestral orchard" of Pakal is one such example of the "borrowing" of agrarian imagery of inherited orchard crops for kingly purposes. Use of this imagery has been broadly misconstrued as an attempt by elites to use imagery that could be understood by the "illiterate masses"; I suggest instead that elites appropriated organic motifs precisely because of their powerful association with agrarian themes of regeneration and inheritance.

The presence of other motifs in mortuary contexts in Formative villages illustrates a similar point—that of appropriation of such images by elites to serve new ends. The quadripartite motif in particular is grounded in agrarian/calendrical expressions of the Formative period. As such, it packs a particular punch when used in the context of divine kingship. In general, then, iconography is a conservative type of expression, and iconographic motifs may be present across significant thresholds of political transformation. That is, the motifs are constant but the contextual meaning of the motifs change as they are manipulated for political and economic ends.

Much of what has been written here challenges untested yet commonplace assumptions about Maya society, questions established wisdom, and I hope, therefore, will swing readers' perspectives away from the prevalent unitary view of Maya society. Excitement over the ongoing decipherment of Maya hieroglyphs has focused attention on the elite sector of Classic Maya society, and current popular publications often present a skewed view of ancient Maya society—one that dwells upon the material expressions of elites. Disregarded is the fact that elites did not invent the solar calendar or ancestor veneration; rather, they appropriated them from an ancient agrarian core of rituals, beliefs, and practices and selectively modified them for the political arena of elite rulership, succession, and competitive interaction. In this book, I have sought to place major ideological tenets of Maya society—such as the link between ancestors and resource rights—in proper historical context. In doing so, I have identified the study of ritual and practice in the residence as requiring further investigation. Through such research, Maya studies will begin to encompass the spirit of social historical research and leave behind the stigma of a terribly skewed, ahistorical perspective.

The Future of the Ancestors
and the Clash between
Science and Human Rights

Just as the clash between kinship and kingship pervaded Maya society in the first millennium A.D., so the opposition between science and human rights will consume archaeological research in the third millennium A.D. This factional and ideological conflict between the perspective of the First Americans and archaeologists of the United States has already fundamentally changed the conduct of archaeological inquiry north of the Río Grande (McGuire 1992). The conflict is focused on one issue: the future of the ancestors. At stake is the privileged right of primarily Anglo archaeologists to reach into the past and touch, examine, and remove ancestral remains and associated burial goods. This is the context in which our zeal to study the past collides with the rights of an ethnic faction to keep their past intact and buried. In many respects it is an unresolvable ideological clash, but it has no doubt been exacerbated by a long and painful history of asymmetrical power relationships between archaeological scientists and First Americans who are the generalized or specific descendants of the progenitors who created what we in the Americas call "the archaeological record." It has been aggravated by the cavalier attitude of archaeologists toward burial remains and a general laziness toward communicating the nature and results of our inquiries to the general public—even less to those linked genealogically to the skeletal material upon which we base our studies. Finally, because few First Americans from north or south of the Río Grande have been included in the process of archaeological research, the practice itself has taken on the unwelcome guise of "an instrument of domination" playing much the same role as did the exclusive, elite-based literacy of the Classic Maya. When access to knowledge becomes circumscribed, it becomes wedded to power in a manner that is not only conducive to abuses but is a flashpoint for resistance and conflict.

To my mind, one thing is certain: it is only a matter of time before the issue of science versus human rights spreads throughout the Americas. It may take two decades or ten, but there will come a time when those wishing to study the ancestral remains of contemporary Maya will be severely restricted in the conduct of their research. I write this as an archaeologist who feels strongly about the critical potential of osteological analysis and mortuary analysis to answer fundamental questions about the course of human life—about changes in diet, decreases in nutritional condition, emergent status distinctions, entrenchment of land rights, and the establishment of divine kingship, to name a few of the questions that we would like to answer about our collective heritage. How ironic it is that just as we are poised to gain true insight into the genealogical linkages among burials through DNA studies, we are at the same time in jeopardy of losing the privilege of studying this most informative class of archaeological material. The ancestors are such a rich source of information about the past that it is heady and intoxicating to archaeologists. Perhaps herein lies the problem and the solution. In the Maya region, and in Latin America in general, we archaeologists have a chance to "sober up" and take action before we lose the privilege to study the past through the remains of those who actually lived in it. The courses of action available to us are not simple and resolution of this conflictive issue not an inevitable outcome, but those of us working in the Maya region need to move now toward ensuring greater participation of contemporary Maya in the research process and toward exhibiting greater sensitivity and professional responsibility toward Maya ancestral remains, which in some cases means reburial. Most of all, we must recognize, as I have tried to show throughout this book, that the ancestral presence gives power, economic clout, dignity, and social identity to descendants. Why do we question the right of descendants to control the disposition of their ancestors? In this light, the endeavor of archaeology—particularly when we reach back into the past to touch the ancients—is more of a sacralized privilege than it is a scientific right. And we should treat it as just that.

Notes

1. A POINT OF DEPARTURE

1. The notion that ancestors are the true owners of resources (both land and home) is echoed in Bunzel's (1952) study of the village of Chichicastenango, where Quiché Maya perceived the home to be under the protection and ownership of specific named ancestors. They used the Spanish term *posada* (temporary lodging) as a metaphor for their occupation of the home.

2. ANCESTOR VENERATION AND LINEAGE ORGANIZATION IN THE MAYA REGION

1. An *encomienda* was a grant of the labor of Maya inhabitants for the purpose of tribute exaction, thus ensuring virtual enslavement of the occupants of the seized lands.

2. Holland (1964:303) notes that the sacred lineage mountains for the Tzotzil are referred to as *ch'iebal* or *ch'ibal*.

3. Juan Xiu is referring to the ill-fated *entrada* of 1624 led by Mirones, which resulted in the massacre of the Spanish troops at Sacalum by Mayas resisting settlement reduction and the imposition of the *encomienda* system (Jones 1989: 155–187). The petition by Juan Xiu reveals two strongly opposed characteristics of Colonial Maya society: (1) the cooperation—some would say collusion—between the Xiu lineage (who had formerly been one of the most powerful lineages in northern Yucatán) with Spanish Colonial powers, as revealed by their willingness to perform mercenary services; and (2) in certain sectors of Maya society, the depth and longevity of Maya resistance to Spanish Colonial imperialism.

4. "The Cehache [a group to the east of the Chontal Maya] appear to have been divided into subdivisions, which were named either for the ruling family or from the predominating lineage of the group" (Scholes and Roys 1968:69).

5. *Hidalgo,* or native nobility, was a term used by the Spaniards to describe Maya elite whose *probanza* or petition to the royal Crown for acknowledgment of their inherited elite status had been granted.

6. "The piece of land which a man receives from his ancestors is sacred; it has its shrine, where offerings are made; in its role as a place where one can approach the supernaturals it is in effect a 'mountain' " (Bunzel 1952:17–18).

7. Use of the term *wits* (mountain) to describe pyramidal structures in Classic Maya hieroglyphic texts (Stuart and Houston 1994) indicates that Vogt's structural analogy was right on the mark.

8. Reverential and protracted treatment of skeletal remains of important deceased lineage members, including the retention of certain skeletal parts in active shrine contexts rather than in burial contexts, is also suggested by the explicit iconography and accompanying hieroglyphic text of Altar 5, Tikal.

9. Papers of don Diego de Quijada (alcalde mayor of Yucatán from 1561 to 1565) relating to the Inquisition include discussion of the ancient things of the lineages in a document entitled "Información hecha en el pueblo de Homun sobre la idolatría de los indios, Septiembre de 1562" (Scholes and Adams 1938: 1:153).

10. See also Roys 1943:92.

11. Well into the twentieth century, caches of icons have been found, such as the discovery of "idols" in a cave near Chalchihuitán (Holland 1964:304).

12. Tedlock (1982:77) gives a slightly more abstract definition of *warabal ja* as "sleeping place [bed or foundation] of the house."

13. For the Early Aztec period in the Basin of Mexico, Brumfiel (1989:133–136) has noted that the archaeological distribution of Aztec II Black-on-Orange coincides with ethnohistorically documented patterns of city-state alliance and intermarriage; she notes that "in this particular case historical records enable us to verify that ceramic style coincides with a regionally demarcated network of social interaction under conditions of political fragmentation and factional competition" (Brumfiel 1989:135).

14. Houston, Stuart, and Taube (1989:722) have translated several phrases on vessels as *u lak* for "his dish," *u hawa(n)te* for "his wide dish," and *yuch'-ib* for "his drinking vessel." The latter refers to vase forms and often has the sign for *cacao* on the vessel also, although sometimes the word *ul* or *sakha* for *atole* or "maize gruel" also occurs. Elsewhere, Taube (1985:176) notes the coincidence between images of the "tonsured young lord" (maize deity) and large, flat polychrome vessel forms, suggesting that these serving platters generally contained prepared maize, such as tamales.

15. In Jones (1989), three "idol-smashing" *entradas* to the southern frontier are described: one led by Garzón (1568) west of Bacalar and south to Tipu, in which Garzón claims to have destroyed many "idols" and books (Jones 1989: 48–49); similar claims by the chronicler of the disastrous *entrada* of Mirones (1622); and finally by the chronicler of a 1631 *entrada* to Dzuluinicob (1989: 173, 200).

16. "Orchard" is one meaning of *pak'al;* "shield" is another (Barrera Vásquez 1980:625).

17. Stephen Houston documents another occurrence of the verb *pasah* on Naranjo Stela 23 (at position F18). In this context, the text is describing the opening of a tomb of a Yaxhá lord (S. Houston, pers. com. 1992).

18. Carlson (1981:201) on cave and ancestors: "In the case of mortuary architecture, one would expect that the placement of the ancestral bones to accumulate vital forces from the Underworld where man was reconstituted would be a prime consideration. Caves are the 'place of emergence' in much of New World creation mythology and hence are focal sacred places, particularly in the context of ancestor worship and lineal descent. We would expect this aspect of a Pre-Columbian geomantic system to manifest itself in kinship structure and terminology and in social organization and community structure." Using central Mexican data, Heyden (1981) also addresses the link between caves and ancestor veneration that may be of particular relevance to the Maya.

19. Reference to the dynamic interaction between real and metaphorical structures and cosmology of ancestral kinship can be found in the work of Vogt (1964:37−38), who refers to the "lineage mountains" of the Tzotzil; Holland (1964:303−304) discusses in specific detail the thirteen levels of the sacred lineage mountain, how these structures correspond to ascending generations, and how the position of an ancestor within the levels rises as the ancestor "matures."

20. Other references to geomancy in Maya architecture include Ricketson (1928) in reference to Group E at Uaxactún and Kubler (1958) in analysis of design space in Maya architecture; Hartung (1977) also discusses geometry and geomancy in Maya architecture. For the Mexican highlands, Millon (1973) discusses the alignment of the Street of the Dead at Teotihuacán in terms of geomantic practices.

21. Becker (1971:181) traces the use of the term *oratorio* for ancestral shrines back to Bishop Diego de Landa.

---

3. CREATING A GENEALOGY OF PLACE

1. Nations and Nigh (1980:15) discuss a similar conceptual difficulty with the meaning of the terms used for "fallow field" among the Lacandón Maya: *acahual*, the Spanish term, which is interpreted as "secondary vegetation on the site of an abandoned milpa," and *pak che kol*, the Lacandón term, which means "planted-tree *milpa*."

2. "I have seen the corn harvest and the Indians say that when they make a new clearing they build a house in it, and the milpa lasts for twenty years without ceasing to give two harvests per year. I have seen in these maize, squash, beans, chiles, pineapples, tobacco, sugar cane, plantains, sweet potatoes, chayotes, cochineal, and cotton, from which the Indian women weave extraordinary and fine quality white and colored fabrics and other things" (Artiga 1699, cited in Jones 1982:287). Marcus (1982) also documents the diversity of cultigens grown on fields of the post-contact period; a translation by Hellmuth (1977:425−426) of

a portion of the *Relación de Nicolás de Valenzuela* recounts the conquest of the Lacandón: "There are in the same town fruit trees, of platano, zapotes, jocotes, anonas of hot lands, guanabanas, trees of round gourds, some achiote trees, very sweet pineapples; and of all this they also have in their milpas and in them much camote, ayote, chayote, yuca, beans, and sweet sugar cane, and in some parts lemons." See also Nations and Nigh (1980:Table 1) for a list of fifty-six plants cultivated in Lacandón *milpa*.

3. A few salient examples: Landa (Tozzer 1941:197) describes a grove of copal trees, scarred for their sap, which was burned: "They raised many trees of the incense of the idols." Tozzer (1941:n.1061) follows with a footnote regarding a description of a large grove of copal trees at Sisimato. Landa (Tozzer 1941:198) also describes the tree from which *balche'* was made (*Lonchocarpus longistylus*), "so almost all of them planted it in their yards or spaces around their houses." Jones (1982:288) notes that Avendaño y Loyola described extensive plantings of fruit trees in Campeche and Cehache: oranges, lemons, coconut palm, *nance*, *guazuma*, various unnamed trees, and some *cacao*. The river valleys of northern Belize continued to provide *cacao* of especially fine quality well into the Colonial period (Jones 1982:282).

4. Roys (1939:21) notes that one of the contested pieces of land in the Ebtun litigations (Tontzimin) was so named for its cenote. The plot resembled a bowl-like hollow with a bit of water at its base, a *cacao* grove in part of the hollow, and a small stone pyramid at the edge of the cenote. Gómez-Pompa, Salvador Flores, and Aliphat Fernández (1990) have documented the presence of *cacao* and other economically important tree species in three collapsed cenotes in northern Yucatán. "Wild" *cacao* has also been found in a sinkhole depression in the Petexbatún region (Dunning, Rue, and Beach 1991).

5. Pioneer swidden has been documented among tropical agriculturalists of South America by Johnson (1983) for the Machiguenga, by Chagnon (1966) for the Yanamamö, and by Carneiro (1961) for the Kuikuru.

6. Coggins (1980, 1988) and Bricker (1983) propose a semantic reading of the "directional" glyphs in terms of a solar cycle rather than cardinality, in the strict sense. East and West refer to the rising and setting sun and North and South to the zenith and nadir respectively.

7. Barrera Vásquez 1980:39.

8. Roys (1967:65, n.1) suggests that this passage does in fact refer to "ancient times."

9. Another bowl with the quincunx motif comes from another Late Formative burial at Tikal (Coggins 1975), and Late Formative caches of small jadeite figurines arranged in a quincunx pattern have been found at Cerros and Nohmul. The Pomoná ear flare, also Late Formative in date, contains four glyphs arranged in a quadripartite pattern (Justeson, Norman, and Hammond 1988).

10. For example, see Barton (1930) on boundary maintenance in the lowland tropics of the Philippines and Hughes (1977) on boundaries and trading networks in highland New Guinea.

11. Careful notation of polity boundaries, in fact, was pervasive throughout Mesoamerica. A large portion of the highland Mexican contact-period text *Historia Tolteca-Chichimeca* is dedicated to the descriptions of boundaries and of the border wars that ensued over contested boundaries (Leibsohn 1993).

12. From Gaspar Antonio Chi: "The lands were in common and (so between the towns there were no boundaries or landmarks to divide them) except between one province (and another, because of wars) and in the case of certain hollows and caves, (plantations of fruit trees and) cacao trees, and certain lands (which had been purchased for the purpose of improving them in some respect)" (Roys 1962:65).

13. Increasingly, archaeological and epigraphic evidence for the importance of lineage structures to the political and economic structure of Classic-period society is being recognized at large sites such as Copán (Fash 1991; Schele and Freidel 1990) and Yaxchilán (Schele and Freidel 1990) as well as at earlier, Formative-period sites such as K'axob (McAnany 1991).

14. In reference to the Postclassic period, Freidel (1983:54) makes a distinction between lands, which may have been held communally by the village, and the products of the land, which are claimed by individuals.

15. Ancestors are specifically referred to as "guardians" among the highland Cakchiquel Maya (Orellana 1984:96).

16. Regarding the 1570 census from Cozumel, Scholes and Roys (1968:472) state that "a census of this date lists the names of the adult occupants of the houses, and we find from two to seven married couples living in each. After the multiple-family houses fell into disuse in colonial Yucatan, groups of married couples, many of them related to one another, apparently continued to live together on the same ground plot, but each couple with their unmarried children occupied a separate house." Hellmuth (1977:438) also notes that "chroniclers consistently report that several families resided together in each house—not just the nuclear family as traditionally claimed in house counts of anthropological writers today. 'Que en muchas de ellas (casas) reconocimos haver a tres y quatro familias y entre esas muchas criaturas' (AGI Escrib. 339-A, Pza. 2, f. 143v)." A now-famous letter written by Bienvenida in 1548 (Cartas de Indias, pp. 77–82) contains a succinct statement on the Maya proclivity toward large residential compounds: "Your Highness shall know that in this land there is hardly a house which contains only a single citizen [male head of household]. On the contrary every house has two, three, six and some still more and among them there is one *paterfamilias* [*ah chun kahil*?] who is the head of the house" (Roys 1943:21).

17. "Among the 275 married couples and widowers listed [in the Matrícula of Tixchel] no relationship is indicated for sixty-seven [about one-quarter of them]. Of the fifty-nine relationship groups, we find twenty-five of only two couples each [about 50 percent], ten of three, thirteen of four, four of five, one of six, four of seven, one of ten, and one of twelve. Although not stated, it would appear that each relationship group was a residence group living either in a multiple-family house or on a single ground plot. To judge by a matrícula compiled at Ppencuyut

in northern Yucatán in 1584, it seems possible that some of the unrelated married couples combined to form larger residence groups, but this is a matter of conjecture" (Scholes and Roys 1968:473).

18. The meaning of the term "slave concubine" is not completely clear.

4. LINEAGE AS A CRUCIBLE OF INEQUALITY

1. Closely related to this study is the work of Carmack (1981) and Fox (1987) on the segmentary lineage structure of the highland Quiché Maya.

2. Elsewhere, Ringle and Andrews (1988) have suggested that the emergence of residentially stable extended-family compounds during the Late Formative at the northern Yucatec site of Komchen is indicative of agricultural intensification.

3. *Cargo,* incidentally, carries all the semantic nuances of *kuch* in that it refers to a burden and an obligation as well as a position of status, although *cargo* operates within a less formalized hierarchy.

4. A classic example of a "lumping" typology is the Copán architectural classification scheme, which leads to statements such as the following regarding large, multistructure architectural units (Type 4): "although the El Bosque and Las Sepulturas zones include architectural units on all levels of the Harvard typology, they can, for several reasons, be regarded as primarily elite occupation areas" (Webster 1989:11).

5. KIN GROUPS AND DIVINE KINGSHIP IN LOWLAND MAYA SOCIETY

1. Jakeman (1945:102) echoes the limited access to knowledge of writing in his slightly different translation of Gaspar Antonio Chi's contribution to the *Relaciones de Yucatán,* Items 14 and 15: "And these [glyphs] had that meaning only to the noble persons, and for this reason all the priests, who were those who were most given to them [the glyphic texts], were important persons." Chi contributed to the *relaciones* of several different *encomenderos,* and Jakeman has compiled the accounts under a section entitled "The 'Historical Recollections' of Gaspar Antonio Chi," pp. 84–105 (text in both Spanish and English). These "recollections" were written about 1577.

2. See Coggins (1992) for expanded discussion of the language of Zuyua.

3. This characterization is based largely upon the urban typology of Richard Fox (1977) and specifically of Fox's description of the regal-ritual centers of the Swazi state, Rajput states of pre-Colonial India, and the Carolingian state.

4. These calculations are based on a 1549 list of tributaries from Maní (Morley 1941); at this time, Spanish political control of the Yucatán had barely been achieved—Mérida had been "founded" in 1542 (Sharer 1983:570) and the terrible inquisitions of Bishop Diego de Landa at Maní and elsewhere (1562) were yet to come.

5. Jones (1989:237) cites tribute and labor demands on Colonial-period

household heads as one of the main reasons for the flight of men from areas of Spanish political domination (such as the Sierra or Puuc Hills) to the southern frontier. In one testimony in particular (Jones 1989:243), Hernando Cal of Oxkutzkab stated that he deserted his home community because his sons had already left and he lacked the financial means and labor support to meet his tribute, *repartimiento*, and church obligations.

6. Ironically, the reconstruction of pre-Hispanic Maya architecture now occupies the stonemasons of Oxkutzkab, many of whom make their living through contracts with the Instituto Nacional de Antropología e Historia (INAH) to restore the monumental core of ancient Maya cities which have become world-class tourist attractions.

7. Tedlock (1992) has argued that the structure and content of the *Popol Vuh* is similar to known hieroglyphic texts (such as the codices) and therefore indicates that the extant European alphabetic version of this epic is based upon an earlier hieroglyphic text.

References Cited

Andrews, E. Wyllys V, and Barbara Fash
 1992 Continuity and Change in a Royal Maya Residential Complex at Copan. *Ancient Mesoamerica* 3:63–88.
Appadurai, Arjun
 1986 Introduction: Commodities and the Politics of Value. In *The Social Life
 of Things: Commodities in Cultural Perspective*, edited by A. Appadurai, pp. 3–63. Cambridge: Cambridge University Press.
Arnold, J. E., and Anabel Ford
 1980 A Statistical Examination of Settlement Patterns at Tikal, Guatemala.
 American Antiquity 45:713–726.
Ashmore, Wendy
 1981 Some Issues of Method and Theory in Lowland Maya Settlement Archaeology. In *Lowland Maya Settlement Patterns*, edited by W. Ashmore, pp. 37–69. Albuquerque: University of New Mexico Press.
 1991 Site-Planning Principles and Concepts of Directionality among the Ancient Maya. *Latin American Antiquity* 2:199–226.
Aveni, Anthony F.
 1977 Concepts of Positional Astronomy Employed in Ancient Mesoamerican
 Architecture. In *Native American Astronomy*, edited by A. F. Aveni,
 pp. 3–19. Austin: University of Texas Press.
Awe, Jaime Jose
 1992 Dawn in the Land between the Rivers: Formative Occupation at Cahal
 Pech, Belize and Its Implications for Preclassic Development in the
 Maya Lowlands. Ph.D. dissertation, Institute of Archaeology, University
 of London.
Awe, Jaime Jose, Cassandra Bill, Mark Campbell, and David Cheetham
 1990 Early Middle Formative Occupation in the Central Maya Lowlands:
 Recent Evidence from Cahal Pech, Belize. *Papers from the Institute of
 Archaeology* (University College, London) 1:1–5.
Ball, Joseph W., and Richalene Kelsay
 1992 Prehistoric Intrasettlement Land Use and Residual Soil Phosphate Levels in the Upper Belize Valley, Central America. In *Gardens of Prehistory: The Archaeology of Settlement Agriculture in Greater Meso-*

america, edited by T. W. Killion, pp. 234–262. Tuscaloosa: University of Alabama Press.

Ball, Joseph W., and Jennifer T. Tascheck
1991 Late Classic Lowland Maya Political Organization and Central-Place Analysis. *Ancient Mesoamerica* 2:149–165.

Barrera Vásquez, Alfredo (Ed. and Trans.)
1957 *Códice de Calkini*. Biblioteca Campechana 4. Campeche: Biblioteca Campechana.

Barrera Vásquez, Alfredo, et al.
1980 *Diccionario Maya Cordemex*. Merida, Yucatan, Mexico: Ediciones Cordemex.

Barton, R. F.
1930 *The Half-way Sun: Life among the Headhunters of the Philippines*. New York: Brewer and Warren.

Becker, Marshall J.
1971 The Identification of a Second Plaza Plan at Tikal, Guatemala, and Its Implications for Ancient Maya Social Complexity. Ph.D. dissertation, Department of Anthropology, University of Pennsylvania.
1992 Burials as Caches; Caches as Burials: A New Interpretation of the Meaning of Ritual Deposits among the Classic Period Lowland Maya. In *New Theories on the Ancient Maya*, edited by E. C. Danien and R. J. Sharer, pp. 185–196. Philadelphia: The University Museum, University of Pennsylvania.

Berdan, Frances F., and Patricia R. Anawalt (Eds.)
1992 *The Codex Mendoza*. Berkeley: University of California Press.

Berlin, Heinrich
1968 The Tablet of the 96 Glyphs at Palenque, Chiapas, Mexico. Middle American Research Institute Publication 26:135–149. New Orleans: Tulane University.

Binford, Lewis R.
1983 *In Pursuit of the Past: Decoding the Archaeological Record*. New York: Thames and Hudson.

Bishop, Ronald L., Dorie J. Reents, Garman Harbottle, Edward V. Sayre, and Lambert Van Zelst
1985 The Area Group: An Example of Style and Paste Compositional Co-variation in Maya Pottery. In *Fifth Palenque Round Table, 1983*, edited by M. G. Robertson and V. M. Fields, pp. 79–84. San Francisco: The Pre-Columbian Art Research Institute.

Blaikie, P., and H. Brookfield
1986 *Land, Degradation, and Society*. New York: Methuen.

Brady, James E.
1989 An Investigation of Maya Ritual Cave Use with Special Reference to Naj Tunich, Peten, Guatemala. Ph.D. dissertation, Department of Anthropology, University of California, Los Angeles.

Braudel, Fernand

1980   *On History*. Translated by Sarah Matthews. Chicago: University of Chicago Press.

Brenner, Mark, Barbara Leyden, and Michael W. Binford

1990   Recent Sedimentary Histories of Shallow Lakes in the Guatemalan Savannas. *Journal of Paleolimnology* 4(3):239–252.

Bricker, Victoria R.

1966   El hombre, la carga y el camino: Antiguos conceptos Mayas sobre tiempo y espacio y el sistema Zinacanteco de cargos. In *Los Zinacantecos*, edited by E. Z. Vogt, pp. 355–370. Mexico City: Instituto Nacional Indígenista.

1983   Directional Glyphs in Maya Inscriptions and Codices. *American Antiquity* 48:347–353.

Brown, Cecil H.

1991   Hieroglyphic Literacy in Ancient Mayaland: Inferences from Linguistic Data. *Current Anthropology* 32:489–496.

Brown, James A.

1981   The Search for Rank in Prehistoric Burials. In *The Archaeology of Death*, edited by R. Chapman, I. Kinnes, and K. Randsborg, pp. 25–37. Cambridge: Cambridge University Press.

Brumfiel, Elizabeth M.

1989   Factional Competition in Complex Society. In *Domination and Resistance*, edited by D. Miller, M. Rowlands, and C. Tilley, pp. 127–139. London: Unwin Hyman.

1991   Weaving and Cooking: Women's Production in Aztec Mexico. In *Engendering Archaeology*, edited by J. M. Gero and M. W. Conkey, pp. 224–251. Oxford: Basil Blackwell.

1993   Factional Competition and Political Development in the New World: An Introduction. In *Factional Competition and Political Development in the New World*, edited by E. M. Brumfiel and J. W. Fox, pp. 3–13. Cambridge: Cambridge University Press.

Bullard, William R., Jr.

1965   *Stratigraphic Excavations at San Estevan, Northern British Honduras*. Occasional Paper 9. Toronto: Royal Ontario Museum, University of Toronto.

Bunzel, Ruth

1952   *Chichicastenango: A Guatemalan Village*. American Ethnological Society 22. Seattle: University of Washington Press.

Carlsen, Robert S., and Martin Prechtel

1991   The Flowering of the Dead: An Interpretation of Highland Maya Culture. *Man* (n.s.) 26:23–42.

Carlson, John B.

1981   A Geomantic Model for the Interpretation of Mesoamerican Sites: An Essay in Cross-Cultural Comparison. In *Mesoamerican Sites and*

World-Views, edited by E. P. Benson, pp. 143–215. Washington, D.C.: Dumbarton Oaks.

Carmack, Robert M.

1981 *The Quiche Mayas of Utatlan*. Norman: University of Oklahoma Press.

Carneiro, Robert L.

1961 Slash-and-Burn Cultivation among the Kuikuru and Its Implications for Cultural Development in the Amazon Basin. In *The Evolution of Horticultural Systems in Native South America*, edited by J. Wilbert, pp. 47–67. Caracas: Sociedad de Ciencias Naturales.

1970a A Theory of the Origin of the State. *Science* 169:733–738.

1970b Scale Analysis, Evolutionary Sequences, and the Rating of Cultures. In *A Handbook of Method in Cultural Anthropology*, edited by R. Naroll and R. Cohen, pp. 833–871. Garden City, N.Y.: The Natural History Press.

Carrasco, Pedro

1976 The Joint Family in Ancient Mexico: The Case of Molotla. In *Essays in Mexican Kinship*, edited by H. G. Nutini, P. Carrasco, and J. M. Taggart, pp. 45–64. Pittsburgh: University of Pittsburgh Press.

1978 La economía del México prehispánico. In *Economía política e ideología en el México prehispánico*, edited by P. Carrasco and J. Broda, pp. 13–76. Mexico City: Editorial Nueva Imagen.

Caso, Alfonso

1938 *Exploraciones en Oaxaca; Quinta y sexta temporadas, 1936–37*. Tacubaya, Mexico: Instituto Panamericano de Geografía e Historia.

1969 *El tesoro de Monte Albán*. Mexico City: Instituto Nacional de Antropología e Historia.

Chagnon, Napoleon A.

1966 Yanomomö Warfare, Social Organization and Marriage Alliances. Ph.D. dissertation, Department of Anthropology, University of Michigan.

Chapman, Robert, Ian Kinnes, and Klavs Randsborg (Eds.)

1981 *The Archaeology of Death*. Cambridge: Cambridge University Press.

Chase, Arlen F.

1992 Elites and the Changing Organization of Classic Maya Society. In *Mesoamerican Elites: An Archaeological Assessment*, edited by D. Z. Chase and A. F. Chase, pp. 31–49. Norman: University of Oklahoma Press.

Chase, Diane Z., and Arlen F. Chase (Eds.)

1992 *Mesoamerican Elites: An Archaeological Assessment*. Norman: University of Oklahoma Press.

Chase, Diane Z., Arlen F. Chase, and William A. Haviland

1990 The Classic Maya City: Reconsidering the "Mesoamerican Urban Tradition." *American Anthropologist* 92:499–506.

Ciudad Real, Antonio de

1984 *Calepino maya de Motul*. Mexico City: Universidad Nacional Autónoma de México.

Clastres, Pierre
   1977   *Society against the State.* Translated by Robert Hurley. New York: Urizen Books.

Clendinnen, Inga
   1987   *Ambivalent Conquests: Maya and Spaniard in Yucatan, 1517–1570.* Cambridge: Cambridge University Press.

Cliff, Maynard B., and Cathy J. Crane
   1989   Changing Subsistence Economy at a Late Preclassic Maya Community. In *Prehistoric Maya Economies of Belize,* edited by P. A. McAnany and B. L. Isaac, pp. 295–324. Research in Economic Anthropology, Supplement 4. Greenwich, Conn.: JAI Press.

Codex Dresdensis (Codex Dresden). See Deckert, Helmut.

Codex Tro-Cortesianus (Codex Madrid)
   1967   Introduction and Summary by F. Anders. Graz, Austria: Akademische Druck-u.

Coe, Michael D.
   1956   The Funerary Temple among the Classic Maya. *Southwestern Journal of Anthropology* 12:387–394.
   1965   A Model of Ancient Community Structure in the Maya Lowlands. *Southwestern Journal of Anthropology* 21:97–114.
   1973   *The Maya Scribe and His World.* New York: The Grolier Club.
   1988   Ideology of the Maya Tomb. In *Maya Iconography,* edited by E. P. Benson and G. G. Griffin, pp. 222–235. Princeton: Princeton University Press.
   1992   *Breaking the Maya Code.* New York: Thames and Hudson.

Coe, William R.
   1965   Tikal, Guatemala, and Emergent Maya Civilization. *Science* 147:1401–1419.
   1990   *Excavations in the Great Plaza, North Terrace and North Acropolis of Tikal.* University Museum Monograph 61 (Tikal Report 14). Philadelphia: The University Museum, University of Pennsylvania.

Coggins, Clemency C.
   1975   Painting and Drawing Styles at Tikal: An Historical and Iconographic Reconstruction. Ph.D. dissertation, Department of Fine Arts, Harvard University.
   1980   The Shape of Time: Some Political Implications of a Four-Part Figure. *American Antiquity* 45:727–739.
   1988   Classic Maya Metaphors of Death and Life. *RES* 16:64–84.
   1992   Pure Language and Lapidary Prose. In *New Theories on the Ancient Maya,* edited by E. C. Danien and R. J. Sharer, pp. 99–107. Philadelphia: The University Museum, University of Pennsylvania.

Coggins, Clemency C., and Orrin C. Shane III (Eds.)
   1984   *Cenote of Sacrifice: Maya Treasures from the Sacred Well at Chichén Itzá.* Austin: University of Texas Press.

Colby, Benjamin N.

1976 The Anomalous Ixil—Bypassed by the Postclassic? *American Antiquity* 41:74–80.

Collier, George A.

1975 *Fields of the Tzotzil: The Ecological Bases of Tradition in Highland Chiapas*. Austin: University of Texas Press.

1982 Maya Subsistence: A Commentary. In *Maya Subsistence: Studies in Memory of Dennis E. Puleston*, edited by K. V. Flannery, pp. 345–347. New York: Academic Press.

Córdova, Fray Juan de

1942 *Vocabulario Castellano-Zapoteco*. Facsimile of 1578 Vocabulario en Lengua Zapoteca. Mexico City: Instituto Nacional de Antropología e Historia.

Culbert, T. Patrick (Ed.)

1991 *Classic Maya Political History: Hieroglyphic and Archaelogical Evidence*. School of American Research Advanced Seminar Series. Cambridge: Cambridge University Press.

Culbert, T. Patrick, Pamela C. Magers, and Mara L. Spencer

1978 Regional Variability in Maya Lowland Agriculture. In *Pre-Hispanic Maya Agriculture*, edited by P. D. Harrison and B. L. Turner II, pp. 157–161. Albuquerque: University of New Mexico Press.

Culbert, T. Patrick, and Don S. Rice (Eds.)

1990 *Precolumbian Population History in the Maya Lowlands*. Albuquerque: University of New Mexico Press.

Deckert, Helmut

1989 *Der Dresdner Maya-Handschrift*. Graz, Austria: Akademische Druck-u.

de Certeau, Michel

1984 *The Practice of Everyday Life*. Berkeley: University of California Press.

Demarest, Arthur A.

1992 Ideology in Ancient Maya Cultural Evolution: The Dynamics of Galactic Polities. In *Ideology and Pre-Columbian Civilizations*, edited by A. A. Demarest and G. W. Conrad, pp. 135–157. Santa Fe: School of American Research Press.

Demarest, Arthur A., Takeshi Inomata, Hector Escobedo, and Joel Palka (Eds.)

1991 *Proyecto arqueológico regional Petexbatún: Informe preliminar #3, tercera temporada 1991*. Nashville: Department of Anthropology, Vanderbilt University.

Diamanti, Melissa

1991 Domestic Organization at Copan: Reconstruction of Elite Maya Households through Ethnographic Models. Ph.D. dissertation, Department of Anthropology, Pennsylvania State University.

Douglas, Mary

1966 *Purity and Danger: An Analysis of Concepts of Pollution and Taboo*. London: Routledge and Kegan Paul.

Dunning, Nicholas P.

1989   *Archaeological Investigations at Sayil, Yucatan, Mexico: Intersite Re-connaissance and Soil Studies during the 1987 Season.* University of Pittsburgh Anthropological Papers 2. Pittsburgh: University of Pittsburgh.

Dunning, Nicholas P., David Rue, and Timothy Beach

1991   Ecología y patrón de asentamiento en la región de Petexbatún: Resultados preliminares de la temporada 1991. In *Proyecto arqueológico regional Petexbatún: Informe preliminar #3, tercera temporada 1991,* edited by A. Demarest, T. Inomata, H. Escobedo, and J. Palka, pp. 829–847. Nashville: Department of Anthropology, Vanderbilt University.

Eaton, Jack D.

1987   Group A-11: An Elite Residential Complex at Rio Azul, Guatemala. In *Rio Azul Reports, No. 3, The 1985 Season,* edited by R. E. W. Adams, pp. 66–86. San Antonio: University of Texas at San Antonio.

Edmondson, Munro S.

1982   *The Ancient Future of the Itza: The Book of Chilam Balam of Tizimin.* Austin: University of Texas Press.

Evans, Susan T.

1992   The Productivity of Maguey Terrace Agriculture in Central Mexico during the Aztec Period. In *Gardens of Prehistory: The Archaeology of Settlement Agriculture in Greater Mesoamerica,* edited by T. W. Killion, pp. 92–115. Tuscaloosa: University of Alabama Press.

Fahsen, Frederico

1988   *A New Early Classic Text from Tikal.* Research Reports on Ancient Maya Writing 17. Washington, D.C.: Center for Maya Research.

Farrington, Ian S.

1985   The Wet, the Dry and the Steep: Archaeological Imperative and the Study of Agricultural Intensification. In *Prehistoric Intensive Agriculture in the Tropics,* Part 1, edited by I. S. Farrington, pp. 1–10. BAR International Series 232. Oxford: British Archaeological Reports.

Farriss, Nancy M.

1983   Indians in Colonial Yucatan: Three Perspectives. In *Spaniards and Indians in Southeastern Mesoamerica,* edited by M. J. MacLeod and R. Wasserstrom, pp. 1–39. Lincoln: University of Nebraska Press.

1984   *Maya Society under Colonial Rule: The Collective Enterprise of Survival.* Princeton: Princeton University Press.

Fash, William L.

1991   *Scribes, Warriors and Kings.* London: Thames and Hudson.

Fash, William L., and David S. Stuart

1991   Dynastic History and Cultural Evolution at Copan, Honduras. In *Classic Maya Political History: Hieroglyphic and Archaeological Evidence,* edited by T. P. Culbert, pp. 147–179. School of American Research Advanced Seminar Series. Cambridge: Cambridge University Press.

Fedick, Scott L.

1994 Ancient Maya Agricultural Terracing in the Upper Belize River Area: Computer Aided Modeling and the Results of Initial Field Investigations. *Ancient Mesoamerica* 5:107–127.

Feeley-Harnik, Gillian

1985 Issues in Divine Kingship. *Annual Review of Anthropology* 14:273–313.

Feuchtwang, Stephan D. R.

1974 *An Anthropological Analysis of Chinese Geomancy.* Taipei: Vithagna, Southern Materials Center.

Flannery, Kent V., and Joyce Marcus

1976 Formative Oaxaca and the Zapotec Cosmos. *American Scientist* 64:374–383.

1983 *The Cloud People: Divergent Evolution of the Zapotec and Mixtec Civilizations.* New York: Academic Press.

Folan, William J., L. A. Fletcher, and E. R. Kintz

1979 Fruit, Fiber, Bark, and Resin: Social Organization of a Maya Urban Center. *Science* 204:697–701.

Folan, William J., Ellen R. Kintz, and Laraine A. Fletcher

1983 *Coba: A Classic Maya Metropolis.* New York: Academic Press.

Fortes, Meyer

1953 The Structure of Unilineal Descent Groups. *American Anthropologist* 55:17–41.

1965 Some Reflections on Ancestor Worship. In *African Systems of Thought,* edited by M. Fortes and G. Dieterlen, pp. 122–144. London: Oxford University Press.

1976 An Introductory Commentary. In *Ancestors,* edited by W. H. Newell, pp. 1–16. Paris: Mouton.

1987 *Religion, Morality and the Person: Essays on Tallensi Religion.* Cambridge: Cambridge University Press.

Fortune, R. F.

1935 *Manus Religion.* Memoirs of the American Philosophical Society 3. Philadelphia: American Philosophical Society.

Fowler, William R., Jr.

1984 Late Preclassic Mortuary Patterns and Evidence for Human Sacrifice at Chalchuapa, El Salvador. *American Antiquity* 49:603–618.

Fox, John W.

1987 *Maya Postclassic State Formation: Segmentary Lineage Migration in Advancing Frontiers.* Cambridge: Cambridge University Press.

Fox, John W., Dwight T. Wallace, and Kenneth L. Brown

1992 The Emergence of the Quiche Elite: The Putun-Palenque Connection. In *Mesoamerican Elites: An Archaeological Assessment,* edited by D. Z. Chase and A. F. Chase, pp. 169–190. Norman: University of Oklahoma Press.

Fox, Richard G.

1977   *Urban Anthropology: Cities in Their Cultural Settings*. Englewood Cliffs, N.J.: Prentice-Hall.

Freedman, Maurice

1966   *Chinese Lineage and Society: Fukien and Kwangtung*. London School of Economics Monographs on Social Anthropology 33. New York: The Athlone Press.

1970   Ritual Aspects of Chinese Kinship and Marriage. In *Family and Kinship in Chinese Society*, edited by M. Freedman, pp. 163–188. Stanford: Stanford University Press.

Freidel, David A.

1983   Lowland Maya Political Economy: Historical and Archaeological Perspectives in Light of Intensive Agriculture. In *Spaniards and Indians in Southeastern Mesoamerica*, edited by M. J. MacLeod and R. Wasserstrom, pp. 40–63. Lincoln: University of Nebraska Press.

1985   New Light on the Dark Age: A Summary of Major Themes. In *The Lowland Maya Postclassic*, edited by A. F. Chase and P. Rice, pp. 285–309. Austin: University of Texas Press.

1986a   Maya Warfare: An Example of Peer Polity Interaction. In *Peer Polity Interaction and Socio-political Change*, edited by C. Renfrew and J. F. Cherry, pp. 93–108. Cambridge: Cambridge University Press.

1986b   Terminal Classic Lowland Maya: Successes, Failures, and Aftermaths. In *Late Lowland Maya Civilization: Classic to Postclassic*, edited by J. A. Sabloff and E. W. Andrews V, pp. 409–430. Albuquerque: University of New Mexico Press.

1993   The Maya Cultural Tradition: Archaeological Applications at K'axob. Comment on papers presented in a symposium entitled "Ancestors, Agriculture and the Archaeology of Place" at the 58th Annual Meeting of the Society for American Archaeology, St. Louis.

Freidel, David A., and Jeremy A. Sabloff

1984   *Cozumel: Late Maya Settlement Patterns*. New York: Academic Press.

Freidel, David A., and Linda Schele

1988   Kingship in the Late Preclassic Maya Lowlands. *American Anthropologist* 90:547–567.

1989   Dead Kings and Living Temples: Dedication and Termination Rituals among the Ancient Maya. In *Word and Image in Maya Culture*, edited by W. F. Hanks and D. S. Rice, pp. 233–243. Salt Lake City: University of Utah Press.

Fried, Morton

1967   *The Evolution of Political Society*. New York: Random House.

Gailey, Christine W.

1987   *Kinship to Kingship: Gender Hierarchy and State Formation in the Tongan Islands*. Austin: University of Texas Press.

Gallareta Negrón, Tomás, Anthony P. Andrews, and Rafael Cobos Palma

    1989 Preliminary Report of the Cupul Survey Project: An Archaeological Reconnaissance between Chichen Itza and the North Coast of Yucatan. *Mexicon* 11:91–95.

Geertz, C.

    1980 *Negara: The Theatre State in Nineteenth-Century Bali*. Princeton: Princeton University Press.

Gero, Joan M., and Margaret W. Conkey (Eds.)

    1991 *Engendering Archaeology: Women and Prehistory*. Oxford: Basil Blackwell.

Gibson, Eric C.

    1989 The Organization of Late Preclassic Maya Lithic Economy in the Eastern Lowlands. In *Prehistoric Maya Economies of Belize*, edited by P. A. McAnany and B. L. Isaac, pp. 115–138. Research in Economic Anthropology, Supplement 4. Greenwich, Conn.: JAI Press.

Giddens, Anthony

    1981 *Power, Property and the State*. Vol. 1 of *A Contemporary Critique of Historical Materialism*. Berkeley and Los Angeles: University of California Press.

Glazier, Jack

    1984 Mbeere Ancestors and the Domestication of Death. *Man* (n.s.) 19: 133–148.

Godelier, Maurice

    1986 *The Mental and the Material: Thought Economy and Society*. Translated by Thom Martin. Thetford, Norfolk, Great Britain: The Thetford Press. First published by Librairie Arthème Fayard, 1984.

Goldstein, Lynne

    1981 One-Dimensional Archaeology and Multi-Dimensional People: Spatial Organisation and Mortuary Analysis. In *The Archaeology of Death*, edited by R. Chapman, I. Kinnes, and K. Randsborg, pp. 53–69. Cambridge: Cambridge University Press.

Gómez-Pompa, Arturo, José Salvador Flores, and Mario Aliphat Fernández

    1990 The Sacred Cacao Groves of the Maya. *Latin American Antiquity* 1:247–257.

Goody, Jack

    1962 *Death, Property and the Ancestors: A Study of the Mortuary Customs of the LoDagaa of West Africa*. London: Tavistock.

Gossen, Gary H.

    1974 *Chamulas in the World of the Sun: Time and Space in a Maya Oral Tradition*. Cambridge: Harvard University Press.

Gossen, Gary H., and Richard M. Leventhal

    1993 The Topography of Ancient Maya Religious Pluralism: A Dialogue with the Present. In *Lowland Maya Civilization in the Eighth Century A.D.*, edited by J. A. Sabloff and J. S. Henderson, pp. 185–217. Washington, D.C.: Dumbarton Oaks.

Grube, Nikolai

  1991 An Investigation of the Primary Standard Sequence on Classic Maya Ceramics. In *Sixth Palenque Round Table, 1986*, edited by M. G. Robertson and V. M. Fields, pp. 223–232. Norman: University of Oklahoma Press.

Guaman Poma de Ayala, Felipe

  [1615] 1980 *Nueva crónica y buen gobierno*. Translated by Jorge L. Urioste. 3 vols. Mexico City: Siglo XXI.

Hammond, Norman (Ed.)

  1991 *Cuello: An Early Maya Community in Belize*. Cambridge: Cambridge University Press.

Hammond, Norman, and Charles Miksicek

  1981 Ecology and Economy of a Formative Maya Site at Cuello, Belize. *Journal of Field Archaeology* 8:259–269.

Handy, E. S. Craighill, and Mary Kawena Pukui

  1972 *The Polynesian Family System in Ka'-u, Hawai'i*. Rutland, Vt.: Tuttle.

Hanks, William F.

  1990 *Referential Practice: Language and Lived Space among the Maya*. Chicago: University of Chicago Press.

Harrison, Peter D.

  1970 *The Central Acropolis, Tikal, Guatemala: A Preliminary Study of the Functions and Its Structural Components During the Late Classic Period*. Ph.D. dissertation, University of Pennsylvania. Ann Arbor: University Microfilms.

Harrison, Peter D., and B. L. Turner II (Eds.)

  1978 *Pre-Hispanic Maya Agriculture*. Albuquerque: University of New Mexico Press.

Hartung, Horst

  1977 Ancient Maya Architecture and Planning: Possibilities and Limitations for Astronomical Studies. In *Native American Astronomy*, edited by A. F. Aveni, pp. 111–129. Austin: University of Texas Press.

Haviland, William A.

  1968 Ancient Lowland Maya Social Organization. In *Archaeological Studies in Middle America*, pp. 93–117. New Orleans: Middle American Research Institute, Tulane University.

  1981 Dower Houses and Minor Centers at Tikal, Guatemala: An Investigation into the Valid Units in Settlement Hierarchies. In *Lowland Maya Settlement Patterns*, edited by W. Ashmore, pp. 89–117. Albuquerque: University of New Mexico Press.

  1988 Musical Hammocks at Tikal: Problems with Reconstructing Household Composition. In *Household and Community in the Mesoamerican Past*, edited by R. R. Wilk and W. Ashmore, pp. 121–134. Albuquerque: University of New Mexico Press.

Haviland, William A., and Hattula Moholy-Nagy

  1992 Distinguishing the High and Mighty from the Hoi Polloi at Tikal, Guatemala. In *Mesoamerican Elites: An Archaeological Assessment*, edited by D. Z. Chase and A. F. Chase, pp. 50–60. Norman: University of Oklahoma Press.

Headrick, Annabeth
1993 Iconographic Expression in the Agrarian Context of K'axob, Belize. Paper presented at the 58th Annual Meeting of the Society for American Archaeology, St. Louis.

Hellmuth, N.
1977 Cholti-Lacandon (Chiapas) and Peten-Ytza Agriculture, Settlement Pattern and Population. In *Social Process in Maya Prehistory: Studies in Honour of Sir Eric Thompson*, edited by N. Hammond, pp. 421–448. London: Academic Press.

Heyden, Doris
1981 Caves, Gods, and Myths: World-View and Planning in Teotihuacan. In *Mesoamerican Sites and World-Views*, edited by E. P. Benson, pp. 1–39. Washington, D.C.: Dumbarton Oaks.

Hodder, Ian
1986 *Reading the Past*. Cambridge: Cambridge University Press.

Hodder, Ian (Ed.)
1982 *Symbolic and Structural Archaeology*. Cambridge: Cambridge University Press.
1987 *The Archaeology of Contextual Meanings*. Cambridge: Cambridge University Press.

Holland, William R.
1964 Contemporary Tzotzil Cosmological Concepts as a Basis for Interpreting Prehistoric Maya Civilization. *American Antiquity* 29:301–306.

Houston, Stephen D.
1989 *Maya Glyphs*. Berkeley and Los Angeles: University of California Press/British Museum.
1993 *Hieroglyphs and History at Dos Pilas: Dynastic Politics of the Classic Maya*. Austin: University of Texas Press.
1994 Literacy among the Precolumbian Maya: A Comparative Perspective. In *Writing without Words: Alternative Literacies in Mesoamerica and the Andes*, edited by E. H. Boone and W. D. Mignolo. Durham: Duke University Press, pp. 27–49.

Houston, Stephen D., and Peter Mathews
1985 *The Dynastic Sequence of Dos Pilas, Guatemala*. Pre-Columbian Art Research Institute Monograph 1. San Francisco: Pre-Columbian Art Research Institute.

Houston, Stephen D., and David Stuart
1989 *The Way Glyph: Evidence for "Co-essences" among the Classic Maya*. Research Reports on Ancient Maya Writing 30. Washington, D.C.: Center for Maya Research.

Houston, Stephen D., David Stuart, and Karl A. Taube
1989 Folk Classification of Classic Maya Pottery. *American Anthropologist* 91:720–726.

Hughes, Ian
1977 *New Guinea Stone Age Trade*. Terra Australis 3. Canberra: Department of Prehistory, Research School of Pacific Studies, Australian National University.

Humphreys, S. C.
1981 Death and Time. In *Mortality and Immortality: The Anthropology and Archaeology of Death*, edited by S. C. Humphreys and H. King, pp. 261–283. London: Academic Press.

Hunt, Eva
1977 *The Transformation of the Hummingbird: Cultural Roots of a Zincantecan Mythical Poem*. Ithaca: Cornell University Press.

Jackson, Lorren
1992 K'axob Project 1992, Operation I. Report on the 1992 Field Season at K'axob, Belize.

Jakeman, M. Wells
1945 *The Origins and History of the Mayas. Part 1: Introductory Investigations*. Los Angeles: Research Publishing.

Johnson, Allen W.
1983 Machiguenga Gardens. In *Adaptive Responses of Native Amazonians*, edited by R. B. Hames and W. T. Vickers, pp. 29–63. New York: Academic Press.

Johnson, Allen W., and Timothy Earle
1987 *The Evolution of Human Societies: From Foraging to Agrarian State*. Stanford: Stanford University Press.

Johnston, Kevin, Fernando Moscoso Moller, and Stefan Schmitt
1992 Casas no-visibles de los mayas Clásicos: Estructuras residenciales sin plataformas basales en Itzán, Petén. In *V simposio de investigaciones arqueológicas en Guatemala, Museo Nacional de Arqueología e Ethnologica*, pp. 147–162. Guatemala: Ministerio de Cultura y Deportes, Instituto de Antropología e Historia.

Jones, Christopher, and Linton Satterthwaite
1982 *The Monuments and Inscriptions of Tikal: The Carved Monuments*. University Museum Monograph 44 (Tikal Report 33, Part A). Philadelphia: The University Museum, University of Pennsylvania.

Jones, Grant D.
1982 Agriculture and Trade in the Colonial Period Southern Maya Lowlands. In *Maya Subsistence: Studies in Memory of Dennis E. Puleston*, edited by K. V. Flannery, pp. 275–293. New York: Academic Press.

1983 The Last Maya Frontiers of Colonial Yucatan. In *Spaniards and Indians in Southeastern Mesoamerica*, edited by M. J. MacLeod and R. Wasserstrom, pp. 64–991. Lincoln: University of Nebraska Press.

1989   *Maya Resistance to Spanish Rule: Time and Resistance on a Colonial Frontier.* Albuquerque: University of New Mexico Press.

Joyce, Rosemary

1990   The Construction of Gender in Classic Maya Sculpture. Paper presented at the 89th Annual Meeting of the American Anthropological Association, New Orleans.

Justeson, John S., William M. Norman, and Norman Hammond

1988   The Pomona Flare: A Preclassic Maya Hieroglyphic Text. In *Maya Iconography*, edited by E. P. Benson and G. G. Griffin, pp. 94–151. Princeton: Princeton University Press.

Karttunen, Frances

1983   *An Analytical Dictionary of Nahuatl.* Austin: University of Texas Press.

Kerr, Justin

1992   The Myth of the Popol Vuh as an Instrument of Power. In *New Theories on the Ancient Maya*, edited by E. C. Danien and R. J. Sharer, pp. 109–121. Philadelphia: The University Museum, University of Pennsylvania.

Killion, Thomas W.

1987   *Agriculture and Residential Site Structure among Campesinos in Southern Veracruz, Mexico: A Foundation for Archaeological Inference.* Ph.D. dissertation, Department of Anthropology, University of New Mexico. Ann Arbor: University Microfilms.

1990   Cultivation Intensity and Residential Site Structure: An Ethnoarchaeological Examination of Peasant Agriculture in the Sierra de los Tuxtlas, Veracruz, Mexico. *Latin American Antiquity* 1:191–215.

Killion, Thomas W., Jeremy A. Sabloff, and Gair Tourtellot

1989   Intensive Surface Collection of Residential Clusters at Terminal Classic Sayil, Yucatan, Mexico. *Journal of Field Archaeology* 16:273–294.

Killion, Thomas W., Inez Verhagen, Dirk Van Tourenhout, Daniela Triadan, Lisa Hamerlynck, Matthew McDermott, and Jose Genoves

1991   Reporte de la temporada 1991 del Recorrido Arqueológico Intersitio de Petexbatún (RAIP). In *Proyecto arqueológico regional Petexbatún: Informe preliminar #3, tercera temporada 1991*, edited by A. Demarest, T. Inomata, H. Escobedo, and J. Palka, pp. 588–645. Nashville: Department of Anthropology, Vanderbilt University.

Kintz, Ellen R.

1983   Neighborhoods and Wards in a Classic Maya Metropolis. In *Coba: A Classic Maya Metropolis*, edited by W. J. Folan, E. R. Kintz, and L. A. Fletcher, pp. 179–190. New York: Academic Press.

Kubler, George

1958   The Design of Space in Maya Architecture. In *XXXI Congreso Internacional de Americanistas, 1954*, 1:515–531. Mexico City: Universidad Nacional Autónoma de México.

Kurjack, Edward B.

1974   *Prehistoric Lowland Maya Community and Social Organization: A Case Study at Dzibilchaltun, Yucatan, Mexico.* Middle American Research Institute Publication 38. New Orleans: Tulane University.

Kurjack, Edward B., and Silvia Garza T.

1981   Pre-Columbian Community Form and Distribution in the Northern Maya Area. In *Lowland Maya Settlement Patterns*, edited by W. Ashmore, pp. 287–309. Albuquerque: University of New Mexico Press.

Laporte, Juan Pedro, and Lilian Vega de Zea

1986   Aspectos dinásticos para el Clásico Temprano de Mundo Perdido, Tikal. In *Primer simposio mundial epigrafía maya*, pp. 127–140. Guatemala City: Ministerio de Cultura y Deportes, Instituto de Antropología e Historia de Guatemala, Asociación Tikal; Washington, D.C.: National Geographic Society.

Lawrence, P., and M. J. Meggitt

1965   Introduction. In *Gods, Ghosts and Men in Melanesia*, edited by P. Lawrence and M. J. Meggitt, pp. 1–26. Oxford: Oxford University Press.

Leibsohn, Dana

1993   The Historia Tolteca Chichimeca: Recollecting Identity in a Nahua Manuscript. Ph.D. dissertation, Department of Art History, University of California, Los Angeles.

León-Portilla, Miguel

1988   *Time and Reality in the Thought of the Maya.* Translated by Charles L. Boiles, Fernando Horcasitas, and the author. 2d ed. Norman: University of Oklahoma Press.

Leventhal, Richard M.

1983   Household Groups and Classic Maya Religion. In *Prehistoric Settlement Patterns: Essays in Honor of Gordon R. Willey*, edited by E. Z. Vogt and R. M. Leventhal, pp. 55–76. Cambridge: Peabody Museum of Archaeology and Ethnology, Harvard University; Albuquerque: University of New Mexico Press.

1990   The Construction of Power in the Ancient Maya World. Paper presented at the 89th Annual Meeting of the American Anthropological Association, New Orleans.

Leyden, Barbara, and Mark Brenner

1992   Reforestation of Lowland Guatemala after European Contact. Paper presented at the 57th Annual Meeting of the Society for American Archaeology, Pittsburgh.

Lincoln, Charles E.

1991   Dumézil among the Maya. Paper presented at the 90th Annual Meeting of the American Anthropological Association, Chicago.

Lind, Michael, and Javier Urcid

1983   The Lords of Lambityeco and Their Nearest Neighbors. *Notas Americanas* 9:78–111.

Lounsbury, Floyd G.
1974 The Inscription of the Sarcophagus Lid at Palenque. In *Primera Mesa Redonda de Palenque*, Part 2, edited by M. G. Robertson, pp. 5–20. Pebble Beach, Calif.: Robert Louis Stevenson School.

Love, Bruce
1992 Divination and Prophecy in Yucatan. In *New Theories on the Ancient Maya*, edited by E. C. Danien and R. J. Sharer, pp. 205–216. Philadelphia: The University Museum, University of Pennsylvania.

Marcus, Joyce
1976 *Emblem and State in the Classic Maya Lowlands*. Washington, D.C.: Dumbarton Oaks and Trustees for Harvard University.

1978 Archaeology and Religion: A Comparison of Zapotec and Maya. *World Archaeology* 10:172–191.

1982 The Plant World of the Sixteenth- and Seventeenth-Century Maya. In *Maya Subsistence: Studies in Memory of Dennis E. Puleston*, edited by K. V. Flannery, pp. 239–273. New York: Academic Press.

1983 Lowland Maya Archaeology at the Crossroads. *American Antiquity* 48:454–488.

1989 From Centralized Systems to City-States: Possible Models for the Epiclassic. In *Mesoamerica after the Decline of Teotihuacan, A.D. 700–900*, edited by R. A. Diehl and J. C. Berlo, pp. 201–208. Washington, D.C.: Dumbarton Oaks.

1992 *Mesoamerican Writing Systems: Propaganda, Myth and History in Four Ancient Civilizations*. Princeton: Princeton University Press.

1993 Ancient Maya Political Organization. In *Lowland Maya Civilization in the Eighth Century A.D.*, edited by J. A. Sabloff and J. S. Henderson, pp. 111–183. Washington, D.C.: Dumbarton Oaks.

Marcus, Joyce, and Kent V. Flannery
1994 Ancient Zapotec Ritual and Religion: An Application of the Direct Historical Approach. In *The Ancient Mind*, edited by C. Renfrew and E. Zubrow, pp. 55–74. Cambridge: Cambridge University Press.

Martínez Hernández, J.
1929 *Diccionario de Motul: Maya Español*. Merida, Yucatan, Mexico: Compañía Tipográfica Yucateca.

Masson, Marilyn
1993 K'axob Caches and Community Integration: Preclassic Manifestations of a Pervasive Maya Pattern. Paper presented at the 58th Annual Meeting of the Society for American Archaeology, St. Louis.

Mathews, Peter
1991 Classic Maya Emblem Glyphs. In *Classic Maya Political History: Hieroglyphic and Archaeological Evidence*, edited by T. P. Culbert, pp. 19–29. School of American Research Advanced Seminar Series. Cambridge: Cambridge University Press.

Mathews, Peter, and Gordon R. Willey
1991 Prehistoric Polities of the Pasion Region: Hieroglyphic Texts and Their

Archaeological Settings. In *Classic Maya Political History: Hiero-glyphic and Archaeological Evidence*, edited by T. P. Culbert, pp. 30–71. School of American Research Advanced Seminar Series. Cambridge: Cambridge University Press.

McAnany, Patricia A.

1986 *Lithic Technology and Exchange among Wetland Farmers of the Eastern Maya Lowlands*. Ph.D. dissertation, Department of Anthropology, University of New Mexico. Ann Arbor: University Microfilms.

1991 Ancestor Worship and Sanctification of Place: Excavations at K'axob, Belize. *Context* (Boston University Center for Archaeological Studies) 9:12–16.

1992 Agricultural Tasks and Tools: Patterns of Stone Tool Discard near Prehistoric Maya Residences Bordering Pulltrouser Swamp, Belize. In *Gardens of Prehistory: The Archaeology of Settlement Agriculture in Greater Mesoamerica*, edited by T. W. Killion, pp. 184–213. Tuscaloosa: University of Alabama.

1993 The Economics of Social Power and Wealth among Eighth Century Maya Households. In *Lowland Maya Civilization in the Eighth Century A.D.*, edited by J. A. Sabloff and J. S. Henderson, pp. 65–89. Washington, D.C.: Dumbarton Oaks.

n.d. K'axob: A Formative and Classic Period Settlement at Pulltrouser Swamp, Belize. Manuscript in possession of author.

McCormack, Valerie J., Hope Henderson, and Francisco Estrada-Belli

1993 Documenting the Elusive Protoclassic and Early Classic Settlement: Stratigraphic Evidence from K'axob. Paper presented at the 58th Annual Meeting of the Society for American Archaeology, St. Louis.

McGuire, Randall

1992 Archaeology and the First Americans. *American Anthropologist* 94: 816–836.

McQuarie, Harriet

n.d. Buried Structures at Pulltrouser Swamp, Belize. Manuscript in possession of author.

Meggitt, M. J.

1965 *The Lineage System of the Mae-Enga of New Guinea*. New York: Barnes & Noble.

Metcalf, Peter, and Richard Huntington

1991 *Celebrations of Death: The Anthropology of Mortuary Ritual*. 2d ed. Cambridge: Cambridge University Press.

Miksicek, Charles H.

1983 Macrofloral Remains of the Pulltrouser Area: Settlements and Fields. In *Pulltrouser Swamp: Ancient Maya Habitat, Agriculture, and Settlement in Northern Belize*, edited by B. L. Turner II and P. D. Harrison, pp. 94–104. Austin: University of Texas Press.

n.d. Paleoecology and Subsistence at Pulltrouser Swamp: The View from the Float Tank. Manuscript in possession of author.

Miller, Daniel, and Christopher Tilley (Eds.)
1984 *Ideology, Power, and Prehistory.* Cambridge: Cambridge University Press.

Miller, Mary E.
1988 The Boys in the Bonampak Band. In *Maya Iconography*, edited by E. P. Benson and G. G. Griffin, pp. 318–330. Princeton: Princeton University Press.

Millon, René
1973 *The Teotihuacán Map.* Parts 1 and 2 of *Urbanization at Teotihuacán, Mexico.* Austin: University of Texas Press.

Morley, Sylvanus G.
1941 The Xiu Chronicle. Part I: The History of the Xiu. Unpublished manuscript at the Tozzer Library. Harvard University, Cambridge.

Morris, Craig, and Donald E. Thompson
1985 *Huánuco Pampa: An Inca City and Its Hinterland.* London: Thames and Hudson.

Morris, Ian
1991 The Archaeology of Ancestors: The Saxe/Goldstein Hypothesis Revisited. *Cambridge Archaeological Journal* 1:147–169.

Murra, John Victor
1980 *The Economic Organization of the Inka State.* Research in Economic Anthropology, Supplement 1. Greenwich, Conn.: JAI Press.

Nash, June
1970 *In the Eyes of the Ancestors: Belief and Behavior in a Maya Community.* New Haven: Yale University Press.

Nations, James D., and Ronald B. Nigh
1980 The Evolutionary Potential of Lacandon Maya Sustained-Yield Tropical Forest Agriculture. *Journal of Anthropological Research* 36:1–30.

Nimis, Marion M.
1982 The Contemporary Role of Women in Lowland Maya Livestock Production. In *Maya Subsistence: Studies in Memory of Dennis E. Puleston,* edited by K. V. Flannery, pp. 313–325. New York: Academic Press.

Needham, Rodney
1970 Editor's Introduction. In *Kings and Councillors: An Essay in Comparative Anatomy of Human Society* by A. M. Hocart, pp. xiii–xcix. Chicago: University of Chicago Press.

Orellana, Sandra L.
1984 *The Tzutujil Mayas: Continuity and Change, 1250–1630.* Norman: University of Oklahoma Press.

Paxton, Merideth D.
1986 Codex Dresden: Stylistic and Iconographic Analysis of a Maya Manuscript. Ph.D. dissertation, Department of Art History, University of New Mexico.

Pérez Romero, José Alberto

1988 Algunas consideraciones sobre cacao en el norte de la Península de Yucatán. Tesis de Licenciatura en Ciencias Antropológicas, Universidad Autónoma de Yucatán, Mérida.

Pohl, Mary, and Lawrence H. Feldman

1982 The Traditional Role of Women and Animals in Lowland Maya Economy. In *Maya Subsistence: Studies in Memory of Dennis E. Puleston*, edited by K. V. Flannery, pp. 295–311. New York: Academic Press.

Pohl, Mary, and John M. Pohl

1993 Cycles of Conflict: Political Factionalism in the Maya Lowlands. In *Factional Competition and Political Development in the New World*, edited by E. M. Brumfiel and J. W. Fox, pp. 138–157. Cambridge: Cambridge University Press.

Potter, Daniel R., Thomas R. Hester, Stephen L. Black, and Fred Valdez, Jr.

1984 Relationships between Early Preclassic and Early Middle Preclassic Phases in Northern Belize: A Comment on "Lowland Maya Archaeology at the Crossroads." *American Antiquity* 49:628–631.

Proskouriakoff, Tatiana

1960 Historical Implications of a Pattern of Dates at Piedras Negras, Guatemala. *American Antiquity* 25:454–475.

1961 Portraits of Women in Maya Art. In *Essays in Pre-Columbian Art and Archaeology*, edited by S. K. Lothrop, pp. 81–99. Cambridge: Harvard University Press.

1962 Civic and Religious Structures of Mayapan. In *Mayapan, Yucatan, Mexico*, edited by H. E. D. Pollock, R. L. Roys, T. Proskouriakoff, and A. L. Smith, pp. 87–164. Carnegie Institution of Washington Publication 619. Washington, D.C.: Carnegie Institution.

1963 Historical Data in the Inscriptions of Yaxchilan, Part 1. *Estudios de Cultura Maya* 3:149–167. Mexico City: Universidad Nacional Autónoma de México.

1964 Historical Data in the Inscriptions of Yaxchilan, Part 2. *Estudios de Cultura Maya* 4:177–201. Mexico City: Universidad Nacional Autónoma de México.

Pyburn, K. Anne

1989 *Prehistoric Maya Community and Settlement at Nohmul, Belize.* BAR International Series 509. Oxford: British Archaeological Reports.

1990 Settlement Patterns at Nohmul: Preliminary Results of Four Excavation Seasons. In *Precolumbian Population History in the Maya Lowlands*, edited by T. P. Culbert and D. S. Rice, pp. 183–197. Albuquerque: University of New Mexico Press.

Redfield, Robert, and Alfonso Villa Rojas

1962 *Chan Kom: A Maya Village.* Chicago: University of Chicago Press.

Renfrew, Colin

1983 The Social Archaeology of Megalithic Monuments. *Scientific American* 249:152–163.

Renfrew, Colin, and John F. Cherry (Eds.)

1986 *Peer Polity Interaction and Socio-political Change*. Cambridge: Cambridge University Press.

Rice, Don S.

1992 Modern Agricultural Ecology in the Maya Lowlands. Paper presented at the 57th Annual Meeting of the Society for American Archaeology, Pittsburgh.

Rice, Don S., Prudence M. Rice, and Edward S. Deevey

1985 Paradise Lost: Classic Maya Impact on a Lacustrine Environment. In *Prehistoric Lowland Maya Environment and Subsistence Economy*, edited by M. Pohl, pp. 91–105. Papers of the Peabody Museum of Archaeology and Ethnology 77. Cambridge: Harvard University Press.

Ricketson, Oliver, Jr.

1928 Notes on Two Maya Astronomic Observatories. *American Anthropologist* 30:434–444.

Ringle, William M., and E. Wyllys Andrews V

1988 Formative Residences at Komchen, Yucatan, Mexico. In *Household and Community in the Mesoamerican Past*, edited by R. R. Wilk and W. Ashmore, pp. 171–197. Albuquerque: University of New Mexico Press.

Rivera Dorado, Miguel

1990 Introducción: Nuevas perspectivas en la arqueología de Oxkintok. In *Oxkintok 3, Proyecto Oxkintok año 1989*, pp. 7–18. Madrid: Misión Arqueológia de España in México.

Robertson, Merle Greene

1983 *The Temple of the Inscriptions*. Vol. 1 of *The Sculpture of Palenque*. Princeton: Princeton University Press.

1985 *The Late Buildings of the Palace*. Vol. 3 of *The Sculpture of Palenque*. Princeton: Princeton University Press.

1991 *The Cross Group, the North Group, the Olvidado, and Other Pieces*. Vol. 4 of *The Sculpture of Palenque*. Princeton: Princeton University Press.

Robertson, Robin A., and David A. Freidel (Eds.)

1986 *Archaeology at Cerros, Belize, Central America*. Volume 1: *An Interim Report*. Dallas: Southern Methodist University Press.

Robicek, Francis

1972 *Copan: Home of the Mayan Gods*. New York: Heye Foundation, Museum of the American Indian.

Robin, Cynthia

1989 *Preclassic Maya Burials at Cuello, Belize*. BAR International Series 480. Oxford: British Archaelogical Reports.

Roys, Ralph L.

1931 *The Ethno-Botany of the Maya*. Middle American Research Series, Publication 2, New Orleans: Tulane University.

1939   *The Titles of Ebtun.* Carnegie Institution of Washington Publication 505. Washington, D.C.: Carnegie Institution.

1941   The Xiu Chronicle. Part 2: The Xiu Chronicle. Unpublished manuscript at the Tozzer Library, Harvard University, Cambridge.

1943   *The Indian Background of Colonial Yucatan.* Carnegie Institution of Washington Publication 548. Washington, D.C.: Carnegie Institution.

1957   *The Political Geography of the Yucatan Maya.* Carnegie Institution of Washington Publication 613. Washington, D.C.: Carnegie Institution.

1962   Literary Sources for the History of Mayapan. In *Mayapan, Yucatan, Mexico,* edited by H. E. D. Pollock, R. L. Roys, T. Proskouriakoff, and A. L. Smith, pp. 25–86. Carnegie Institution of Washington Publication 619. Washington, D.C.: Carnegie Institution.

1967   *The Book of Chilam Balam of Chumayel.* Originally published in 1933 in CIW series. Norman: University of Oklahoma Press.

Roys, Ralph L., France V. Scholes, and Eleanor B. Adams

1940   Report and Census of the Indians of Cozumel, 1570. In *Contributions to American Anthropology and History,* pp. 1–30. Carnegie Institution of Washington Publication 523. Washington, D.C.: Carnegie Institution.

Ruz Lhuillier, Alberto

1973   *El Templo de las Inscripciones, Palenque.* Colección Científica Arqueología 7. Mexico City: Instituto Nacional de Antropología e Historia.

RY

1983   *Relaciones histórico-geográficas de la gobernación de Yucatán (Mérida, Valladolid y Tabasco).* Instituto de Investigaciones Filológicas Centro de Estudios Mayas, Tomos 1 y 2. Mexico City: Universidad Nacional Autónoma de México.

Sabloff, Jeremy A.

1986   Interaction among Classic Maya Polities: A Preliminary Examination. In *Peer Polity Interaction and Socio-political Change,* edited by C. Renfrew and J. F. Cherry, pp. 109–116. Cambridge: Cambridge University Press.

Sabloff, Jeremy A., and Gair Tourtellot

1991   *The Ancient Maya City of Sayil: The Mapping of a Puuc Region Center.* Middle American Research Institute Publication 60. New Orleans: Tulane University.

Sahlins, Marshall D.

1961   The Segmentary Lineage: An Organization of Predatory Expansion. *American Anthropologist* 63:322–345.

1985   *Islands of History.* Chicago: University of Chicago Press.

Salomon, Frank

1991   Introductory Essay: The Huarochirí Manuscript. In *The Huarochirí Manuscript: A Testament of Ancient and Colonial Andean Religion,* edited by F. Salomon and G. L. Urioste, pp. 1–38. Austin: University of Texas Press.

Sanders, William T.

    1989   Household, Lineage, and State at Eighth-Century Copan, Honduras. In *The House of the Bacabs, Copan, Honduras*, edited by D. Webster, pp. 89–105. Studies in Pre-Columbian Art and Archaeology 29. Washington, D.C.: Dumbarton Oaks.

Sanders, William T., and David Webster

    1988   The Mesoamerican Urban Tradition. *American Anthropologist* 90: 521–546.

Saxe, Arthur A.

    1970   Social Dimensions of Mortuary Practices. Ph.D. dissertation, Department of Anthropology, University of Michigan.

Schele, Linda

    1981   Sacred Site and World-View at Palenque. In *Mesoamerican Sites and World-Views*, edited by E. P. Benson, pp. 87–117. Washington, D.C.: Dumbarton Oaks.

    1984   Human Sacrifice among the Classic Maya. In *Ritual Human Sacrifice in Mesoamerica*, edited by E. H. Boone, pp. 7–48. Washington, D.C.: Dumbarton Oaks.

    1991   The Demotion of Chac-Zutz': Lineage Compounds and Subsidiary Lords at Palenque. In *Sixth Palenque Round Table, 1986*, edited by M. G. Robertson and V. M. Fields, pp. 6–11. Norman: University of Oklahoma Press.

Schele, Linda, and David Freidel

    1990   *A Forest of Kings: The Untold Story of the Ancient Maya.* New York: William Morrow.

Schele, Linda, and Jeffrey H. Miller

    1983   *The Mirror, the Rabbit, and the Bundle: "Accession" Expressions from the Classic Maya Inscriptions.* Studies in Pre-Columbian Art and Archaeology 25. Washington, D.C.: Dumbarton Oaks.

Schele, Linda, and Mary E. Miller

    1986   *Blood of Kings: Dynasty and Ritual in Maya Art.* New York: George Braziller; Fort Worth: Kimball Art Museum.

Scholes, France V., and Eleanor B. Adams

    1938   *Don Diego Quijada: Alcalde Mayor de Yucatán, 1561–1565.* Mexico City: Antigua Librería Robredo, de José Porrua e Hijos.

Scholes, France V., and Ralph L. Roys

    1938   Fray Diego de Landa and the Problem of Idolatry in Yucatan. In *Cooperation in Research*, pp. 585–620. Carnegie Institution of Washington Publication 501. Washington, D.C.: Carnegie Institution.

    1968   *The Maya Chontal Indians of Acalan-Tixchel.* 2d ed. Originally published in 1948 in CIW series. Norman: University of Oklahoma Press.

Service, Elman

    1971   *Primitive Social Organization.* 2d ed. New York: Random House.

Shanks, Michael, and Christopher Tilley
  1987 *Re-Constructing Archaeology: Theory and Practice.* Cambridge: Cambridge University Press.
Sharer, Robert J.
  1978 Special Deposits. In *The Prehistory of Chalchuapa, El Salvador*, edited by R. J. Sharer, pp. 181–193. Philadelphia: University of Pennsylvania Press.
  1983 *The Ancient Maya.* 4th ed., revised from earlier editions by Sylvanus G. Morley (1946) and George W. Brainerd (1956). Stanford: Stanford University Press.
Sheets, Payson
  1992 *The Ceren Site: A Prehistoric Village Buried by Volcanic Ash in Central America.* Fort Worth: Harcourt Brace Jovanovich.
Sherbondy, Jeanette E.
  1982 *The Canal System of Hanan Cuzco.* Ph.D. dissertation, Department of Anthropology, University of Illinois at Urbana-Champaign. Ann Arbor: University Microfilms.
Silverblatt, Irene
  1987 *Moon, Sun and Witches: Gender Ideologies and Class in Inca and Colonial Peru.* Princeton: Princeton University Press.
  1988 Women in States. *Annual Review of Anthropology* 17:427–460.
Smith, A. Ledyard
  1962 Residential and Associated Structures at Mayapan. In *Mayapan, Yucatan, Mexico*, edited by H. E. D. Pollock, R. L. Roys, T. Proskouriakoff, and A. L. Smith, pp. 165–319. Carnegie Institution of Washington Publication 619. Washington, D.C.: Carnegie Institution.
Smith, Carol A. (Ed.)
  1990 *Guatemalan Indians and the State, 1540–1988.* Austin: University of Texas Press.
Smith, Thomas C.
  1959 *Agrarian Origins of Modern Japan.* Stanford: Stanford University Press.
Smyth, Michael P.
  1990 Maize Storage among the Puuc Maya. *Ancient Mesoamerica* 1:51–69.
Southall, Aidan W.
  1957 *Alur Society: A Study of Processes and Types of Domination.* London: W. Heffer and Sons.
Spalding, Karen
  1984 *Huarochirí: An Andean Society under Inca and Spanish Rule.* Stanford: Stanford University Press.
Stein, Julie
  1990 Sedimentation and Maya Agriculture along the Rio Hondo. In *Ancient Maya Wetland Agriculture: Excavations on Albion Island, Northern Belize*, edited by M. Pohl, pp. 323–338. Boulder: Westview.

Stuart, David
  1988   Blood Symbolism in Maya Iconography. In *Maya Iconography*, edited by E. P. Benson and G. G. Griffin, pp. 175–221. Princeton: Princeton University Press.
Stuart, David, and Stephen Houston
  1994   *Classic Maya Place Names.* Washington, D.C.: Dumbarton Oaks.
Tambiah, Stanley J.
  1976   *World Conqueror and World Renouncer: A Study of Buddhism and Polity in Thailand against a Historical Background.* New York: Cambridge University Press.
Taube, Karl A.
  1985   The Classic Maya Maize God: A Reappraisal. In *Fifth Palenque Round Table, 1983,* edited by M. G. Robertson and V. M. Fields, pp. 171–181. San Francisco: The Pre-Columbian Art Research Institute.
  1989   The Maize Tamale in Classic Maya Diet, Epigraphy, and Art. *American Antiquity* 54:31–51.
Taylor, Paul Michael, and Lorraine V. Aragon
  1991   *Beyond the Java Sea: Art of Indonesia's Outer Islands.* Washington, D.C.: The National Museum of Natural History, Smithsonian Institution, in association with New York: Harry N. Abrams.
Tedlock, Barbara
  1982   *Time and the Highland Maya.* Albuquerque: University of New Mexico Press.
Tedlock, Dennis
  1985   *Popol Vuh: The Mayan Book of the Dawn of Life.* New York: Simon & Schuster.
  1992   The Popol Vuh as a Hieroglyphic Book. In *New Theories on the Ancient Maya,* edited by E. C. Danien and R. J. Sharer, pp. 229–240. Philadelphia: The University Museum, University of Pennsylvania.
  1993   Torture in the Archives: Mayans Meet Europeans. *American Anthropologist* 95:139–152.
Thompson, J. Eric S.
  1954   *The Rise and Fall of Maya Civilization.* Norman: University of Oklahoma Press.
  1972   *A Commentary on the Dresden Codex.* Memoirs of the American Philosophical Society 93. Philadelphia: American Philosophical Society.
  1976   *Maya History and Religion.* Norman: University of Oklahoma Press.
  1978   *Maya Hieroglyphic Writing: An Introduction.* 3d ed. Originally published in 1960. Norman: University of Oklahoma Press.
Tilley, Christopher (Ed.)
  1990   *Reading Material Culture: Structuralism, Hermeneutics and Post-Structuralism.* Oxford: Basil Blackwell.
Tourtellot, Gair, III
  1988   Developmental Cycles of Households and Houses at Seibal. In *House-

hold and Community in the Mesoamerican Past, edited by R. R. Wilk and W. Ashmore, pp. 97–120. Albuquerque: University of New Mexico Press.

1990 Burials: A Cultural Analysis. In *Excavations at Seibal, Department of Peten, Guatemala*, pp. 81–142. Memoirs of the Peabody Museum of Archaeology and Ethnology 17:2. Cambridge: Harvard University Press.

Tozzer, Alfred M.

1907 *A Comparative Study of the Mayas and the Lacandones.* New York: Macmillan.

Tozzer, Alfred M. (Trans.)

1941 *Landa's Relación de las Cosas de Yucatán: A Translation.* Papers of the Peabody Museum of American Archaeology and Ethnology 18. Cambridge: Harvard University Press.

Turner, B. L., II

1983 *Once beneath the Forest: Prehistoric Terracing in the Rio Bec Region of the Maya Lowlands.* Dellplain Latin American Studies 13. Boulder: Westview.

Turner, B. L., II, and Peter D. Harrison

1981 Prehistoric Raised Field Agriculture in the Maya Lowlands. *Science* 213:399–405.

Turner, B. L., II, and Peter D. Harrison (Eds.)

1983 *Pulltrouser Swamp: Ancient Maya Habitat, Agriculture, and Settlement in Northern Belize.* Austin: University of Texas Press.

Turner, B. L., II, and William T. Sanders

1992 Summary and Critique. In *Gardens of Prehistory: The Archaeology of Settlement Agriculture in Greater Mesoamerica*, edited by T. W. Killion, pp. 263–284. Tuscaloosa: University of Alabama Press.

Vaughn, Hague H., Edward S. Deevey, and Samuel E. Garrett-Jones

1985 Pollen Stratigraphy of Two Cores from the Peten Lake District, with an Appendix on Two Deep-Water Cores. In *Prehistoric Lowland Maya Environment and Subsistence Economy*, edited by M. Pohl, pp. 73–90. Papers of the Peabody Museum of Archaeology and Ethnology 77. Cambridge: Harvard University Press.

Vogt, Evon Z.

1964 Ancient Maya Concepts in Contemporary Zinacantan Religion. VI*ᵉ Congrès International des Sciences Anthropologiques et Ethnologiques* II-2:497–502. Paris: Musée de l'Homme.

1969 *Zinacantan: A Maya Community in the Highlands of Chiapas.* Cambridge: Belknap Press and Harvard University Press.

1976 *Tortillas for the Gods: A Symbolic Analysis of Zinacanteco Rituals.* Cambridge: Harvard University Press.

1981 Some Aspects of Sacred Geography of Highland Chiapas. In *Mesoamerican Sites and World-Views*, edited by E. P. Benson, pp. 119–142. Washington, D.C.: Dumbarton Oaks.

Walker, Debra S.

 1990 Cerros Revisited: Ceramic Indicators of Terminal Classic and Postclassic Settlement and Pilgrimage in Northern Belize. Ph.D. dissertation, Department of Anthropology, Southern Methodist University, Dallas.

Wallerstein, Immanuel

 1974 *The Modern World System: Capitalist Agriculture and the Origins of the European World-Economy in the Sixteenth Century*. New York: Academic Press.

Watanabe, John M.

 1990 From Saints to Shibboleths: Image, Structure, and Identity in Maya Religious Syncretism. *American Ethnologist* 17:131–150.

Watson, Rubie S.

 1988 Remembering the Dead: Graves and Politics in Southeastern China. In *Death Ritual in Late Imperial and Modern China*, edited by J. L. Watson and E. S. Rawski, pp. 203–227. Berkeley: University of California Press.

Wauchope, Robert

 1938 *Modern Maya Houses: A Study of their Archaeological Significance*. Washington, D.C.: Carnegie Institution.

Weber, Max

 1947 *The Theory of Social and Economic Organisation*. Translated by A. R. Henderson and T. Parsons. New York: Oxford University Press.

 1968 *Economy and Society*. Vol. 3. New York: Bedminster Press.

Webster, David

 1989 The House of the Bacabs: Its Social Context. In *The House of the Bacabs, Copan, Honduras*, edited by D. Webster, pp. 5–40. Studies in Pre-Columbian Art and Archaeology 29. Washington, D.C.: Dumbarton Oaks.

 1993 The Study of Maya Warfare: What It Tells Us about the Maya and What It Tells Us about Maya Archaeology. In *Lowland Maya Civilization in the Eighth Century A.D.*, edited by J. A. Sabloff and J. S. Henderson, pp. 415–444. Washington, D.C.: Dumbarton Oaks.

Webster, David, and Nancy Gonlin

 1988 Households of the Humblest Maya. *Journal of Field Archaeology* 15: 169–190.

Welsh, W. B. M.

 1988 *An Analysis of Classic Lowland Maya Burials*. BAR International Series 409. Oxford: British Archaeological Reports.

White, Jacqueline

 1990 K'axob 1990: Stratigraphy of Operation I. Report on the 1990 Field Season at K'axob, Belize.

Whitecotton, Joseph W.

 1990 *Zapotec Elite Ethnohistory: Pictorial Genealogies from Eastern Oaxaca*. Publications in Anthropology 39. Nashville: Vanderbilt University.

Wilk, Richard R.

1985 Dry Season Agriculture among the Kekchi and Its Implications for Prehistory. In *Prehistoric Lowland Maya Environment and Subsistence Economy*, edited by M. Pohl, pp. 47–57. Papers of the Peabody Museum of Archaeology and Ethnology 77. Cambridge: Harvard University Press.

1988 Maya Household Organization: Evidence and Analogies. In *Household and Community in the Mesoamerican Past*, edited by R. R. Wilk and W. Ashmore, pp. 135–151. Albuquerque: University of New Mexico Press.

Wilson, Richard

1993 Anchored Communities: Identity and History of the Maya-Q'eqchi'. *Man* (n.s.) 28:121–138.

Winter, Marcus C.

1974 Residential Patterns at Monte Alban, Oaxaca, Mexico. *Science* 186: 981–987.

Wisdom, C.

1940 *The Chorti Indians of Guatemala*. Chicago: University of Chicago Press.

Wolf, Eric

1982 *Europe and the People without History*. Berkeley: University of California Press.

Ximénez, Francisco

1929 *Historia de la provincia de San Vicente de Chiapa y Guatemala*. Biblioteca "Goathemala" de la Sociedad de Geografía e Historia, Tomo 1. Guatemala: Tipografía Nacional.

Zier, Christian J.

1992 Intensive Raised-Field Agriculture in a Posteruption Environment, El Salvador. In *Gardens of Prehistory: The Archaeology of Settlement Agriculture in Greater Mesoamerica*, edited by T. W. Killion, pp. 217–233. Tuscaloosa: University of Alabama Press.

Zuidema, R. Tom

1973 Kinship and Ancestorcult in Three Peruvian Communities: Hernández Príncipe's Account of 1622. *Bulletin de l'Institut Français d'Etudes Andines* 2:16–33.

Index

Boldface page numbers refer to illustrations.

Abasolo, 19
Acalan, 93, 132, 151
agriculture
  boundary, 84, 85
  cultigens: *agave*, 77; avocado, 75, 102; *cacao*, 74, 75, 76, 77, 87, 94, 101, 102, 118, 136, 142, 145, 170, 172, 173; chicozapote, 75, 76, 102; guyaba, 75, 102; maize, 72, 73, 101; maize, symbolization of, 73; nance, 75, 102, 172
  deforestation, 69
  fallow, 65, 66, 67, 69, 73, 79, 109, 110, 159, 171; fallow, high bush, 69–70, 70; fallow, low bush, 71, 71. *See also* k'ax
  field hut, 72, 72
  field size, 79
  granary, 72
  household size, 109
  iconography, 75, 81
  methods and practices: *calmil*, 77; double-cropping, 73–74; far fields, 72, 74, 94; fixed-plot, 78, 84, 79, 110, 159; gardens, 74, 77; intensification, 95, 174; milpa, 68, 72, 73; near fields, 99, 100, 110, 159; non-contiguous plots, 79; permanent fields, 74, 75, 91; polycropping, 73; swidden, 68, 78, 95, 109, 110, 159, 172
  orchard, 74, 75, 77, 99, 100, 101, 159, 164; ancestral orchard, 43, 76, 164
  palynology, 69
  Petén, 69
  rituals and, 80, 84
  soil fertility, 73
  weather, 80; drought, 81, 84; risk factors, 79; risk reduction, 79
aguada. See cenote
Aguilar, 122
AHAU. See ahaw
ahaw, 9, 87, 117, 118, 127, 129, 136, 141, 154
ah chun kah, 117, 118, 120, 122, 173. *See also* household, head
ah kuch kab, 9, 24, 32, 33, 87, 92, 93, 95, 96, 117, 132, 135, 140, 143, 151, 152, 153, 163. *See also* lineage, head
AH KULELES, 152
AH TUPILIL, 152
All Saints' Day. *See* Todos Santos
Altun Ha, 53
Alur of Africa, 14, 15
analogy
  ethnographic, 158
  ethnohistoric, 158
ancestors
  bias: age bias, 60; female, 47; gender bias, 60
  cult of, 27
  deified, 23
  enveloping the, 101
  human rights, 167–168
  iconography of, 39, 44, 46; images of, 40; perception of, 29

inheritance: land, 64, 68, 75–76, 120, 143, 161, 164; orchards, 101, 161
material remains: bones, 46, 47, 60; burials, 94 (*see also* burial); exhumation of, 47; missing material remains, 61, 62; placement of, 1, 30, 49, 50, 100, 115
obligations, 161
offerings to, 115
politics, 128, 150, 160, 164; inequality, 111
role of, 16; importance of, 28; meaning of, 1, 161; selection of, 11, 29, 115
royal, 39; cartouche, 43; shrine, 102, 107, 150; tombs, 14
ancestor veneration
archaeological evidence for, 55
in China. *See* China, ancestor veneration
definition of, 10–11
gender: bias, 13, 123; female role, 12, 13; male role, 12, 13, 14
genesis of, 53, 127, 161, 164; chronological changes, 126
noncommoner: elite, 10, 125, 126; royal, 40, 127
physical locale, 13–14; pyramid, 128, 133; residence, 53, 58
politics, 125, 126; kingship, 127
resource rights, 8, 29, 43, 99, 100, 110, 113, 161, 165, 169
rituals, 6, 12, 51, 93, 126, 161; vs. ancestor worship, 10–11; vs. tonalism, 29
See also burial; shrine
ancestral spirit, 11
Andrews, E. Wyllys V, 121
apiary, 70
archaeological methods
artifact distribution patterns, 102
chemical phosphate analysis, 102
settlement pattern analysis, 103
survey, 102
authority symbols
mat, 128, 149
throne, 128
auto da fé, 35–36

auto-sacrifice. *See* bloodletting
Avila, Father Francisco de, 17
ayllu, 18, 137
membership, 17
ranking of, 18
resource rights, 17

Bacalar, 170
balche, 118, 172
BATAB, 87, 90, 92, 93, 96, 117, 118, 136, 137, 140, 152, 154
Belize River Valley, 78. *See also specific sites of Belize*
Benque Viejo, 53
bloodletting, 34, 44, 45
ancestors, 44
Lady Xoc, 34
social status and, 34
bones. *See* ancestors, material remains; burial; shrine
Book of Chilam Balam of Chumayel. See *Chilam Balam of Chumayel*
boundary. *See* polity, boundary
bride service, 107, 120
Brumfiel, Elizabeth M., 140, 146, 151, 170
bundles, 61, 135
Bunzel, Ruth, 113, 120, 169, 170
burial
analysis of, 104
directionality, 52
elite, 123
gender of, 123
group size and, 51
human rights and, 167–168
offerings, 57, 58, 115
patterns, 55, 103
in residences, 104, 126
respect for, 167–168
See also ancestors; ancestor veneration

cacao. See agriculture, cultigens, *cacao*
cacique, 91, 101, 106, 152
Cahal Pech, 145
Cakquichel Maya, 28, 173
chajal, 28
Cal, Hernando, 175. *See also* Oxkutzkab

Calotmul Document, 116
calpulli, 92, 116
Camal, Francisco, 89
Canul lineage, 96
Caracol, 143, 144, 155
cargo, 118, 174
Carlson, John B., 171
Carmack, Robert M., 25–26, 28, 114
Carneiro, Robert L., 6
Carrasco, Pedro, 116
cave, 50, 87, 171
cedar, 37–38
Cehache, 25, 169
Cemé, Catalina, 138
cemeteries, 30
cenote, 74, 87, 142, 172. *See also* Chichén Itzá
ceramics, 115, 134, 170
  Aztec, 170
  iconography and, 133, 134
  incensario, 88, 88
  Jaina, 44
  neutron activation, 32
  ownership, 32
Ceren, El Salvador, 77, 101
  macoyas, 77
Cerros, 88, 114, 123, 137, 160, 172
Chalchihuitán, 170
Chase, Arlen F., 143
Chase, Diane Z., 143
Chi, Francisco, 89. *See also* Xiu
Chi, Gaspar Antonio, 22, 36, 80, 90, 91, 129, 132, 142, 173, 174. *See also* Xiu
ch'ibal, 23, 128
Chichén Itzá, 36, 43, 80, 89, 151
Chichicastenango, 26, 93, 161
Chilam Balam of Chumayel, 23, 27, 64, 80, 89, 128, 130, 140, 149
Chilam Balam of Tizimin, 148
China, 13, 14, 53, 61, 81, 120
  ancestor entombment, 50
  ancestor rituals, 50
  ancestor veneration, 27, 113, 150
  feng-shui, 12, 52, 113, 150
  lineage, 16, 95, 100, 112
Chol Lacandón. *See* Lacandón Maya
Chol Manche, 106

Chuhuhub, 101
Chunchucmil, 94
cloud motif. *See* ancestors, iconography
Cobá, 77, 94, 95, 104
Cocom, 80, 87, 141, 142, 153; Nachi, 88, 142, 143
codex, 129, 153
  Codex Dresden, 21, 35, 35, 81, 82,83, 84, 153
  Codex Grolier, 21
  Codex Madrid, 33, 34, 35, 37, 38, 44, 45, 47, 47, 136
  Codex Mendoza, 136
  Codex Vienna, 18
  Códice de Calkini, 92, 96
Coe, Michael D., 23, 117, 152
Colby, Benjamin M., 29
Colha, 145, 155
collapse, Maya, 146
Collier, George A., 91, 99, 107, 115, 120
commoner, Maya. *See* nonelite, Maya
conflict. *See* warfare
Copán, 52, 53, 85, 88, 123, 148, 151, 153, 155, 173
  altars: Altar Q, 40, 42; Altar T, 148; Altar U, 148
  burial patterns, 103
  factions, 148
  groups: Group 9, 148; Group 9N-8, 123; Group 10L-2, 121
  House of Bacabs, 26, 33, 148
  rulers: 18-Rabbit, 154; Smoke Shell, 153; Yax-Kuk-Mo', 40, 41, 42; Yax Pac, 40, 42, 43, 148
  structures: Structure CV-43, 148; Structure 10L-22A, 153; Temple 11, 40, 41
Cordemex dictionary, 67, 92, 139
council house, 151, 153
councilor. *See* ah kuch kab
Cozumel Island, 79, 94, 101, 106, 107, 173
cremation, 27
cross motif. *See* quadripartite motif
Cuello, 63, 73, 145, 155
Cupul, 87, 148, 154
Cuzco, Peru, 17. *See also* Inka

deities, Maya, 27, 81, 143, 151
descent, 115, 116, 123, 127–128
  genesis of, 114
  See also lineage; patronymic
Diamanti, Melissa, 103
domestic cycle, 107
domestic rituals
  in China, 33
  women and, 33
Dos Pilas, 90
  Ruler 3, 141
  Ruler 4, 90, 155
DZACAB, 128
Dzibilchaltún, 53, 94, 95, 104, 148
Dzuluinicob, 170

Earthquake (son of Seven Macaw), 148
Eaton, Jack D., 121
Ebtun, 172
eccentrics, 46, **46**
education, 130
Ek, Can, 101
Ekbalam, 148
elite, 6, 12, 24, 33, 61, 91, 95, 103, 111,
  112, 116, 125, 126, 127, 129, 130,
  132, 135, 139, 141, 142, 143, 144,
  145, 148, 151, 152, 153, 157, 158,
  160, 164, 174
  almehen, 128
  archaeological signature of, 26
  hidalgo, 25, 138, 169
  land inheritance, 84
encomendero, 174
encomienda, 22, 169
entrada, 16, 36, 75, 79, 169, 170
extended family. *See* household, multiple
  family

fallow. *See* agriculture, fallow
famine food, 141
Farriss, Nancy M., 105, 117, 142, 151
Fash, Barbara, 121
feasting, 31, 32, 87, 101, 118, 133, 153
  female contribution, 32
  occasions for, 31
  social status and, 31
Feuchtwang, Stephan D. R., 81, 113, 150

Fiji, 141
fire-serpent, 19
Flannery, Kent V., 127
Fortes, Meyer, 10–11, 164
Freedman, Maurice, 11, 13, 14, 16, 33,
  50, 95, 100, 112
Freidel, David A., 26, 142
Fuensalida, Friar, 101

Garzón, 170
genealogy, 15, 47, 114, 128, 161
  definition of, 15
  of place, 99, 110, 115, 126
  royal Maya, 99, 127
  unrelatedness, 107
Goody, Jack, 12, 113
Gregorio de Montalvo, Bishop, 74

HALACH UINIC (*halach winik*), 9, 27, 87,
  88, 89, 90, 117, 118, 136, 140, 142,
  152, 154
Hanks, William F., 68, 119
Haviland, William A., 26, 99, 103, 114,
  119, 121, 150
Hellmuth, N., 73
Hernández de Córdoba, Francisco, 27
hidalgo, 25, 138, 169
hieroglyphs, 14, 24, 47, 80, 89, 99, 110,
  117, 126, 127, 128, 130, 144, 155,
  160, 162, 170, 175
  titles, 135, 153
  toponyms, 90, 143
Highland Maya. *See* Cakquichel Maya;
  Ixil Maya; Q'eqchi Maya; Quiché
  Maya; Tzotzil Maya; Tzutujil Maya
Historia Tolteca-Chichimeca, 133, 173
Hocaba, 89
Holland, William R., 171
Holmul, 53
hol pop, 24, 31, 143, 152, 153
household, 105, 117, 118, 120, 133,
  138, 158, 159
  archaeological evidence, 106
  centralization of, 132
  composition of, 106, 107, 121, 122, 173
  external relations, 119
  genesis of, 123

head, 95, 106, 118, 120, 121, 122,
    135, 139, 162, 163, 175. *See also*
    ah chun kah
  kingship and, 131
  linguistics and, 119
  multiple family, 105–106, 108–109,
    119, 123, 162, 173
  organization, 150
  production, 107, 119, 125, 135, 136,
    139, 140
  size, 106, 107, 114, 121
Houston, Stephen D., 32, 43, 129, 130,
    171
huacas, 17, 18
Huarochirí manuscript, 17, 18
Huitzo, 19
Hunacti, 101
Hunahpu, 143, 148

iconography, 126, 130, 133, 141, 149,
    152, 153, 155, 164
  jaguar, 149
  See also ancestors, iconography of
idol, 27, 35, 36, 37, 99, 113, 151, 162,
    170, 172
  carving of, 37
  material for, 37
  misinterpretation of, 27
incensario, 88, 88
incense, 172
inheritance, 94, 96, 99, 110
  genealogy and, 99
  withholding, 107
  See also ancestors, inheritance; elite,
    land inheritance; lineage, resource
    rights
Inka, 16, 17, 137, 140
Isla de Mujeres, 27
Itzá, 106
Ixil Maya, 29, 30

Jaina figurines, 44
Japan, 112
Jimbal, 46

k'ax, 69, 110, 159
  definition/translation of, 67

pharmaceutical qualities of, 71
  resources of, 70
  species in, 70
K'axob, 54, 55, 60, 73, 85, 97, 104,
    114, 115, 116, 124, 126, 145, 155,
    156, 158, 160, 161, 173
  ancestor shrine, 55, 59, 63, 97, 114
  B Group, 56
  burial, 62
  cache, 60, 104, 105
  ceramics, 88
  offerings, 57, 57, 58, 104
  Operation 1, 98
  quincunx pattern, 105
  Structure 18, 58, 88, 97, 115
Kekchi (Q'eqchi) Maya, 120, 190
Killion, Thomas W., 72
kin group. *See* lineage; household, mul-
    tiple family
kingship, 125, 127, 128, 131, 133 145,
    156
  authority and, 131, 149
  conflict and, 149
  divine, 132, 143, 156, 158, 160, 163,
    164
  domination and, 131, 140, 141
  gender and production, 131, 139
  household and, 143, 144
  labor and, 131, 136, 137
  lineage and, 143, 144
  power and, 141, 143, 148, 149, 151
  representation of, 152
  revenue and, 131, 133, 134
  typology of, 144
  variation in, 154
Komchen, 119, 174
kuch, 111, 117, 153, 174
kuchkabal, 143, 153
kuchteel, 91, 153
Kuikuru, 172
kulche', 37. *See also* idol

Lacandón Maya, 37, 69, 71, 72, 106,
    171, 172
Laguna de los Términos, 141
Lamanai, 155
Lambityeco, 19

land
   inherited, 160, 173. *See also* ances-
      tors, inheritance, land
   principle of first occupancy, 96–97,
      112, 116, 162
   social status, 84
Landa, Bishop Diego de, 26, 27, 28, 29,
   32, 34, 36, 37, 39, 80, 96, 97, 99,
   101, 116, 118, 121, 129, 140, 142,
   171, 172, 174
lineage
   agriculture and, 78; subsistence inten-
      sification, 95
   collapse of Maya and, 96
   descent, 49, 113, 123, 128; matrilin-
      eage, 123, 128; membership, 113,
      116; patrilineage, 25, 61, 107, 123,
      128
   inequality, 111, 162; ranking, 23, 25,
      116; status differences, 104, 116;
      subordinate, 25
   obligation, 92, 138, 147; labor, 25,
      138, 147
   organization of, 25, 92, 150, 155,
      173; duration of, 16; founding, 23,
      27, 97, 99 (*see also* principle of first
      occupancy); mobility, 96; residence
      of, 34; segmentary, 26, 133, 147,
      174; size, 114; *xe'al*, 25
   politics, 24; authority, 131; autonomy
      of, 147; boundaries, 91; centraliza-
      tion, 132; Classic Maya, 26; dis-
      pute, 87; faction, 145, 148; leader-
      ship, 25; nonroyal, 158; power,
      125, 163; predatory, 112; protec-
      tion, 89; taxation, 25, 147
   resource rights, 95, 113, 116, 123; in-
      heritance, 123; land rights and, 65,
      67, 78, 91, 92, 95, 96, 150 (*see also*
      ancestors, inheritance, land); land
      tenure, 8–9, 110, 159, 162
   ritual, 92; altar, 100; customs, 16,
      128
   See also Canul lineage; Cocom; Xiu
lineage head, 24, 65, 92, 93, 95, 118,
   123, 131, 139, 152, 153, 163
   c'amal, 25
   chajal, 28

chuchkajaw, 25
hol pop, 24, 31
   residence and, 104
   See also ah kuch kab
literacy, Maya, 129, 130
   education and, 130
   extent of, 129
   scribes, 129, 136, 149
   test of, 130
llacta, 18
LoDagaa, 12, 15, 113

Machiguenga, 172
Mae Enga of New Guinea, 95, 111
Mak-Chanil. See Copán, House of
   Bacabs
Maní, 25, 28, 30, 87, 89, 135, 138, 174
Maní Land Treaty, 87, 89, 91, 116, 142,
   153
mantas, 32
Manus, 11
Marcus, Joyce, 19, 34, 79, 127
matrículas, 107
Mayapán, 53, 85, 94, 96, 116, 129,
   135, 141, 142
Mérida, 135, 174
Mirador, 137
Mirones, 170
Mixtec, 18, 20
   vehe, 20
Monte Albán, 19
Morley, Sylvanus G., 118
Motul dictionary, 92, 139
Mountain Cow, 53
Muna, 137
municipios, 96

Nabalam, 148
nacom, 154
nagualism, 29
Nakbe, 137
Naranjo, 155
   Stela 23, 171
New Year Ceremonies, 23, 93
nobles. *See* elite
Nohmul, 74, 78, 114, 155, 160, 172
nonelite, Maya, 6, 24, 25, 33, 47, 50,
   61, 84, 95, 99, 111, 112, 116, 123,

126, 138, 140, 141, 145, 146, 147,
150, 151, 157, 158, 160. *See also*
YALBA UINICOB
Nuer, 147

Oaxaca, 16. *See also* Mixtec; Zapotec
oratorio, 53, 103, 171
Orbita, Friar, 101
Oxkintok, 52
Oxkutzkab, 137, 175

pacarinas, 18
Palenque, 26, 40, 43, 51, 52, 88, 127
Group of the Cross, 128
royalty: Ac-Kan, 49; Kan Bahlum-
Mo', 75; Kan-Xul, 75; Lady Kan-
Ik, 49, 75; Lady Zac-Kuk, 49, 75,
76; Pakal, 19, 43, 44, 49, 51, 75,
76, 101, 127, 142, 164, 170
patron deities, 23
patronymic, 23, 107, 121
Petén, 142, 145, 146, 150, 163
Petexbatún, 74, 78, 94–95, 147, 172;
Nim Li Naj, 95
Piedras Negras, 39
place names. *See* hieroglyphs, toponyms
polity
autonomy of, 155
boundary: dispute, 89, 90, 91;
marker, 89; zone 86–87, 88, 89,
173
Classic period, 88
Postclassic, 88
polygyny, 107
Pomoná, 85, 172
Popol Vuh, 27, 143, 148, 175
population movement. *See reducción*
posada, 169
Ppustunich, 99
prestation economy, 31, 118, 136
principal, 24, 92, 93, 96
principle of exclusionary closure, 130
principle of first occupancy, 96–97, 99,
112, 116
probanza, 137, 169
prophecy, Maya, 149
Pulltrouser Swamp, 74, 77, 102, 115
pyramids, funerary, 22, 23, 52, 160

Q'eqchi (Kekchi) Maya, 90, 120
quadripartite motif, 57, 58, 85, 86, 104,
114, 160, 164, 172
Quiché Maya, 18, 20, 24, 25–26, 28,
29, 30, 49, 61, 85, 96, 100, 113, 114,
120, 133, 147, 148, 161, 169, 174
Quijada, Diego de, 28, 137, 170
quincunx pattern, 104, 105, 172

recitation literacy, 130. *See also* literacy
reducción, Spanish policy of, 80, 132,
169
regal-ritual center, 147, 174
regidor. See ah kuch kab
relaciones geográficas, 22, 129
Relación de Cansahcab, 22
Relación de Dzonot, 89, 151
Relación de Nicolás de Valenzuela 72,
172
Relaciones de Yucatán, 92, 148, 152,
154, 174
residence, 14, 50, 97, 111, 119, 121, 125
boundary of, 94
distribution of, 74
inheritance of, 99; land tenure and,
65; land use and, 65; orchards,
101, 102
longevity of, 97, 99; principle of first
occupancy, 96–97, 99, 112, 116.
See also land
organization: multiple family. *See*
household, multiple family
ritual, 101, 104; burials, 104; dedicatory deposits, 66, 104; feasting,
101; sacrifice, 101
structures: alpha, 104; arrangement,
102; clusters, 104; development
cycle, 99, 107; mobility of, 78; orientation of, 102; platform, 102; remodeling of, 66, 103, 104, 113,
126, 161; size, 97, 139; type, 124;
variation in, 158
residence pattern, 119, 120
patrilocal, 107
Río Azul, 121
Río Bec, 78, 94
Roys, Ralph L., 23, 24, 27, 71, 89, 91,
94, 96, 121, 141, 149. 151, 170

sacrifice, 101
  animal, 35
  auto-sacrifice. See bloodletting
  human, 62–63, 101, 107, 122, 148
Sahlins, Marshall D., 95, 141, 147
Sanders, William T., 33, 74, 77
San Estevan, 74, 155
San José Mogote, 19
Sayil, 89
Schele, Linda, 26
Scholes, France V., 151
scribes, 129, 136, 149
segmentary lineage, 147, 174. See also
  lineage, segmentary
segmentary state, 147
Seibal, 53, 60, 90, 123
servants, 121
Service, Elman, 15
Seven Macaw, 148
Sheets, Payson, 101
Sherbondy, Jeanette E., 17
shrine, 26, 29, 30, 107, 114
  burials within, 102, 161
  development cycle and, 55
  domestic, 30, 35, 66, 100, 128
  K'axob, 55, 59, 63
  refurbishing, 51
  royal funerary, 51, 128, 137
sinkhole. See cenote; Chichén Itzá
skull-and-crossbones motif. See ancestors, iconography of
slash-and-burn agriculture. See swidden
  agriculture
slave, 121, 122
slavery, 107, 148, 169
sleeping house. See warabal ja
Southall, Aidan W., 14, 15
space-time continuum, 85, 160
Spaniards, 22, 122, 135, 169
Spanish Inquisition, 27–28, 101, 170
  torture, 28
stela
  Copán, 40
  Naranjo, 171
  Tikal, 41
stonemason, 137, 175
Stuart, David, 32, 43

swidden agriculture, 68, 78, 95, 109,
  110, 159, 172

Tah Itzá, 74–75, 93, 101
  Can Ek, 75
Tallensi, 10, 15
Tamarindito, 90
Taube, Karl, 32
Tedlock, Barbara, 85, 114
Tedlock, Dennis, 25
Tenochtitlan, 151
Teotihuacán, 171
Thai monarchy, 131
Thompson, J. Eric, 145, 153
Ticul, 99
Tierras Largas, 19
Tikal, 16, 26, 49, 51, 53, 61, 85, 88, 99,
  105, 114, 119, 130, 132, 155
  Altar 5, 47, 48, 170
  groups: Group 6B-41–6B-44, 121;
    Group 6E-1, 119; Group 7F-1,
    103; Group 7F-35–36, 121; Group
    2G-1, 103
  North Acropolis, 52
  rulers: Ruler A, 49; Scroll-Ahau-
    Jaguar, 40; Yax-Moch-Xoc, 48
  Stela 29, 41
  structures: Structures 6B-30, 6B-33,
    6B-44, 121; Structures 5D-6–5D-9,
    121
Tipu, 170
Titles of Ebtun, 66, 90, 94
Tiv, 147
Todos Santos, 30, 31
Tomaltepec, 19
tomb-guardians, 33
tonalism, 29
Tonga, 140
Tontzimin dispute, 90
totems, 11
Tourtellot, Gair, 123
trade, 145
tribute, 89, 92, 93, 117, 118, 119, 121,
  133, 135, 136, 138, 139, 140, 169,
  175
  cloth, 139
  patan, 139

turkey, 136
Turner, B. L. II, 74, 77
Tus, Lorenzo, 67
Tzotzil Maya, 26, 30, 61, 85, 87, 99,
    107, 143, 169, 171
Tzut of Yaxakumche, Diego, 138
Tzutujil Maya, 28, 43, 162

Uaxactún, 137, 171
Uayeb, 23, 93, 152
UAYMIL, 71, 71. *See also* agriculture,
    fallow
Uc, Francisco, 101
Ucanal, 46
Utatlán, 25, 85, 114, 133. *See also*
    Quiché Maya

vacant terrain, 65, 101–102
Vogt, Evon Z., 118, 171

warabal ja, 18, 100, 170. *See also*
    Quiché Maya
warfare, 6, 89, 90, 112, 121, 133, 141,
    145, 146, 148
    class conflict, 146, 150
    factional conflict, 146, 150, 151
    iconography of, 122
way glyph, 24
Webster, David, 123
were-jaguar, 19
Wilk, Richard R., 120
writing. *See* hieroglyphs; literacy

Xbalanque, 143, 148
Xicalango, 151

Xiu, 24, 25, 30, 80, 87, 116, 118, 137,
    142, 169
Alonso, 138
Francisco de Montejo, 87, 137, 139,
    142–143, 153
Juan, 101, 138, 169
See also Chi, Francisco; Chi, Gaspar
    Antonio

YALBA UINICOB, 10
Yanamamö, 172
Yaxchilán, 34, 39, 40, 43, 47, 173
    royalty: Bird Jaguar 40; Lady Balam-
    Ix, 44; Lady Eveningstar, 40; Lady
    Xoc, 34, 44; Shield Jaguar, 40
Year Bearer, 153, 154
Yoruba, 130–131
Yucatán, 20, 26, 65, 66, 68, 71, 73, 79,
    81, 87, 92, 94, 117, 121, 122, 132,
    135, 136, 142, 144, 147, 153, 154,
    159, 163, 173, 174
Yucatec Maya, 35, 37, 94, 119, 128,
    152
    almehen, 24
    ch'ibal, 23
    drought and famine, 80
    yax ch'ibal, 23

Zapotec, 18, 127
    deities, 19
    penigolazaa, 19
    residences, 19
    See also Oaxaca
Zipacna, 148